WESTERN RIVER TRANSPORTATION

THE JOHNS HOPKINS UNIVERSITY STUDIES IN
HISTORICAL AND POLITICAL SCIENCE

NINETY-THIRD SERIES (1975)

1. The Barristers of Toulouse in the Eighteenth
Century (1740–1793)

By Lenard R. Berlanstein

2. Western River Transportation: The Era of Early Internal
Development, 1810–1860

By Erik F. Haites, James Mak, and Gary M. Walton

WESTERN RIVER TRANSPORTATION:

THE ERA OF EARLY INTERNAL DEVELOPMENT, 1810–1860

Erik F. Haites, James Mak,
and Gary M. Walton

THE JOHNS HOPKINS UNIVERSITY PRESS
BALTIMORE AND LONDON

Copyright © 1975 by the Johns Hopkins University Press

Manufactured in the United States of America

The Johns Hopkins University Press, Baltimore, Maryland 21218
The Johns Hopkins University Press Ltd., London

Library of Congress Catalog Card Number 75–12568
ISBN 0–8018–1681–5

Library of Congress Cataloging in Publication data will
be found on the last printed page of this book.

CONTENTS

PREFACE

The economic growth of the United States in the nineteenth century was strategically influenced by the spread of a market economy. Manufacturing development, in particular, and levels of overall productivity, in general, were largely dependent on the size of the market. This, in turn, was limited by the costs of moving goods and negotiating exchanges. Historically, transportation has been the most important component of these costs.

Economic historians generally agree that improvements in transportation were a significant aspect of nineteenth-century U.S. development, and the dramatic fall in transportation costs before the Civil War has been given special emphasis by a number of scholars.[1] During this early period of the era of internal improvements the nation initiated and committed itself to the construction of an internal transportation network that especially influenced regional development. Nowhere was this impact more evident than in the regions west of the great Appalachian barrier.

Investments in canals, in railroads, and in watercraft, most notably the steamboat, are the outstanding transportation developments of this era. Scholarly interest in canals and railroads as contributors to U.S. economic

---

[1] Perhaps the most dramatic indications of a transportation revolution have been given by Taylor (1951) and by North (1965).

development is evidenced by the abundance of recent research on these facilities.[2] By comparison, relatively little research and almost no economic analysis has focused on the development of the river transportation system in the American West. Because the river system was the principal carrier of freight in that widespread area throughout much of the ante-bellum period, the void recounting the history of river transport requires filling.

The main purpose of this study is to provide a systematic quantitative analysis of early western river transportation. It should be stressed that the emphasis on quantification and economic analysis distinguishes it considerably from the excellent classic history of western steamboats by Louis C. Hunter.[3] As our repeated use of his work amply illustrates, his study has proved invaluable to our own. But to complement the recent investigations of nineteenth-century canals and railroads requires a study of a different scope and with an alternative analytical approach.

An additional purpose of this study is to illustrate the actual workings of a particular market within a definite historical context. Despite the widespread recognition of the important role of the market system in U.S. economic development, much of the analysis of the market's role has been at too high a level of aggregation to clearly illustrate the interaction of supply and demand forces and the progress achieved by the adoption and spread of new improvements in the production process. By concentrating here on a single market for river transportation services our analysis permits a close view of the evolution of market forces and the effects of productivity-raising improvements as a vehicle of growth during a period of tremendous change.

Finally, this study sheds further light on the role of private initiative vis-à-vis public engagement in the economic development of the early West. How did the development of a western river transportation system compare with that of canals and railroads during this era of internal improvements? Was it representative of the so-called "American System" of government partnership with private enterprise?[4] In touching on these issues we enlarge on·the examination by Carter Goodrich and others on the mixture of public and private enterprise in canals, railroads, and other internal improvements in the nineteenth century.[5]

Our study being limited primarily to the economics of western river transportation, 1810–60, we clearly disclaim any intent to provide a general economic history of the period. Indeed, our study is not even exhaustive of

---

[2] For examples of recent research on these subjects see Scheiber (1969a); Ransom (1964): 365–76; Ransom (1967): 12–35; Ransom (1970): 1041–60; Fogel (1964); Fishlow (1965); and Boyd and Walton (1972): 233–55.

[3] Hunter (1949).

[4] The term "the American System" was coined in the interesting review of the role of government in the ante-bellum economy by Lively (1955): 81–96.

[5] Goodrich (1960, 1961, 1967).

all developments of western river transportation, but instead focuses on the major and typical developments. Undoubtedly, future research will modify and add to our efforts. Nevertheless, we believe that our inquiry is sufficiently complete and our conclusions adequately supported to merit the scrutiny of other scholars at this time.

We have accumulated many academic debts in the course of our research. Louis C. Hunter, Stanley L. Engerman, Thomas A. Berry, Harry N. Scheiber, Lance E. Davis, Donald N. McCloskey, James F. Shepherd, Douglass C. North, Richard Easterlin, and an anonymous outside reviewer read earlier drafts of the manuscript. We greatly appreciate their many helpful suggestions and detailed comments. In addition, various portions of the manuscript have been presented to economic history workshops at Indiana University, the University of Illinois, the University of Chicago, the University of Pennsylvania, and the University of Hawaii. We are grateful to many of these workshop participants for their comments. Randall Weir provided able research assistance and Freda Hellinger and Cathie Crecelius provided able clerical assistance. Marion Impola and Nancy Gallienne worked over the manuscript and greatly improved its readability. We are especially indebted to Jeremy Atack for unearthing the sample of steamboats from the 1850 Census. We are also grateful to *Business History Review, Journal of Economic History,* and *Explorations in Economic History* for permission to reprint portions of our earlier research that have already appeared in article form.

Finally, the estimates and calculations in this study occasionally diverge from ones previously published in the above journals. New evidence, such as that from the 1850 Census, which became available to us subsequent to our previous publications, has resulted in some updating and improvements in the estimates. Such refinements and changes are minor and the basic findings remain unaltered; however, it should be made clear that the estimates below do represent the most complete and up-to-date estimates that the available data presently allow.

WESTERN   RIVER   TRANSPORTATION

1

RIVER TRANSPORTATION
IN THE ANTE-BELLUM WEST

"Steam navigation colonized the west! It furnished a motive for
settlement and production by the hands of eastern men, because
it brought the western territory nearer to the east by nine tenths
of the distance. . . . Steam is crowding our eastern cities with
western flour and western merchants, and lading the western
steamboats with eastern emigrants and eastern merchandise. It
has advanced the career of national colonization and national production, at least a century!"

James H. Lanman, 1841

From the turn of the nineteenth century to the embittered days of the
Civil War, the United States underwent a literal transfiguration. During
this early period the frontier raced westward, leaping the Appalachians,
snatching up vast stretches of new territory that now are the midwest and
south-central regions. As the wilderness became homeland, agriculture bud-
ded, bloomed, and enriched the soil for commercial enterprises, which in turn
prospered. Thus the early predominantly self-sufficient pioneer activities of
barter and exchange were increasingly supplanted by market-oriented enterprise. Both the West and the nation had entered a path of irreversible
development.[1]

To bridge the gap between the largely unsettled fertile western regions and
the more densely populated seaboard, the nation now undertook internal
improvements designed to overcome the barriers of mountains, distance, and
inaccessibility. Efforts to construct canals and railroads were important

---

[1] For estimates of the rate of economic growth for the United States during this
period, see David (1967): 151–97. Also, see the classic interpretive study by North
(1961).

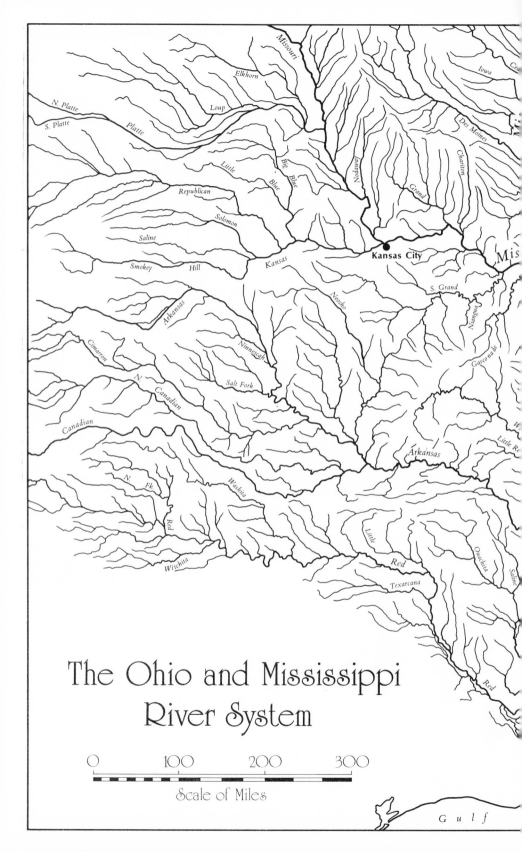

The Ohio and Mississippi
River System

Scale of Miles

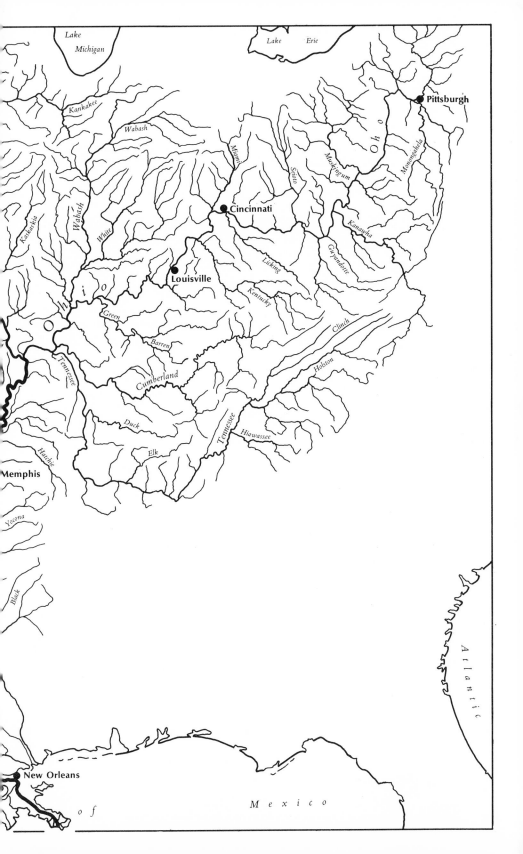

aspects of this era, but in the West, or more specifically in the trans-Appalachian West,[2] the carriage of freight went primarily by the natural waterways, the western rivers.

The comment by the contemporary observer, James Lanman, that "steam navigation colonized the west"[3] undoubtedly exaggerates the role of the rivers, but the implication is echoed by Douglass North: "Although early western settlement had occurred soon after the Revolutionary War, what really inaugurated a change in its status was the opening of a far-reaching transportation network. The first link of this was forged from the interconnected rivers that bound together the Mississippi, the Missouri, and the Ohio; by this route, the products of the West could flow to the South."[4] Similarly, George Taylor stresses the importance of the rivers to the West: "No section of the country was so completely dependent upon steam for effective transportation, and in no other part of the world were so many steamboats built and operated."[5] Similar to Lanman, another contemporary, James Hall, said: "Of all the elements of the prosperity of the West—of all the causes of its rapid increase in population, its growth in wealth, resources, and improvement, its immense commerce, and gigantic energies, the most efficient has been the navigation by steam."[6]

[2] "The West" and "the trans-Appalachian West," as used interchangeably in our descriptions, include all or parts of the states of Ohio, Indiana, Illinois, Michigan, Wisconsin, Iowa, Missouri, Kentucky, Tennessee, Arkansas, Mississippi, Louisiana, New York, Pennsylvania, and Virginia. In our trade estimates, below, however, New York, Pennsylvania, and Virginia are not included because only small portions of their populations lived west of the Appalachians. This considerable degree of aggregation is relaxed in various sections of the analysis below, where the western border states of Kentucky and Tennessee, and the Southwest, which includes for our purpose Arkansas, Mississippi, and Louisiana, are treated separately from the remaining Northwest region.

[3] *Hunt's Merchant's Magazine*, vol. 6: 124.

[4] North (1966): 80. His assertion that the South was a major market of western produce has sparked a lively debate which, as yet, is unsettled. Whether exports from the West were actually consumed in the South, on the seaboard, or abroad need not detour us here; our concern is with the means by which the goods were transported from the interior. For examples of this debate, see Fishlow (1964): 352–64; Fogel (1964): 377–89, plus postscripts on this exchange by both Fishlow and Fogel in Andreano, ed. (1965): 209–24; Parker, ed. (1970); Hutchinson and Williamson (1971): 591–612. It should be emphasized that almost this entire debate has centered on the post-1840 period, because only for these years are statistics available. North's assertions, however, were for the pre-1843 period, and for this period there are no reliable statistics on goods purchased or the consumption of western foodstuffs in the Southwest. North, by the way, never argued that the South Atlantic states were large consumers of western foodstuffs. Post-1840 evidence would bear on the issue of the South as a market for western foodstuffs if the relative prices of the major commodities did not change significantly over the period. As pointed out by Douglas Shetler, however, "The relative price of western corn to southern cotton had more than doubled between 1840 and 1860"; Shetler (1972): 3. Based on his model of the demand relationships for foodstuffs in the West, he concludes that the South was an important buyer of western foodstuffs in the pre-1840 period.

[5] Taylor (1951): 63.

[6] Hall (1848*a*): 41.

In general, the growth of cities in the West underscores the commerical significance of the rivers. Landlocked cities grew only painfully slowly until released by the railroad, whereas riverside towns and cities grew apace throughout the ante-bellum period.[7]

To give some perspective on how goods were shipped in the West, a brief survey of trade patterns and transportation systems will allow us to focus on the main routes and alternative transportation systems, and to assess their relative importance in terms of actual use. It must be stressed, however, that the quantitative information presently available is woefully deficient and must be interpreted with great caution. Though it supports the overall importance of the rivers, any comparisons must obviously be tentative and imprecise.

During the ante-bellum period, three "natural gateways" linked the West with the rest of the nation and the outside world. The first ran eastward from the Great Lakes, either down the St. Lawrence River or along the Hudson or Mohawk river valleys, the latter being the more popular route, with New York City as its eastern terminus. The second gateway linked Pittsburgh and Wheeling on the Ohio River to Philadelphia and Baltimore on the east coast. The third gateway, at New Orleans, was the main Southern entrepôt. Albert Kohlmeier has termed these the northern, the northeastern, and the southern gateways, respectively, and we do likewise.[8]

The major development on the northern gateway, the opening of the Erie Canal in 1825, was followed by the building of the Welland Canal, by improvements in the St. Lawrence Seaway system, and, finally, by the completion of the New York Central and the New York and Erie railroads in 1852.

The northeastern gateway, which stirred up lively rivalry between Pittsburgh and Wheeling on the one end and Philadelphia and Baltimore on the other, justified the completion of the National Road to Wheeling in 1817. This was soon followed by the opening of the Pennsylvania Turnpike to Pittsburgh. The Pennsylvania Canal system, linking Pittsburgh and Philadelphia, was opened in 1834, but its anticipated competitor, the Chesapeake and Ohio canal system, was never finished. When the coming of the railroad renewed the rivalry, the Pennsylvania and the Baltimore and Ohio railroads reached Pittsburgh and Wheeling within months of each other in 1853.

The major event on the southern gateway was the development of steamboat services on the Mississippi after 1811. However, improvements in ocean travel also permitted the establishment of regular packet lines running between New York and New Orleans by the early 1820s.[9]

---

[7] *U.S. Twelfth Census,* vol. 1, Table 6: 430–33, and Serial set 5250, Senate Exec. Doc. 325, 33–93.

[8] Kohlmier (1938):2.

[9] Albion (1938), contains an excellent discussion of the changes in ocean travel during this period. Also, see North (1968): 953–70. In general, throughout this period

Of course, which gateway best served any particular area in the West depended on the relative costs of shipment and on seasonal factors affecting their operations. Since both these determinants were subject to wide variations during the period, and since other supply and demand elements were also changing, it is not surprising that the areas served and the volumes of trade passing over the different routes were constantly in flux.

From the crude estimates in Appendix A we are able to draw rough contours of outbound shipments from the interior.[10] In 1810 these shipments totaled approximately 65,000 tons for all three gateways combined. That the total tonnage had risen to about 4,690,000 tons by 1860 documents the impressive development that was taking place in the West.

A breakdown of the absolute amounts of shipments through each gateway, given in Figure 1, shows the southern gateway to have been dominant throughout most of the period. Calculations of the relative shares in percentage terms (Table 1) show that until the late 1830s the southern gateway accounted for over 80 percent of these shipments. Thereafter, its position was steadily eroded until by the end of the period it serviced slightly less than one-half of the total.

Prior to the opening of the Erie Canal in 1825, the northern gateway had handled virtually no outbound traffic. Most of the canal's early freight still originated in western New York, and the immediate impact of the new waterway on western shipments was small. By the late 1830s, however, the picture had changed radically, and by 1860 the development of feeder systems and other improvements had enabled the northern route to edge past the southern gateway in terms of the percentage of shipments from the interior. As indicated in Figure 1 and Table 1 the greatest gains occurred primarily in the last two decades of the period.

The northeastern gateway played only a minor role in the carriage of

---

ocean-going vessels became larger, faster, and more efficient, and in the later decades of the ante-bellum period, ocean-going steamships were introduced. *The New Orleans Price Current,* for example, first tallied the arrivals of steamships separately during the year ending August 31, 1847. In that year it counted 109 steamship arrivals, compared to 2,872 arrivals of sailing ships, *The New Orleans Prices Current* (September 2, 1848): 3.

[10] It should be clarified that the receipts at New Orleans overstate outbound shipments from the trans-Appalachian West via the southern gateway. A small portion of these shipments were eventually shipped back upstream, and toward the end of the ante-bellum period fairly sizable proportions of certain western commodities were being consumed in New Orleans rather than reexported to the eastern seaboard or to Europe. (See, for example, Fishlow (1965): 280–81. As a consequence, our estimates of trade flows by the southern gateway (Table 1, Appendix A; and Figure 1 and Table 1 below) are a mixture of interregional and intraregional trade flows. This is necessarily the case because we have included Louisiana, hence New Orleans, as part of the western region. This, however, does not vitiate the use of the data for our purpose, which is to show the dominance of the river system as a carrier of total traffic in the West. It is perhaps more correct to view these shipments via the southern gateway, as we do below, as shipments from the interior, rather than as outbound shipments.

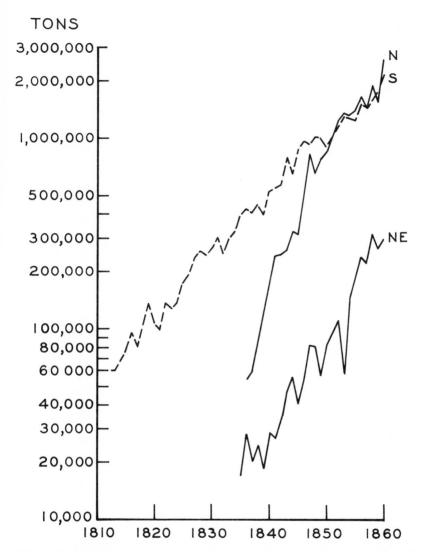

Fig. 1. Freight shipments from the interior by the Western gateways, 1810–16.
Source: Appendix A.

shipments from the West, never accounting for more than 7 percent of the total and generally for less than 5 percent.

Unfortunately, very little information is available on the inbound trade, especially in the early decades of the ante-bellum period. Perhaps the scarcity of data can be attributed to the typically odd-sized, unstandardized nature of the goods shipped, since manufactures of various shapes and sizes were an important part of the total. For instance, a contemporary French observer,

Table 1. Shares of Freight Shipments from the Interior by the Western Gateways, 1810–60 (percent)

Year	Northern[a]	Southern	Northeastern[b]
1810–14	0	100	0
1815–19	1	99	0
1820–24	0	100	0
1825–29	0	100	0
1830–34	1	99	0
1835–39	13	83	4
1840–44	28	68	4
1845–49	38	58	4
1850–54	49	47	4
1855–60	48	45	7

Source: Appendix A.

[a]The calculations for the years 1825–35 may be biased downward slightly because they do not include possible freight shipments, if any, by the Erie Canal, from areas west of New York State, 1825–35 (see Appendix A).

[b]These calculations do not include freight shipped via the National Road and the Pennsylvania Turnpike. The crude calculations indicate, however, that they were only a very small portion of the total amounts shipped (see Appendix A).

M. Chevalier, has suggested that furniture and farm machinery accounted for about 20 percent of westbound shipments on the Erie Canal during the mid-1830s.[11]

Tabulations of the inbound shipments of several major commodities (sugar, salt, iron, molasses, coffee, groceries, and miscellaneous merchandise) by each gateway for several benchmark years have been made and these are given in Table 2. Unfortunately, it is not possible to determine the exact importance of these shipments relative to total inbound freight; but in terms of tonnage, they probably accounted for more than one-half of the total. For instance, Kirkland maintains that coffee, sugar, and molasses formed the chief upstream long distance shipments into the interior.[12] In any case, the total volume of inbound shipments was much smaller than those outbound, and even if the estimates in Table 2 were doubled they would hardly amount to one-half the volume flowing from the interior.

Although the evidence is extremely tenuous, it does suggest that the southern route was the major route for inbound shipments in the 1830s,[13] accounting for approximately 45 percent of the total. By the 1850s, its share had dwindled to only 25 to 30 percent of the total, with the offsetting rise, in percentage terms, going to the northern route, which rose from 32 percent to

[11] Chevalier (1840), vol. 1: 236.

[12] Kirkland (1969): 143.

[13] The following description is based on the assumption that the pattern of shipment of goods excluded would not have differed markedly from that of the goods included.

Table 2. Shipments of Selected Commodities[a] into the Trans-Appalachian West for Various Years, 1835–57

Year	Amounts (000 Tons)				Percent		
	Northern gateway	North-eastern gateway	Southern gateway	Total	Northern gateway	North-eastern gateway	Southern gateway
1835	50	35	69	154	32	23	45
1839	61	52	71	184	33	28	39
1844	77	52	86	215	36	24	40
1849	175	65	125	365	48	18	34
1853	470	90	225	785	61	11	29
1856	500	–	–	965[b]	52[b]	23[b]	25[b]
1857	–	225	240				

Sources: Kohlmeier (1938): 4–7, 20, 21, 32–35, 51–57, 82, 83, 92–94, 115–26, 146–61; Dixon (1909): 24–35; Berry (1943): 5; Sadove (1950): 193; Serial set 2552, House Exec. Doc. 6, pt. II, 191–220; Serial set 622, Senate Exec. Doc. 112, 625–35.

[a]The commodities included are sugar, salt, iron, molasses, coffee, groceries, and miscellaneous merchandise.

[b]To permit comparison, the observations for 1856 and 1857 have been combined.

52 percent of the total inbound freight between 1835 and the 1850s. This shift of the inbound trade, which reduces the southern gateway to about half of the northern gateway by the 1850s, is supported somewhat by an alternative calculation for 1851. Kirkland gives an estimate suggesting that the value of property sent into the interior via the Hudson River was about double that sent by the Mississippi; approximately $81 million as compared to $39 million.[14]

Despite the crudeness of the estimates, and even if we allow much room for error, it is quite clear that when both inbound and outbound shipments are taken together the southern gateway dominated most of the ante-bellum period and that prior to 1845 it received more cargo than passed through the other two gateways combined. It is this finding that urges an emphasis on the importance of the river system in the West. In the pre-1845 period, the main commerical link between the West and the seaboard and abroad was through the Crescent City (New Orleans), and it was by river that goods moved to and from the southern gateway.

As the evidence shows, however, the preeminence of the river routes and the southern gateway was being displaced in the last two decades of the ante-bellum period.[15] First the canals in the 1830s and then the railroads in

[14] Kirkland (1969): 153.
[15] A consideration of trade flows between the western subregions and within these regions would not alter this general conclusion. Unfortunately, only scattered pieces of

the 1850s brought about a redirection of traffic from a predominantly
southern orientation to an East–West routing.[16] Starting in the Ohio Valley
and the northwestern grain regions, these developments arrested the rate of
growth of river commerce. By the 1850s the Mississippi River system had lost
much of its interregional orientation and had become increasingly regional in
character.

Nevertheless, the evidence indicates that despite its relative decline the
southern route did not suffer in absolute terms. The spread of railroads,
roads, and canals, in combination with developments of the Great Lakes,
more closely bound together the Northwest and provided an alternative to
the Crescent City as a link to the East and abroad. But the resulting
alterations in trade patterns and redirection of interregional traffic was more
than offset by the growth of river trade, especially in the South. As we show
below, shipping activity on the western rivers continued to increase throughout the entire ante-bellum period, despite the displacement effect of the iron
horse.

Of course, had the onslaught of the iron horse come earlier, the importance of the rivers probably would have diminished much sooner in the
ante-bellum period. As emphasized by Albert Fishlow, however, the major
influence of the railroad came after the outbreak of hostilities:

A basic conclusion following from this discussion of internal commerce is the
limited contribution of the railroad before 1860 in two of the three major
axes of trade. Only in the flow between East and West, and to a smaller
degree in the opposite direction, did the trunk lines carry a large volume of
traffic, and even these with minor benefits. Almost all the trade emanating
from or destined for the South was quite independent of developments in the
railroad sector, in part because the overland connections between that region

---

information exist on these trade flows, and it is not possible to assess in the aggregate the
patterns or magnitudes of such movements. However, among the western subregions and
among the states and territories this traffic was carried primarily by two major components, both of them water systems. The Great Lakes system formed one route and the
rivers–the Mississippi, the Missouri, the Ohio, and others–comprised the other. Canals,
such as the Welland, which connected Lake Ontario to the other Great Lakes, and the
Louisville and Portland canal around the falls on the Ohio River, were important
complements to these systems. But even the relatively successful Ohio Canal, linking the
Ohio River to Lake Erie, was condemned to the role of feeder. Similarly, the railroads
did not change the West's general reliance on these two components in the ante-bellum
period, except perhaps in the final few years. Wagon and overland transport were of
moderate importance for short hauls, but more distant overland freighting was imprac-
tical until the advent of the railroad. Consequently, when trade within the interior is
considered in addition to trade from and into the interior, the river system remains an
important and probably dominant element of the overall commerce of the West.

[16] For excellent treatment of different aspects of this redirection of trade and from
different perspectives see Fishlow (1964): 352–64; Kohlmeier (1938); Scheiber (1969a),
chap. 12; and Clark (1966): 221–36.

and the others were poorest, but more fundamentally, because competitive water routes represented barriers so formidable that integration would have made little difference and hence received little attention.[17]

Moreover, improvements in river transportation maintained it as the superior medium throughout much of the West, despite attempts by canal promoters in some areas to lessen their dependence on the river. For instance, in the case of Cincinnati, which played a pivotal role in the direction of traffic to the East and South, Harry Scheiber notes that

Despite the availability of both the railroad and the canal route to the lake, most of Cincinnati's export trade remained southern in orientation. As late as 1850 fully 90 per cent of Cincinnati flour exports and 85 per cent of whiskey were shipped to the South or New Orleans. In summary, then, western Ohio's canals had made Toledo prominent in the grain trade, altered the pattern of commerce in southern groceries and in merchandise, and stimulated manufacturing at Cincinnati. The export commerce of the Queen City itself, however, continued to look southward in 1850. Declining freight rates on the rivers and on coastwise routes from New Orleans to the east, linked with expanding demand for foodstuffs in the plantation country of the lower Mississippi Valley, meant that the southern third of Ohio—including the Miami Valley south of Piqua as well as the Scioto country—simply did not seek or need that "liberation" from the southern market which the early canal advocates had postulated as essential to growth.[18]

Finally, it should not be overlooked that according to one estimate the total amount of freight and number of passengers carried in 1849 by western river steamboats was 3.32 billion freight-ton miles and 1.1 billion passenger miles.[19] In that one year, western river steamboats carried about 1 billion freight-ton miles more and only about 700 million passenger miles less than the amounts carried by railroads in the *entire* United States in one year a *whole decade later.*[20]

In short, the western rivers were the dominant medium of trade throughout most of the ante-bellum period and formed a vigorous part of the transportation network, especially in the South, right up to the eve of the War itself. It was undoubtedly these considerations that led Hunter to assert that "the rivers formed the backbone of the transportation system of the West prior to the Civil War."[21]

[17] Fishlow (1965): 288.
[18] Scheiber (1969a): 255.
[19] Serial Set 619, Senate Exec. Doc. 42, 114.
[20] Fishlow (1965): 337.
[21] Hunter (1933–34): 23.

2

AN HISTORICAL SKETCH OF
WESTERN RIVER TRANSPORTATION
BEFORE THE CIVIL WAR

"When I was a boy, there was but one permanent ambition
among my comrades in our village on the West bank of the
Mississippi River. That was to be a steamboatman."

Mark Twain, 1874

Early explorers, traders, and settlers of the vast continental reaches of
the United States relied heavily on the waterways for transportation at
lower cost than they could find by any land route. Emigrants moving
across the Appalachian barrier in search of new economic opportunities
found the rivers particularly well suited to the movement of people and
belongings. Consequently, during the early ante-bellum period, settlement of
the transmountain region proceeded mainly along the Mississippi and its
tributaries, a relatively inexpensive highway network of approximately forty-
five rivers extending over 16,000 miles.[1]

Among the first white men to travel the Mississippi River system were the
missionary and military explorers of France, Spain, Great Britain, and the
United States. Parts of this territory were claimed, and sometimes controlled
by each of these countries, and the European powers sometimes traded off
such claims in settlement of various conflicts. Of course, the most significant
and final transfer of much of the region came in 1803 with the Louisiana
Purchase, which gave the United States title to that portion of the system it
did not already control.

---

[1] The navigable portions of the Mississippi River system in 1890 totaled approximately 16,090 miles. As listed here, they did not differ markedly from the navigable
miles during the ante-bellum period. See *Hunt's Merchants' Magazine*, vol. 18: 492–94.

Trappers and fur traders following the tracks of the explorers were in turn succeeded by settlers who thinned the stock of game and pressed the trappers farther west. Typically, the early trans-Appalachian settlers crossed the mountains to Pittsburgh, where they purchased supplies and built, or bought, a family flatboat to load with their belongings. When the stage of the river was sufficiently high they floated to their destination or until they found a suitable location for settlement downstream from Pittsburgh.

Another route favored by the early settlers was overland through the Cumberland Gap to eastern Kentucky, from which point many again took to the rivers, moving northwest along the Kentucky and Licking to the banks of the Ohio. Since the Spanish (and French) who controlled New Orleans before 1803 did little to encourage the northern movement of settlers upstream, the settled portions of the Mississippi watershed by 1810 consisted of the valleys of the Ohio River and its tributaries and the New Orleans area.

EARLY FORMS OF RIVER TRANSPORTATION

Types of river craft varied widely according to the different requirements of those using them. Explorers, for instance, favored the birchbark canoe, a light, small craft that could travel on almost any inland body of water and

Name of river	Miles	Name of River	Miles
Missouri	3,127	Cache (Arkansas)	160
Mississippi	2,161	Macon	130
Ohio	1,021	Allegheny	123
Red	986	Deer Creek	116
Arkansas	884	Monogahela	110
White	779	Kentucky	105
Tennessee	759	Kenawha	94
Cumberland	609	Muskingum	94
Yellowstone	474	Tensas	92
Ouachita	384	Iowa	80
Wabash	365	Current	80
Osage	303	Big Hatchie	75
Minnesota	295	Rock	64
Boeuf	280	Black (Louisana)	61
Sunflower	271	Chippewa	57
Illinois	270	St. Croix	55
Yazoo	228	Big Horn	50
Bartholmew	113	Clinch	50
Black (Arkansas)	212	Little Red	49
Green	200	Big Cypress and Lake	44
St. Francis	180	Big Black	35
Tallahatchie	175	Dauchite	33
Wisconsin	160		

Source: Serial set 2552, House Exec. Doc. 6, pt. II, 563.

was easy to maneuver, to paddle, and to portage. In contrast, trappers and fur traders required a larger vessel to transport their pelts to market. If the river was shallow or swift, or imposed a long portage, they used a longer and broader version of the birchbark canoe. However, if the weight of the boat was not important, they sometimes used a pirogue, or dugout canoe constructed from two logs, each shaped as a side. Properly constructed, the boat could be expanded by the insertion of planks between the two halves. Although it, too, was quite limited in carrying capacity, the pirogue was much larger and stronger than the birchbark canoe.

The early settlers relied on still larger craft. They wanted a boat that was easily managed, inexpensive, simple, and could make at least one downstream journey with a large quantity of supplies. The flatboat—which was also called an ark, New Orleans boat, Kentucky boat, broadhorse, broadbeam, sneak box, or raft—was well suited to the task. Basically, it was a large, oblong, wooden box that floated with the river current. The typical early flatboat, although not a thing of esthetic charm, could carry 30 to 40 tons of freight and cost only about $50 to $60.[2]

The flatboat was built on sills or gunwales of heavy timbers about six inches thick and was strengthened by sleepers. The gunwales were a foot or two high, and on top of them were mortised studs, perhaps three inches thick and four to six inches wide. At the top of these studs were fastened the rafters that were to bear the roof. The planks of the floor were about two inches thick, but the siding boards were of ordinary thickness. . . . The calking [sic] was tow or any other substance that would answer the purpose.[3]

Flatboats customarily floated down the rivers only during high water. To keep in the current and away from obstructions, they were equipped with a large "sweep" on either side and a long oar at the stern. Occasionally, poles were also used to avoid trouble. Some boats rigged a square sail to take advantage of favorable winds, but most were simple craft, and none had a keel.

The dangers of navigating the rivers with such crude equipment are easily imagined. According to one contemporary: "[Flatboats] can be managed only slowly and with difficulty, and are not, therefore, well adapted to avoid the obstacles which suddenly present themselves; they cannot at all contend with the current. Their pilots are seldom well acquainted with the habits of the river."[4] Despite these problems, the flatboat was typically chosen over the costly alternative of land transportation. Little time and skill were required for its construction, and at the voyage's end it could be used as a temporary house or dismantled to construct a permanent home.

[2] See Appendix E, Table E–1.
[3] Baldwin (1941): 48.
[4] Serial set 78, House Doc. 35, 22.

The overall simplicity of the flatboat also assured its success in commerce. Since most early settlements were located along navigable rivers, and since lumber was plentiful, it was easy for a settler, either by himself or with the help of his neighbors, to build a flatboat and float his produce, and perhaps his neighbor's, to market. This was most often done after the harvest in the fall or during the spring when the rivers ran high. The major market during the ante-bellum period was New Orleans, and as often as not the trip was over 1,000 miles. A typical voyage from the Ohio Valley to New Orleans during the early 1800s took one month, at the end of which the farmer sold his produce and his boat and usually returned home by land—an additional three to four months beset with the hardship and danger of any expedition through the wilderness.[5]

Some variations in the flatboat did develop as their commercial use spread. For example, a comparison of two flatboats at Pittsburgh, one going only as far as the lower Ohio Valley and a second destined for New Orleans, would reveal that the second boat was of stronger construction and better timber, was caulked more fully and higher all around, had a longer and stronger cable, and was better and more completely roofed. Aside from such improvements, however, the major differences were in size and carrying capacity. Flats ranged in width from 12 to 20 feet and in length from 20 to 150 feet.[6] Their carrying capacity ranged from 30 tons initially to nearly 300 tons by the end of the ante-bellum period.[7]

Since a flatboat traveled only with the current downstream, some vehicle was needed to carry cargo and passengers upstream. Before the advent of the steamboat, this task was fulfilled by vessels built on a keel, their ribs covered with plank:

The ordinary keelboat was forty to eighty feet long and from seven to ten feet in beam, had a shallow keel, and was sharp at both ends. It drew about two feet of water when loaded. The middle part of the boat might be left open, but usually it was covered in whole or in part by a cabin or a cargo box that had an inside clearance of about six feet. Here the goods were stored and here the passengers found shelter. All around the gunwales ran a cleated footway, twelve to eighteen inches wide, where the crew walked when poling the boat. At the bow were the seats for the rowers, four to twelve in number, who sometimes received assistance from a square sail. The sail, however, was useless except on comparatively broad waters, so that many keelboats carried none. Steering was done by means of a long oar pivoted at the stern and extending ten or twelve feet beyond the boat. The steersman, who was usually the boat's captain, or patroon, as he was called in the West, stood upon the roof of the cabin or upon a block made of a length of log upended

---

[5] For a description of the difficult return trip, see Baldwin (1941), chap. V.
[6] Baldwin (1941): 47.
[7] Serial set 2552, House Exec. Doc. 6, pt. II, 195.

and with notches cut in the side to enable him to mount. The keelboat's burden ranged between fifteen and fifty tons, but was usually less than thirty.[8]

Keelboats probably came into general use on the Ohio River about 1780,[9] but the barge, a near relative of the keelboat, was not commonly used until about 1800.[10] Although it was similar in construction to a keelboat, it was intended for use only on the larger main trunk river routes. Usually not much longer than a keelboat, the barge was about twice as wide and drew from three to four feet of water. Its larger size accommodated a much greater load, and capacities ranged from 50 to 150 tons, with about 100 tons being most common. The barge was also distinguished by always carrying one mast and often two, fitted with square sails or rigged like a schooner or hermaphrodite brig. Nevertheless, it was little more than a large keelboat equipped to take advantage of the wind, and it operated only on the lower Ohio and the Mississippi rivers.[11]

Propelling a loaded keelboat against the current was a tedious task. The first rule was to take advantage of nature whenever possible. If conditions were suitable, the boat was sailed upstream. The returning current or eddy, which sometimes occurs below points of land, occasionally allowed boats to drift up the river. However, if nature could not be made to do the work, the boat's manpower was called upon.

When a crew powered a boat upstream, they always kept to the slow current near shore and suited their techniques to conditions. If the river bottom were not too soft or the water too deep, they poled the boat. To do this, a crewman would start at the bow, stick a long pole into the bottom, place the other end against his shoulder and then walk (or crawl) to the stern along the cleated footway. There he would withdraw his pole, move to the front of the boat and start again. This required careful supervision to coordinate the efforts of the crew and to use the limited deck space.

When the bottom was unsuitable, the crew might "cordelle" the boat, provided shore conditions made it possible. A cordelle, or towline, several hundred feet long was attached to the boat and taken ashore by the crew, who then walked along pulling the boat behind them. If both the bottom and the shore were unsuitable, the crew would resort to "warping," which required two skiffs. One would carry a cordelle upstream where it was fastened to a snag or a tree. Then the crew at the bow of the keelboat would haul in

[8] Baldwin (1941): 44–45.
[9] Ibid., p. 44.
[10] Goodwin (1907): 335.
[11] Today, the term "barge" connotes a vessel more like that of a flatboat rather than a vessel with a hull and rigging, similar to those of the ocean-going sailing ships of the period. Therefore, to avoid confusion, both keelboats and barges will be referred to here as keelboats.

the line, thus pulling the vessel forward, while a second skiff would be carrying another cordelle farther upstream.

If there were a large number of low overhanging branches (usually encountered only when the river was very high), the crew would "bushwack" the boat upstream, each man in turn grabbing a branch at the bow, walking to the stern, releasing it, and returning to the bow to repeat the performance. Only if there were no other way could the crew row the keelboat upstream.

With a strong favoring wind, a keelboat might sail 30 miles upstream in a day, but under normal conditions 15 miles was a good average. A trip from New Orleans to Louisville, a distance of 1,350 miles, took approximately three to four months, as contrasted to the downstream voyage of one month.[12]

More than twice as many men were required to operate a keelboat on the upstream journey as on the downstream trip; since longer times and higher costs naturally resulted in a rate differential, the ratio of upstream to downstream rates on freight was on the order of five to one before the advent of the steamboat.[13]

Needless to say, the rigors and high costs of moving a loaded keelboat upstream encouraged the search for other methods of propulsion. One rather bizarre attempt was to put horses to walking on a treadwheel to turn a set of paddle wheels. This venture began in the summer of 1807 from New Orleans, and the destination was to have been Louisville. "The trip was begun but never completed. Before arriving at Natchez some twelve to twenty horses were used up on the treadwheel, and the voyage was abandoned near that city."[14]

The first effort to operate a steamboat on the Mississippi River came in 1803 and ended in failure:

Captain James McKeever of the U.S. Navy and M. Louis Valcour became interested in the steam engine designed by Oliver Evans of Philadelphia. They united to build a steamboat 80 feet length, 18 feet beam to ply between New Orleans and Natchez. The river quickly subsided from flood level, leaving the boat high and dry. There was no prospect of the river's rising for six months, and, their capital exhausted, the owners allowed William Donaldson to erect the engine in a saw mill, where it cut up 3,000 feet of boards every 12 hours.

The partners had confidence in their steamboat plans, but were ruined when incendiary fires, started by hand sawyers, destroyed the mill and their engine. The firm lost $15,000 and was not able to realize its ambition to be the first steamboat operator on the Mississippi River.[15]

---

[12] Baldwin (1941): 66.
[13] See Appendix D, Table D–1.
[14] *New Orleans Gazette,* July 23, 1807, quoted in Leahy (1931): 60.
[15] Dayton (1925): 333–34.

Several years later, steam navigation on the Mississippi became, haltingly, a reality. In September of 1811 the steamboat *New Orleans*, built by Robert Fulton and Robert Livingston, departed from Pittsburgh, but its proud progress toward its namesake city was delayed at Louisville until the end of November because the river was not high enough to allow passage over the Falls of the Ohio. Later, as the *New Orleans* was proceeding downstream, an earthquake struck the area and altered the course of the river somewhat. Despite this, the voyage was successfully completed on January 13, 1812,[16] and the *New Orleans* continued to ply between New Orleans and Natchez until it was sunk by a snag in 1814.[17]

In 1815 the *Enterprise*, under Captain Shreve's command, was the first steamboat to travel upstream as far as Louisville. The *Aetna* (360 tons) a Fulton–Livingston boat, made the same journey in 1815, repeated it twice in 1816, and then once again in 1817. During the winter of 1816–17 the *Washington* (403 tons), the largest steamboat then in operation, also made the upstream journey to Louisville, and her second journey to Louisville, under Shreve's command in the spring of 1817, chalked up the record time of twenty-five days. Supposedly, this voyage convinced the public, and the successful introduction of steamboating on the western rivers is thus dated from that year.[18]

Structurally, the first steamboats in the West did not differ much from the seagoing vessels of the time:

Hulls were deep and well-rounded, with projecting keels and a marked sheer fore and aft. They were heavily framed and planked and had a low ratio of breadth to length and [a high ratio] of depth to length. Sitting low in the water, the early steamboat hulls housed not only cargo but also machinery, furnaces, and boilers, and usually passenger quarters as well. Bowsprits and figureheads were for many years ordinary equipment, and some of the early boats even had portholes. In a few cases, at least, the steering wheel occupied its traditional position aft on the main deck. Masts and sails were occasionally carried in order to take advantage of the wind when it was in the right quarter.[19]

The design of the early steamboats was found, however, to be inappropriate for the shallow western rivers, and within the first twenty-five years of its introduction a new look was added. The keel disappeared entirely, and

---

[16] For a detailed description of the voyage of the *New Orleans*, see Latrobe (1871).

[17] A snag was a tree whose roots had become anchored in the riverbed after it had fallen into the river. The top of the tree remained near the surface, and the action of the current usually caused it to face downstream. A vessel moving upstream could easily be speared and sunk by a snag.

[18] Landon (1960): 45.

[19] Hunter (1949): 65. The words in brackets indicate a correction that was probably a clerical error in Hunter's text.

unctional evolution finally produced a long, narrow, flat-bottomed vessel, sually with giant paddle-wheels enclosed in circular housings fitted on the ides. The newer and more modern steamboats carried their machinery and ome heavy cargo (for ballast) below the decks, but most of the cargo emained topside. These decks supported a superstructure that gave the boat he famous top-heavy appearance it carried to the end of its days.

Craft other than those described above were also to be found on the rivers t various times. Among these were the batteaux, market boats, schooners, nd sloops—the latter two being used primarily on the lower Mississippi.[20])verwhelmingly, however, the keelboats, flatboats, and steamboats ruled the iver commerce, and it is these craft that occupy our attention.

THE CHANGING STRUCTURE OF RIVER TRANSPORTATION

The story of the comparative rise and decline of the three major modes of ransportation cannot be told in precise quantitative terms. The data base, specially on keelboating and flatboating, is simply too weak to permit any ccurate reconstruction of their relative development. Nevertheless, from ragmentary data and qualitative information we can trace the general outline f their evolution.

It is not known exactly when the first keelboat came into use on the vestern rivers, but very early ones were used near Pittsburgh on the upper)hio to carry mail, passengers, and freight. By 1805 approximately 50 eelboats of about 30 tons each were plying between Pittsburgh and Cincinati; a decade later nearly 150 of these craft were engaged in the "upper Ohio rade."[21] The round trip from Pittsburgh to Louisville, a distance of approxinately 1,200 miles, took nearly two months, and each boat typically made at east three round trips a year.[22] Trade between New Orleans and the Ohio alley also commenced at this time. The early nineteenth-century observer, ames Hall, noted: "Previous to the year 1817, the whole commerce from Jew Orleans to the upper country was carried in about twenty barges, veraging one hundred tons each, and making but one trip in the year."[23] Most keelboats were smaller than those operating in the Ohio valley—New)rleans trade. The size distribution of keelboats registered at New Orleans Table 3) shows that most of the vessels were less than one hundred tons, and hese probably worked the lower tributaries of the Mississippi River.

According to Hall's estimate, the upstream freight traffic on the Mississippi River before the advent of the steamboat was only 6,500 tons per year. By

---

[20] Serial set 2552, House Exec. Doc. 6, pt. II, 197–98.
[21] Baldwin (1941): 178.
[22] Ibid.
[23] Hall (1848*a*): 13.

Table 3. Size Distribution of Keelboats Registered at New Orleans, 1804–20

Size (tons)	Number
20–29	59
30–39	46
40–49	21
50–59	16
60–69	3
70–79	6
80–89	4
90–99	2
over 100	4

Source: Louisiana (1941) I: 141.

comparison, prior to 1817, shipments into New Orleans by river totaled over 60,000 tons per year.[24] Thus, the vast majority of all river traffic prior to 1817 moved downstream, and this aspect continued throughout the entire ante-bellum period. For all western rivers combined, the peak annual number of keelboats in operation was only about three hundred,[25] and their importance in terms of tonnage never matched that of flatboats.

The introduction of the steamboat on western rivers promptly ended keelboat operations on the major trunk routes. As one contemporary observed for the Mississippi route: "The up freight of the river was much smaller than that down and the steam-boats could easily handle all of it; hence the keel boats were superfluous and were no longer needed to carry freight up the country."[26] Another account states that steamboats "have almost entirely superseded the use of Barges, which were formerly the largest boats in use."[27] Within a decade of the introduction of steamboating, keelboating had ended on the major trunk routes.

After the 1820s, some smaller keelboats continued to operate, but their use was restricted to the shallower waters of the upper Mississippi, the Ohio, the Missouri, and their remote tributaries, where the steamboat did not make its presence felt until later.[28]

[24] Serial set 2552, House Exec. Doc. 6, pt. II, 199.
[25] Baldwin (1941): 181.
[26] Serial set 2552, House Exec. Doc. 6, pt. II, 197.
[27] Serial set 78, House Doc. 35, 22.
[28] For instance, note the following numbers of steamboat and keelboat arrivals at St. Louis from the upper Mississippi:

Year	Steamboats	Keelboats
1841	143	108
1842	195	88
1843	244	55

Serial set 434, Senate Doc. 179, 29.

Data on flatboating, like those on keelboating, are fragmentary and come only from the incomplete records of flatboat arrivals at New Orleans. As given in Table 4, these show a substantial expansion of flatboating, even after the advent of the steamboat. In 1816, the year before the first successful steamboat navigation of the western rivers, 1,287 flatboats arrived in New Orleans. The number increased to 2,792 in the commercial year 1846–47 and then declined rapidly to 541 in the commercial year 1856–57. Thereafter, flatboat arrivals were no longer officially published,[29] but one source indicates that they continued to arrive at New Orleans, though infrequently, until 1870.[30]

Table 4. Annual Arrivals of Flatboats at New Orleans for Selected Years, 1806–57

Year	Number of arrivals	Year	Number of arrivals
1806	455	1849–50	1,184
1808	1,049	1850–51	1,145
1816	1,287	1851–52	1,468
1825–26	981	1852–53	1,047
1835	1,365	1853–54	701
1845–46	2,763	1854–55	614
1846–47	2,792	1855–56	718
1847–48	2,111	1856–57	541
1848–49	1,196		

Source: Records for the years 1806 and 1808 are from Babin (1953): 87–88; those for 1826 and the commercial years 1845–46 to 1856–57 are from Serial set 2552, House Exec. Doc. 6, pt. II, 198 and 222.

Although the total number of arrivals at New Orleans continued to rise after the introduction of steam, flatboats lost ground fairly quickly in terms of the relative proportion of freight carried. According to Switzler: "In 1826, 57 per cent of the freight was carried to New Orleans by the steam-boats and only 43 per cent by other (largely flatboats) means."[31]

Estimates indicate that by around 1840, flatboats carried only about 20 percent of the downstream freight arriving at New Orleans,[32] and by 1860 they could not have carried much more than 5 percent of the freight tonnage arriving from the interior.[33]

[29] Serial set 2552, House Exec. Doc. 6, pt. II, 222.
[30] New Orleans, *Register of Flatboats.*
[31] Serial set 2552, House Exec. Doc. 6, pt. II, 198. The year of 1826 was probably a poor one for flatboating, however, and only 981 flatboats arrived in New Orleans, compared to 1,287 in 1816 and 1,049 in 1808. Our guess is that steamboats achieved parity around 1830.
[32] Scheiber, in Ellis, ed. (1969): 288.
[33] This is calculated assuming 500 flatboat arrivals each carrying 150 tons—the approximate average size of flatboats (see Appendix E) arriving in New Orleans during the 1850–60 decade.

It is important to stress the limitations of the New Orleans records. Though they provide the best overall source of flatboat activity, the number of arrivals understates the magnitude of flatboating on the Mississippi. Accidents enroute took their toll, and boats and cargoes were sometimes sold before reaching the southern gateway. Contemporary sources indicate that only three-fourths to four-fifths of the flats destined for New Orleans actually reached there.[34] Moreover, the rise in the number of arrivals understates the growth of activity because, as noted above, the size of the boats was increasing.

Still more important, the overall magnitude of flatboating included other trades than that to New Orleans. Many flats carried freight between the interior cities and from farms located on various tributary rivers not serviced by steamboats; such produce was often then transhipped by steamboats to other markets outside the region.

If we are willing to accept estimates made by contemporary observers which probably are educated guesses rather than actual counts, it would appear that the number of flatboats engaged in the New Orleans trade represented roughly 50 to 60 percent of the total number of flatboats operating on the western rivers during any given year. One estimate, made in 1828, suggests a figure of 7,000 flatboats operating on the western rivers, each carrying on the average 40 tons of freight,[35] but another, in 1832, states that only 4,000 flats of 40 tons each were in operation.[36] Another estimate for 1842, gives a figure of 4,000 flatboats, each carrying on the average 75 tons of freight;[37] and toward the end of that decade 4,000 flats still were alleged to have descended the Ohio and Mississippi rivers.[38]

Records of flatboat arrivals at Cincinnati, while not always consistent with contemporary estimates of the total number of flatboats operating on the western rivers, further support the contention that flatboats in the New Orleans trade represented no more than one-half of the total number of flatboats operating annually on the western rivers. In 1847, the peak year of flatboat arrivals in New Orleans, 3,336 flatboats arrived in Cincinnati, of which 700 departed for destinations further downstream (including New Orleans).[39] In contrast to the subsequent sharp decline of arrivals in New Orleans, the number of flatboat arrivals in Cincinnati rose to nearly 6,000 in 1853 and still reached about 5,000 in 1854.[40]

[34] Serial set 2552, House Exec. Doc. 6, pt. II, 221.
[35] Serial set 178, House Report 213, 2. This estimate was probably exaggerated in the effort to obtain Congressional help for river improvements.
[36] *Louisville Directory* (1832): 127.
[37] Serial set 415, Senate Doc. 129, 3.
[38] Scheiber, in Ellis, ed. (1969): 290.
[39] Ibid., p. 288.
[40] Ibid.

Clearly, it is not possible to pinpoint any exact date of decline of flatboat operations for western rivers overall. We can be certain though, that the flatboat resisted longer on the major trunk routes than did the keelboat, and its use actually increased, even after the advent of the steamboat. Available evidence suggests that the flatboat trade was dual in nature. Important to its continuation was the interior component, consisting largely of local and feeder routes, serving farms located on tributary rivers inaccessible to steamboats; this freight was taken to local markets to be processed and subsequently transhipped onto steamboats. The development of this component of the flatboat trade was largely determined over time by the availability of alternative feeder carriers, such as canals and railroads. By contrast, the development of the New Orleans flatboat trade was to be largely dictated by competition from steamboats, as will be shown in Chapter 3.

Unquestionably, the craft of greatest significance to western river commerce was the steamboat. In many respects its introduction represented a "transportation revolution," and, as indicated in Figure 2, the remarkable record of the expansion of steamboating on the western rivers evinces both the early recognition by westerners of the economic potential of this new technology and their willingness to adopt it.

Several alternative measures can be used to document the magnitude of ante-bellum steamboating on the western rivers. One is the number of steamboat arrivals (or departures) at major terminal points on the river system. Except for New Orleans, however, the data are too incomplete to support an overall index of this activity. The available evidence does suggest that steamboating expanded on the New Orleans and St. Louis trades throughout the ante-bellum period, but in the Pittsburgh and Cincinnati trades, expansion came to an end around the 1850s and the traffic declined absolutely thereafter,[41] no doubt due to the competition of the railroads, which had then reached the Ohio valley.[42]

By far the best available measure of the progress of western river steamboating is the series on aggregate tonnage given in Figure 2. As shown, total annual tonnage in operation on all western rivers had expanded a hefty forty-three-fold from the first tentative decade of steamboat operations to the last decade of the ante-bellum period. The rate of expansion, however, was not constant throughout this period. Decade rates of growth were 395.9 percent, 1811–20; 199.1 percent, 1820–30; 139.5 percent, 1830–40; 96.3 percent, 1840–50; and 37.7 percent, 1850–60. Like most industries, steamboating had enjoyed an initial period of rapid expansion followed by secular retardation. Also, while the direction of the secular trend was unmistakably upward, the impressive record of sustained growth in tonnage was marred by

---

[41] Hunter (1949), Table 2: 644–45.
[42] See, for instance, Fishlow (1965), chap. VII.

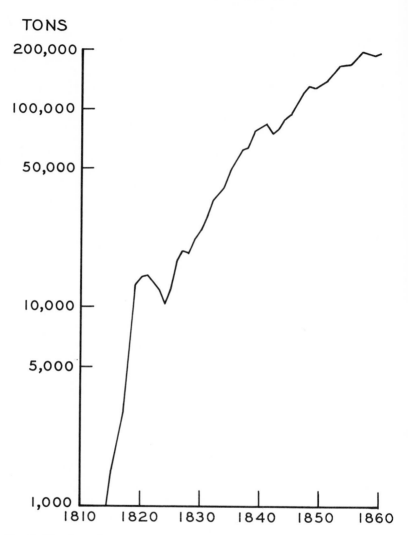

Fig. 2. Tonnage of steamboats in operation on Western rivers, 1814–60. *Source:* Appendix B, Table B-1.

significant fluctuations in annual construction and even by an occasional year or more of contraction, as in 1822–24, 1828, 1842–43, 1849, 1854, and 1858–59.

Strikingly, this timing closely parallels the expansion and contraction of general economic activity in the West.[43] According to Thomas S. Berry, ante-bellum western economic activity tended to "surge and recede in tides of

[43] Berry (1943), chaps. XII–XVII.

fairly equal lengths (eighteen to twenty-two years)."[44] Roughly speaking, the interval between 1785 and 1861 witnessed four of these tides, but with phases not so neatly divided. The flood period generally averaged about sixteen years, the ebb only three or four years. The former reached peaks in 1795–98, 1816–19, 1835–39, and 1854–57; the latter reached troughs in 1802–05, 1821–24, and 1860–61.[45]

A comparison of the movements in general economic activity with movements in aggregate western river steamboat operating tonnage (Table 5) reveals a remarkable correspondence in their movements, both in the direc-

Table 5. Time Periods of Peaks and Troughs in General Economic Activity in the West and in Aggregate Operating Tonnage of Western River Steamboats before the Civil War

Peaks		Troughs	
General economic activity	Aggregate[a] operating tonnage	General economic activity	Aggregate operating tonnage
1816–19	1819–21	1821–24	1822–24
1835–39	1839–41	1841–43	1842–43
1854–57	1855–57	1860–61	1858–60

Sources: Peaks and troughs in general economic activity in the West are obtained from Berry (1943): 530; peaks and troughs in aggregate operating tonnage are obtained from Appendix B, Table B–1.

[a]During periods of monotonically rising tonnage, the dating of the initial year of the peak interval is somewhat arbitrary. The peak intervals could just as well read 1816–21 and 1835–41.

tion and in the timing at which they reach their heights and depths (with perhaps a slight lag in the tonnage series).[46] Of the six periods of contraction in steamboat operating tonnage, three (1822–24, 1842–43, and 1858–60) are clearly explained by periods of general economic recession.[47] Of the remaining three, both 1828 and 1849 can be accounted for by short-term economic

---

[44] Ibid., p. 530.

[45] Ibid. For an explanation of these movements, see North (1956): 493–505; also, North (1961).

[46] Except for 1858–60, movements in the tonnage series appear either to coincide with or to lag slightly in timing the movements in the level of general economic activity. Table 5 shows the trough in operation tonnage, 1858–60, preceding a trough in the level of general economic activity. This is somewhat deceptive, however, due to the imprecise dating process for the terminal period. Aggregate steamboat tonnage reached a peak in 1857, when general economic activity reached its peak phase, 1854–57. A sharp economic crisis in the latter part of 1857 brought an equally drastic contraction in operating tonnage beginning in 1858. The economy appeared to show signs of recovery in 1860, but this was quickly reversed (1860–61) by the Civil War. See Berry (1943): 470–529, and North (1956): 497–98.

[47] The remarkably quick adjustment of operating tonnage to movements in general

fluctuations;[48] for 1854 the only apparent explanation is the suspension of navigation due to low water.[49]

The evidence presented here thus indicates that despite a slowing in rate of growth, steamboating on the western rivers did expand continually throughout the ante-bellum period, interrupted only occasionally by adverse economic or navigational conditions. The westward thrust of the iron horse brought about a reduction in total tonnage in operation in certain regions, most notably in the Ohio valley during the 1850s, but there was no such decline of steamboating for the entire western region before the outbreak of hostilities.[50] This conclusion challenges the popular belief that railway competition during the decade of the 1850s brought about an absolute decline in steamboating on the western rivers before the Civil War.[51]

---

economic activity was due to the ease of entry into the market, the short time required to build a steamboat, and the vessel's short life.

[48] Berry (1943): 409, 427, and 470.

[49] Contemporary observers noted disruptions in navigation on three occasions between 1811 and 1860: 1819–20, 1838–39, and 1854–56; but in only one year (1854) was the disturbance important enough to reverse the expansion path of aggregate steamboat tonnage (Berry [1943] : 535). Since all three periods fell within peak intervals in general economic activity (see Table 3), one might deduce that navigational difficulties that might have discouraged the building of steamboats were more than offset by the climate of economic good times.

[50] In an unpublished paper, Richard Vedder attempts to show the effect of the spread of the railroad on the construction of steamboats in the late ante-bellum period. See Richard K. Vedder, "Steamboating on Antebellum Western Rivers: Further Evidence," Ohio University, 1974. It seems fairly obvious that the railroad reduced steamboat construction below what it otherwise might have been, but other forces countered and maintained positive additions to the working stock of steamboats in operation.

[51] Davis, Easterlin, Parker, et al. (1972): 487–88.

3

COMPETITION ON THE
TRUNK RIVERS

"I have known a man to purchase a steamboat without a dollar in hand, drop her down to the wharf, stick up his "shingle" for New Orleans, get a full cargo, . . . negotiate a bill of exchange on his agent in New Orleans to pay charges and outfit here, make a successful trip or two, pay for his boat and in sixty days be on the lookout for another similar speculation."

Sketch Book of St. Louis, 1858
quoted by Gould

U.S. westward expansion and commercial development were paralleled by a tremendous growth of river-craft operations between 1810 and 1860. In the process, competition among a widely varied array of craft of different sizes and capabilities became a Darwinian study in survival of the fittest.

As described in Chapter 2, the steamboat had been preceded by keelboats and flatboats. Following a trial period (1811–20), which tested the utility of steam power, this newcomer among river craft promptly supplanted the lumbering dinosaur of the keelboat, which depended on human brute strength and the occasional help of nature to work its way upstream. Some keelboats were able to prolong their service lives by retreating to the more shallow rivers and remote backwaters, but essentially the species became extinct in the trunk river sections of the Mississippi, the Ohio, and the Missouri during the 1820s. By contrast, flatboating, which profited from the natural force of river currents, not only survived the stiff competition of the steamboat, but even forged ahead to reach a peak of activity on the lower Mississippi in the mid-1840s.

This contrast of failure and success by the older craft on the trunk rivers is analyzed here by a comparison of their costs and revenues. More generally, however, our objective is to determine the comparative profitability of all the craft—steamboats, keelboats, and flatboats—on the major trunk rivers and to assess the overall conditions of this market for river transportation services in the ante-bellum period. To complete the analysis for western river transportation as a whole, our findings here for the trunk rivers are appropriately qualified in Chapter 4, along with an analysis of contrasting developments on the tributaries and more remote river trades.

Observations by informed contemporaries suggest several major developments in western steamboating. For instance, after his tour of the trans-Appalachian West in 1818, Estwick Evans reported: "The profits attending the business of steamboats upon the western rivers are almost beyond belief; but the competition arising from this circumstance is daily lessening them."[1] Later, in 1834, Morgan Neville noted that "although the benefits conferred on our country, by steam navigation, were incalculable, the stock invested in boats was, as a general rule, a losing investment. In a few cases, owing to fortuitous events, or to the exercise of more than usual prudence, money has been made; but the instances are so few as not to affect the rule."[2] Attempts to alter this situation by merger and combination apparently did not succeed.

Impressive in their number and variety, the Ohio River steamboat combinations were in operation distinguished mainly by the brevity of their careers and by the ineffectiveness of their efforts, . . . Few of them lasted longer than a season and the existence of many was limited to a few weeks. . . . [E]ven the most durable of the combinations could only restrain and not eliminate competition. Their success consisted for the most part in preventing rates from falling to very low levels rather than in raising them above what were popularly regarded as "fair" and "living" rates.[3]

One major development was the emergence of an up-river backhaulage problem in the 1840s,[4] and a contemporary steamboat captain, Davis Embree, noted: "The return loading . . . is almost a clear gain upon the shipments downward, to which steamboats owe their livelihood, and most of them their existence."[5]

Thus, the major developments on the trunk rivers before 1860 were the introduction of the steamboat, the rapid demise of keelboats, a period of high but declining profits for steamboats which were allegedly minimized by the 1830s, a failure of combinations and mergers, a gradual decline of flatboating

---

[1] E. Evans (1904): 325.
[2] Hall (1848a): 134.
[3] Hunter (1933–34): 121–22.
[4] Serial set 2552, House Exec. Doc. 6, pt. II, 221.
[5] Embree (1848–49): 109.

after 1845, and a backhaulage problem after 1840. One interesting speculation is why the steamboat industry did not produce a class of expansive cigar-smoking tycoons comparable to the railroad capitalists of the following era. The answer apparently lies in the characteristics of the market for river transport.

To simplify the analysis of these events and to make it more systematic, our investigation is for several reasons limited to the single route between Louisville and New Orleans. First, that was the main traffic artery during most of the ante-bellum period. As Hunter states: "With the expansion of steamboat tonnage after 1817 the Louisville—New Orleans trade at once became the principal field of operations in the West and from this time to the fifties maintained its preeminence despite rapid extension elsewhere."[6] Second, data relating to this route are more plentiful and span a longer period than those relating to any other. Also, keelboats, flatboats, and steamboats all operated on this major trunk route during the period, and this was not often the case. Finally, as we show elsewhere, the Louisville—New Orleans route was in many respects typical of major trunk routes.

Despite this simplification, data limitations make it necessary to limit the calculations of cost and revenues to decade periods. Only a partial explanation of the estimates is given here, but a detailed discussion of the data and the assumptions on which the estimates are based can be found in Appendixes C, D, and E. It should be stressed that the estimates are averages. The typical experience is sought, and exceptional cases are not revealed, except as they influence the averages. Bearing in mind, then, that the calculations are intended only as reasonable approximations, we can proceed, taking each craft separately.

ANNUAL STEAMBOAT COSTS

The average total cost estimates include depreciation, repairs, insurance, labor, fuel, stores, and "other" costs. Calculations of these itemized costs, along with their totals, for an average steamboat in each decade are given in Table 6.

Construction costs were a function of the size of the vessel, the quality of its machinery, and the splendor of its furnishings. While construction costs per ton were falling slightly, the average size of vessels was increasing significantly, leading to higher construction costs per vessel. Regardless of the method used to calculate depreciation, the average amount must equal the original cost divided by the average lifespan of the steamboat. The average lifespan of steamboats in the Louisville—New Orleans trade averaged about six

---

[6] Hunter (1949): 35.

Table 6. Average Annual Costs of Steamboat Operations in the Louisville–New Orleans Trade, by Decade, 1810–60

Period	Average annual depreciation charge	Average annual repair costs	Average annual insurance premiums
Before 1820	$4,583	$3,300	$4,950
1820–29	5,317	3,828	4,785
1830–39	5,683	4,092	4,092
1840–49	5,580	3,348	2,790
1850–60	6,000	4,320	3,240

Period	Average annual labor costs	Average annual fuel costs	Average annual stores and "other" costs	Average annual total costs
Before 1820	$ 5,320	$ 2,228	$ 3,235	$23,600
1820–29	6,850	5,445	5,269	31,500
1830–39	13,610	9,920	10,084	47,500
1840–49	12,265	12,594	10,653	47,200
1850–60	15,720	15,862	13,535	58,700

Source: Appendix C.

*Rounded to the nearest hundred dollars.

years over most of the period, except in the 1840s, when it was nearer to five years.[7]

According to one informed contemporary, total repairs over the life of a vessel typically amounted to one-half of the original construction costs. This plus other evidence, suggests yearly repair bills of about 12 percent of original costs.[8]

The hazards of steamboating were many, including explosions, fires, and snagging. Coupled with the short life span of the boats, these dangers resulted in insurance rates so high that many operators carried no insurance,[9] and those who did could purchase commercial insurance only up to two-thirds or three-quarters of the value of the boat.[10] Nevertheless, the cost of insurance on the full value of the steamboat is the relevant cost for risk of loss; our

[7] The decline in the average life span of steamboats over 200 tons during the 1840–49 decade probably was the result of the suspension (1838) of the federal government's river improvement work. The increase in the average life span of such steamboats during the 1850–60 period resulted from the strict inspection and safety regulations required by the Act of 1852.

[8] See the statement made in 1829 by Morgan Neville, in Hall (1848a): 129.

[9] J. L. Wilmers of Neare, Gibbs and Co., River Marine Underwriters, Cincinnati, Ohio in a letter dated March 20, 1967, estimated that of steamboats five years old or less, 45 percent carried insurance prior to 1830, 60 percent carried insurance between 1830 and 1850, and 80 percent carried insurance after 1850. He also estimated that of vessels over five years old, 20 percent carried insurance prior to 1830, 40 percent carried insurance between 1830 and 1850, and 55 percent carried insurance after 1850.

[10] Hunter (1949): 366.

calculations are thus based on reported commercial rates applied to the original cost of the boat.

Throughout the period, an average steamboat was handled by about twelve crewmen for each one hundred tons of measurement. At least seven of these were officers; the rest worked the deck and cabins.[11] The captain and clerk were retained throughout the year at annual salaries, but officers and other crew members were paid monthly and were, typically, laid off after the normal navigation season.

The average annual fuel expense for each period has been calculated by multiplying the average daily fuel consumption per vessel, times the average running time per year, times the average price of wood. These expenses rose significantly as the vessels and engines increased in size and power. In addition, fuel consumption per ton rose because of greater average running time per year. The price per cord of wood increased only slightly.

Stores and "other" costs were primarily food for cabin passengers and crew, but also covered such unrelated items as supplies for the kitchen, dining hall, and passenger cabins (linen, dishes, utensils, etc.), utility equipment for the boat (ropes, account ledgers, receipt books, etc.), wharfage charges, and canal tolls. These food and miscellaneous expenses totaled about 30 percent of the annual operating expenses, plus labor and fuel expenses.

Steamboats received the bulk of their revenues from the carriage of passengers and freight, especially in the Louisville–New Orleans trade; therefore, our estimates are limited to these major revenue sources and ignore such inconsequential sources of revenue as mail contracts,[12] barge towing, barroom operations, and government charters.[13]

Passenger revenues were earned on two classes of service. Cabin passengers enjoyed excellent meals and accommodations comparable to those of the best hotels of the time, but deck passengers were left to make themselves as comfortable as possible among the freight and to provide their own food. Our estimates in Table 7 show that the fares paid by these two classes of passengers differed as widely as the apparent services they received.

Throughout the ante-bellum period, large numbers of immigrants and flatboatmen traveled upstream from New Orleans, far exceeding the roster of passengers going in the other direction. Unfortunately, the exact proportions are unknown, and we have assessed that the downstream passengers for each period averaged about three-quarters the number going upstream (Appendix D., Table D–4). This assessment, plus information on the proportion of deck

---

[11] Ibid., p. 443; Huber (1959): 97; Serial set 619, Senate Exec. Doc. 42, 13–14.

[12] Mail contracts were awarded only to the fastest boats. Even then the data presented in footnote 1 in Appendix D indicates that a mail-carrying boat's income from this source would have been $500 per year on the Louisville–New Orleans route.

[13] Hunter (1949): 373–74.

Table 7. Fares for Deck and Cabin Passage and Freight Rates on Cargo between Louisville and New Orleans, 1810–60

	Passenger fares (per person)				Freight rates (per 100 pounds)	
	Upstream		Upstream		Downstream	Downstream
Period	Cabin	Deck	Cabin	Deck		
Before 1820	$125	$25	$75	$18	$5.00	$1.00
1820–29	50	10	25	6	1.00	0.625
1830–39	25	6	25	6	0.50	0.50
1840–49	20	4	20	4	0.25	0.30
1850–49	15	3	15	3	0.25	0.325

Source: Appendix D.

to cabin passengers, permits the calculation of passenger earnings. These earnings are presented in Table 8.

Annual average cargo earnings depended on the rates charged and on the quantity and distance of cargo carried. At any given time the freight rates varied with the stage of the river, the number of boats in port, the nature and amount of freight to be shipped, the qualitative differences in the vessels, the relative bargaining skills of the operators, and other factors. Our estimates of the average rates are also given in Table 7; like the passenger fares, they fell significantly during the period.

The volume of freight carried per boat, by decade, is not easily determined, but available evidence suggests that downstream loads averaged about 75 percent of capacity throughout the period (Appendix D, n. 62). This is an arithmetic mean over the whole season, because during the peak shipping periods of fall and spring steamboats undoubtedly carried capacity loads downstream. Multiplication of the average tonnage capacity by 75 percent and by the average number of trips made per year gives the annual tonnage volume of downstream freight. The product of these utilized tonnages and the appropriate (decade) freight rates give the annual downstream freight revenues per steamboat shown in Table 8.

Throughout the ante-bellum period, upstream freight never matched the volume of that shipped downstream. For instance, according to Johnson, "[Shipments up the Mississippi] never attained more than one-half the volume of the trade downstream, notwithstanding the ability of the steamboat to stem the current of the water, and, with the exception of such bulky articles as sugar and coffee and occasionally some heavy machinery, very few commodities were sent as far north as the Ohio Valley."[14] Allowing for the

[14] Johnson (1915), vol. 1: 213.

difference between upstream and downstream carrying capacity suggests that the upstream utilization would have been, at most, the same as that downstream. Therefore, 75 percent has been accepted as the average upstream utilization rate before 1840 although, as suggested here and indicated in Appendix D, (p. 159 and n.62) this rate is probably biased upward. After 1840, the imbalance between upstream and downstream volumes developed into a serious backhaulage problem on the Louisville–New Orleans route.[15] No independent evidence on utilization exists for these latter two decades, but assuming that only normal profits were being earned by this period, residuals of utilization can be calculated.[16] These are 44 percent for the 1840s and 12 percent for the 1850s.

STEAMBOAT PROFITS

Table 8 summarizes the estimates of steamboat revenues and costs by decade. The annual profits are profits in an accounting sense. They do not include the opportunity cost of the capital invested in the steamboat operation.

The profit rate is defined as the annual profits expressed as a percentage of the invested capital. It can be shown that this is equivalent to the rate of return earned on an investment over its lifetime.[17] The appropriate definition of invested capital for this calculation is the original cost of the vessel plus the working capital required. We have assumed that the working capital required is equal to the out-of-pocket costs for the round trip.

Two profit rates are shown. The lower rates in column (7) are calculated on the assumption that the boat is fully insured. Thus they represent the returns to capital and the risk of operations. The higher rates in column (8) are based on the assumption of no insurance coverage, and these include a risk premium for the possible loss of the vessel. Of course, actual historic profit rates would depend on the amount of insurance purchased, and would therefore fall within the bounds defined by our estimates. Since the fraction of vessels with insurance coverage increased over time, the *actual decline* in profits *would be greater* than that exhibited by either one of our series taken alone. To illustrate, suppose only 20 percent of all steamboats carried insurance before 1820, but that 80 percent were insured after 1850, and that the coverage was two-thirds of the value during both periods; the average observed profit rate would be 42 percent before 1820 and 14 percent after 1850. In any case, and despite their approximate nature, the estimates vividly

---

[15] See for instance, Morrison (1958): 248 and Embree (1848–49): 109.
[16] Evidence in support of the assumption that only normal profits were earned after the 1830s is presented below.
[17] Knight (1936): 409–17.

Table 8. Estimates of the Annual Total Costs, Total Revenues, and Profits of Steamboats in the Louisville–New Orleans Trade, 1810–60

Period	(1) Average annual passenger revenue*	(2) Average annual downstream freight revenue*	(3) Average annual upstream freight revenue*	(4) Average annual total revenue* (1)+(2)+(3)	(5) Average annual total cost*	(6) Average annual profits* (4)–(5)	(7) Profit rate, fully insured[a]	(8) Profit rate, no insurance[b]
Before 1820	$16,100	$ 4,900	$12,400	$33,400	$23,600	$9,800	29%	44%
1820–29	17,000	10,900	8,700	36,600	31,500	5,100	14	27
1830–39	23,600	18,600	9,300	51,500	47,500	4,000	10	21
1840–49	22,600	22,300	5,500	50,400	47,200	3,200	10	19
1850–59	23,600	36,900	2,200	62,700	58,700	4,000	10	18

Source: See text, Table 7 and Appendix D.

*Rounded to the nearest hundred dollars.

[a] Column 6 divided by the original cost of the vessel plus operating costs for one round trip voyage; also see text.

[b] Annual profits plus insurance costs both divided by the original cost of the vessel plus operating costs for one round trip voyage; also see text.

portray that during the early part of the period steamboating in the Louis-ville–New Orleans trade was highly profitable. We see from column 7 that the average rate of return adjusted for risk prior to 1820 was 29 percent. During the 1820 decade the average rate adjusted for risk was 14 percent, but by the 1830s the picture changed; the rate of return was reduced to just 10 percent. Other studies have found this to be the normal return to capital during this period.[18] In other words, admitting the approximate nature of the calcula-tions, after 1830 steamboating on average had been reduced to the level of normal returns to capital in competitive enterprises. In view of these esti-mates, the contemporary reports of the "unprofitability" of steamboating are best explained by Hunter's conjecture that "complaints of this kind [the unprofitability of steamboating] are not, of course, to be taken at face value; perhaps they reflected rather the failure to realize oversanguine hopes than actual failure to show profits."[19]

Why did the profit position of steamboating change over time? To explain this, one has to examine the characteristics of the market for steamboat services. Throughout the ante-bellum period, the carrying capacity of any particular steamboat was small relative to the total volume of freight, and the number of boats in operation at any one time was relatively large. The ownership and the control of these boats were widely distributed. Given the absence of any legal or institutional restraints, and with capital requirements typically small and readily obtainable, entry into the market was easy and rapid. The construction time of vessels was a few months at most. Finally, all steamboats basically provided the same services, and although individual vessels generally plied their own designated trades, they were capable of moving between trades to exploit "exceptional" profit opportunities.

Clearly, these conditions are all characteristic of a purely competitive market, and according to economic theory a purely competitive firm (a steamboat in this case) does not earn "economic" profits in long-run equilib-rium. Rather, it is expected that it can earn a return equal to those in other competitive industries, adjusted for risk. The elimination of profits in the Louisville–New Orleans trade during the 1820s merely achieved the long-run equilibrium expected of purely competitive industries, whereas, the "excess"

---

[18] Fogel and Engerman (1974), vol. 1: 70, report that "on average, slaveowners earned about 10 percent on the market price of their bondsmen. Rates of return were . . . approximately the same across regions . . . and over the period from 1820 through 1860, there was no secular trend in the level of profits away from the average." They also indicate that these rates of return are equal to, or greater than, those obtained in a variety of nonagricultural enterprises during the ante-bellum period. By contrast, rates of return to investments in southern manufacturing industries–sawmills, flour mills, blacksmiths, boat and shoe manufacture, leather products, and wagonmaking–in 1860 averaged 28 percent. Bateman, Foust, and Weiss (1975).

[19] Hunter (1949): 357.

profits earned on an average before 1830 were entrepreneurial rewards to early risk-takers in the industry.

It is important to note that the profit position attained during the 1830–39 decade was a long-run phenomenon resulting from adjustments within the market rather than a short-run consequence of fluctuations in business activity. Considerable qualitative evidence indicates that this profit equilibrium persisted throughout the ante-bellum period,[20] and the 1850 census reports on vessels operating in the Louisville–New Orleans trade provide important quantitative support for this proposition. The average rate of return for the twenty-two vessels calculated, using the procedures described above, was 7.8 percent.

Despite the fact that steamboats yielded, on average, only normal profits, the industry continued to expand after the 1830–39 decade.[21] The expansion of capacity was in part because of the growth of demand for transport services generated by the rapid economic growth of the Ohio and Mississippi valleys. As we shall see in Chapter 5, it was also in response to improvements in steamboat operations and in the construction and design of the vessels, which significantly reduced the round-trip costs of river transportation. The keen competition among operators spurred a parallel downward movement of costs and of freight rates and fares. Undoubtedly, alterations in demand and supply caused temporary fluctuations in profits as well, but the ease of entry assured that short periods of excess profits were soon eliminated.

THE PROFITABILITY OF FLATBOATING

Data on flatboating are even more sparse than those on steamboating, but reasonable approximations can be made of their average costs and earnings. Our estimates of these costs[22] by decade are given in Table 9.

Available evidence indicates that flatboats arriving at New Orleans increased in size from an average capacity of 30 tons during the 1810–29 decades to 146 tons during the 1850–60 period. The cost of construction rose proportionately, since the outlay per ton, or per foot, remained approximately the same. Flatboats less than 75 tons typically required a crew of five, including the captain, who was paid $75 for the four-week trip. The others received $40 each. A 100-ton boat was manned by a crew of six, at $40 each, plus a captain, who earned $100 for the trip. A 150-ton flatboat was manned by a captain, who was paid $125, a second-in-command, paid $75, and eight other crewmen, each paid $40.

---

[20] See ibid., pp. 384–89 and Serial set 619, Senate Exec. Doc. 42, 114.
[21] See Palmer (1932): 69, Figure 2 in Chapter 2 above, and Appendix B, Table B–1.
[22] The sources to the cost estimates are given in Appendix E.

Table 9. Average Costs of Flatboats in the Louisville–New Orleans Trade, 1810–60

Period	Average flatboat capacity (tons)	Average flatboat cost (at $1.50 per ton)	Average crew size	Average total wages	Average food costs	Wharfage charges	Average total costs
1810–19	30	$45	5	$235	$5	$6	$291
1820–29	41	62	5	235	6	6	309
1830–39	56	84	5	235	9	10	338
1840–49	93	140	7	340	12	10	502
1850–60	146	219	10	520	22	15	776

Source: Appendix E.

To determine the average costs of food we accepted declarations in the existing literature that flatboatmen consumed a rather hardy diet. Therefore, we have assumed that the diet was approximately that of a male adult slave in the antebellum South.[23] These rations are converted to dollar values by using Berry's Cincinnati prices.[24]

Wharfage charges at New Orleans were of some small importance, as indicated in Table 9.

Flatboat freight rates normally were less than downstream steamboat rates. The risk of loss was higher by flatboat, and their slower pace may have encouraged preference for the steamboat, at least for perishable commodities. There may also have been some qualitative differences in the services, but, aside from these slight variations, it seems reasonable to assume that traders would have been impartial between shipping by the steamboat or the flatboat for the same overall expense of insurance and freight. Given this assumption average, long-run rates can be derived by subtracting from the steamboat freight rates, the difference between the (higher) insurance costs by flatboat and those by steam. Though this procedure would be inadequate for obtaining monthly rates, it serves well as a means of viewing the long-run trend of flatboat rates.

Our estimates of these average rates are given in Table 10, along with our estimates of revenues and costs. Because of the longer shipment time by flats, plus possible qualitative factors, and other reasons indicated in Appendix E, these rates are biased upward. Consequently, the revenue estimates, which are

Table 10. Average Flatboat Freight Rates, Revenues, and Costs in the Louisville–New Orleans Trade, 1810–60

Period	Average flatboat freight rates ($/ton)	Average flatboat revenue (including salvage revenues)	Average flatboat costs[a]
1810–19	$16.55	$501	$291
1820–29	10.50	436	309
1830–39	8.65	492	338
1840–49	5.20	498	502
1850–60	5.55	832	776

Source: Appendix E.

[a]From Table 9.

[23] Fogel and Engerman (1974), vol. 2: 97, gives the per capita food consumption of slaves in 1860. This diet is shown to have a higher caloric value than the diet of the average person in 1879.

[24] Berry (1943), Table 16: 183 and 545–48. Converting the Fogel and Engerman diet into dollar values gives an 1860 cost of about $30 per person per year. The differences in costs for the other years are due to price changes.

the product of the rates and average flatboat capacity,[25] are also biased upward. In addition to the cargo earnings, salvage revenues from the sale of the boat at New Orleans resulted in modest revenues of approximately $6, 1810–29, and $8, $14, and $22 in each respective decade from 1830 to 1860.

The larger "apparent profits" earned by flatboat operators in the early decades of the nineteenth century should be interpreted cautiously. As noted, the estimates are crude, especially for revenues that have been deliberately overstated and therefore lead to exaggerated differences between revenues and costs. Moreover, it is doubtful that such excess of revenues can be termed profits in the usual sense, since a large part of the excess (perhaps all of it) was in the form of opportunity cost payments to the flatboat owners for time and money spent on the return trip upriver.

Before the era of steam, returning flatboat owners faced several months of difficult overland travel. For some this meant neglecting their farms or some other occupation during critical periods, such as the planting season. Originally, these opportunity costs were so high as probably to preclude any excess profits. As Odle reports, "the farmer-merchants found that their marketing trips were arduous and that they lost valuable time needed for spring planting."[26] As late as 1844 farmers in Knox County, Indiana were complaining that

The uncertainty of the time of shipment, and the short period during each season [of the spring rise of the Wabash River], have prevented the merchants of this country embarking as regular dealers in the produce business. The consequence has been, the farmers have, much to their injury, been compelled to ship their own products . . . and too often does it happen that they lose one year's cropping in disposing of the cropping of the previous year, and that, too, at a ruinous sacrifice, both in their health and their fortunes.[27]

After the arrival of the steamboat the opportunity costs of the return trip, though not entirely eliminated, were substantially reduced. This is consistent with our estimates in Table 10, and, given the opportunity costs involved and the general overstatement in our estimates of earnings, we conclude that only normal or very limited excess profits were being earned in flatboating from 1810 to 1840. By the late 1840s flatboats were probably unprofitable on an average, after account is taken of the opportunity costs of the return trek, and the decline of flatboating on the Louisville–New Orleans route was unmistakably evident after the mid-1840s.[28] Though some flatboats probably

---

[25] Flatboats typically carried a full load of freight downstream. See Hall (1848a): 204, for example.

[26] Odle (1952), pt. V: 249–50.

[27] Ibid.

[28] See Table 4, Chapter 2 for data on the annual arrivals of flatboats at New Orleans. According to the New Orleans, *Register of Flatboats* some flatboats apparently were in

earned revenues sufficient to cover their costs, this was the exception by the late 1840s. The steamboat had won the day, and the lumbering old flat was disappearing from the wide brown highway of the Mississippi.

THE PROFITABILITY OF KEELBOATS

It is simply impossible to derive any systematic estimates of keelboat costs, because the handful of data cannot support them. However, in Table 11 we set out two sets of estimates calculated as upperbound and lowerbound measures, which may be viewed as extremes which probably bracket the average costs of operation.

Keelboat freight rates were generally slightly below those of steamboats, but we have assumed parity prior to 1820. This upward bias is maintained for the 1820s as well by using *upperbound* rates of $1.25 per 100 pounds upstream and 62.5¢ per 100 pounds downstream, as quoted in *Wholesale Prices Current at Cincinnati.* [29]

On the Louisville—New Orleans route keelboats reportedly averaged around 100 tons capacity and, typically, made one round trip per year. [30] Before 1820 a fully loaded vessel therefore yielded an annual revenue of $12,000, of which $10,000 was earned on the upstream trip. Such revenues for a fully utilized keelboat would have approximated the upperbound cost estimate ($11,446). Consequently, keelboats were probably earning at least normal profits before the age of steam.

We have seen how the success of the first steamboats led to a boom in their construction; as total carrying capacity increased, freight rates predictably declined. Since steamboats served the same upstream functions as keelboats, relative efficiency would determine which survived. By the early 1820s, upstream freight rates had fallen so drastically (viz., from $5.00 per hundred lbs. to less than $1.25 per hundred lbs.) that even if our low cost estimate were the correct one, the total revenues of $3,750 were still shy of

---

operation as late as 1870. The destruction of steamboats during the Civil War was accompanied by a temporary jump in freight rates, which would explain this extension, due primarily to short-run rather than long-run economic forces. The diversion of total freight from flats to steam also altered its composition considerably. For instance, during a five-month period of 1843–44, flatboats were estimated to have carried 32 percent of the pork, 38 percent of the whiskey, and 81 percent of the flour shipped from Cincinnati to New Orleans. Hunter (1949): 56. For an average of the 1850s it was estimated that they carried less than 1 percent of the pork, 6 percent of the whiskey, and only 26 percent of the flour. Ibid., p. 56. Ranked by value per unit of weight these commodities are pork, whiskey, and flour. Toward the end of the ante-bellum period flatboats arriving at New Orleans carried mostly coal from Pittsburgh and hay from Indiana. Serial set 2552, House Exec. Doc. 6, pt. II, 222.

[29] Wholesale Prices Current at Cincinnati, Ohio (1823): 3.

[30] Gould (1951): 67.

Table 11. High and Low Cost Estimates of Operating a Keelboat in the Louisville–New Orleans Trade before the Civil War

	High estimates ($)	Low estimates ($)
Wages		
Downstream	800	300
In port	800	300
Upstream	8,000	2,625
Captain	600	250
Food	246	134
Depreciation	800	200
Repairs	200	200
Totals	11,446	4,009

Notes:
1 Depreciation was calculated assuming a minimum life span of 5 years and maximum life span of 20 years. The initial construction cost of a keelboat on the Louisville–New Orleans route was $4,000 (100 tons).

2. For the wage bills, the upperbound cost estimate assumes a crew of 50 men for the upstream journey and 20 for the downstream journey. The lowerbound estimate assumes crews of 35 and 12 for the upstream and downstream voyages respectively. In each case there was a captain in addition to the crew. Upperbound wages were assumed to be $40 per month for crewmen and $100 per month for the captain. The downstream trip was assumed to take one month, with 5 months spent on the upstream voyage. Lowerbound wages were assumed to be $25 for crewmen and $50 per month for the captain. Again the downstream voyage was assumed to take one month, with the upstream voyage taking 3 months. In both cases the keelboat was assumed to spend one month in port, with only its downstream crew retained.

3. Food costs were calculated in the same manner as for flatboats.

4. Repairs were estimated at 5 percent of the original cost of the boat.

covering the out-of-pocket expenses of wages, food, and repairs (see Table 11). Keelboats had reached the end of their run on the major trunk route of the Mississippi.

It should be noted that this demise of keelboating on the Louisville–New Orleans route was due primarily to the lowering of rates for upstream freight, which critically affected their profits. For example, had downstream rates remained unchanged at $1.00 per hundred lbs. in the early 1820s, the yearly total revenue received by a keelboat still would have fallen short of the low cost estimate because of the lower upstream rates. Putting it in another way, keelboats were primarily in the business of carrying merchandise upstream, and before 1820 approximately five-sixths of their total revenues were earned on the northbound passage. When more efficient steamboats competed for upstream freight, keelboats had to yield the right of way.

After the 1820s, smaller keelboats continued to ply their way, but only along the shallower waters of the upper Mississippi, Ohio, and Missouri, and their tributaries, where steamboats could not yet intrude.

THE BACKHAULAGE PROBLEM

With the continuing rise of steamboat capacity, a backhaulage problem began to appear, and this grew more and more serious during the late forties and throughout the fifties. As shown in Table 7, upstream rates were typically higher than those downstream, but by the 1840s this rate structure reversed itself. We have suggested that normal returns overall were fairly common, but excess capacity on the upstream voyage would logically have induced greater competition for upstream freight and fluctuations in shipping rates.

In that steamboats earned a normal rate of return after 1840 (that total costs, including normal profits, equaled total revenues),[31] it is possible to estimate the utilized volume of upstream carrying capacity as 44 percent for the 1840s and only 12 percent for the 1850s. Clearly by the 1850s and possibly by the late 1840s this unused space on the upstream voyage was a special concern to owners.

The emergence of the backhaulage problem was actually a testimonial to the changing role of the steamship in the development of the West. Initially the new vessels had followed in the wake of the old keelboats, engaging primarily in the business of carrying merchandise upstream. This freight was typically high in value and low in bulk compared to downstream freight, and the growth in its volume did not keep pace with the expanding carrying capacity of the steamboat fleet. As a result, the owners came to depend more and more on downstream revenues to cover larger shares of the round-trip costs until, by the last two ante-bellum decades, a steamboat's main source of livelihood was the transport of agricultural produce out of the West.

ECONOMIC CONCENTRATION

After this look at the competitive character of the market for Mississippi River transportation services, it is now possible to answer the interesting question of why the steamboat transport industry did not spawn a class of financial and industrial tycoons (capitalists) comparably to those who manipulated railroads in the era that followed, and who waxed prosperous in other industries during the last decades of the nineteenth century.

Capital "immobilities" to use a term by Lance Davis,[32] distorted the pattern of growth in the United States throughout the entire nineteenth century, but they exerted the greatest impact in the decades after the Civil War, when the stars of such financial capitalists as Carnegie and Rockefeller

---

[31] See Chapter 4, Table 14.

[32] According to Lance Davis, "Capital can be said to be immobile if savers are unwilling or unable to make their accumulations available to capital users whose activities yield the highest return." Davis (1967): 582.

were rising. Immobilities grew more pressing as the demand increased for external finance. This phenomenon, according to Lance Davis, was in turn due "to the shift of industry from the East to the West, to a series of technological innovations in manufacturing that increased both total capital requirements and the minimum size of initial investment and to new develop-ments in agriculture that required greater amounts of capital equipment." [33] The rapid rise in demand for long-term finance meant ultimately a deperson-alization of capital—that is, capital generally could no longer be provided in sufficient amounts by a proprietor's personal funds or even by the pooled resources of two or three partners in a business venture. Short of formalized capital markets, such long-term external finance was primarily met through the intervention of financial entrepreneurs whose personal contacts or excep-tional business acumen allowed them to move capital across industrial and geographical lines.

In the early days, capital requirements in the West had been met almost entirely from limited local sources, but two major exceptions to this rule occurred before the Civil War. Partly from eastern savers but largely from abroad, funds had moved to the West in the 1830s and again in the 1850s in response to large-scale demands for long-term finance to build western canals and railway systems. Although the steamboat industry did not share in these capital inflows directly, it no doubt benefited from lower interest rates resulting from such an influx of capital.

For its direct needs, the steamboat industry required relatively small initial investments to enter the market. Financing could remain primarily local and was usually concentrated in river towns. Any movements of eastern capital in this direction were generally negligible in amount, and limited to the whole-sale, commission, and forwarding merchants who were "parties at interest" and principal users of steamboat transport services. Some additional finances were supplied by farmers, by steamboat captains and agents, by builders and insurance agents, and from retained earnings.[34] In 1851 one contemporary source stated that "The greater portion of steamboat stock (say two-thirds) is owned on board by officers, on shore by boat-builders, by boat-store keepers, and by engine builders. . . . The other portion of stock is principally owned by commission-merchants, or by persons who wish to place relatives as officers on boats. There are but few instances of persons holding steamboat stock for the purpose of making money, independent of other interest."[35] In short, the methods of finance differed little from those typical of other business enterprises in the West, and with comparatively low capital require-

---

[33] Ibid., p. 583.
[34] Hunter (1949):357–61.
[35] Serial set 619, Senate Exec. Doc. 42, 119.

ments for the purchase and operation of steamboats, financial consideration
were not a major barrier to entry into the industry.

One possibility for monopoly in the steamboat industry appeared before
the Civil War. To review the background, the first steamboat to operate or
the western rivers was the *New Orleans,* owned by Robert Fulton and Robert
Livingston. Before building this boat, the two men had sought to protect
their investment by obtaining exclusive steam navigation rights from all the
states bordering the Ohio and Mississippi rivers.[36] Although only Louisiana
acceded to their request, that one grant could have ensured effective control
of navigation on the Ohio and Mississippi rivers, since New Orleans was the
principal transhipment point for surplus western agricultural produce des
tined both for the eastern seaboard cities and for foreign countries.

The first interlopers into Louisiana waters to test the monopoly grant
came in 1815 from a Brownsville group headed by Daniel French and Henry
M. Shreve. They had entered the business on the Ohio River in 1813. Under
Shreve's command the *Enterprise* sailed to New Orleans, where it was seized
thus beginning a series of legal skirmishes. The trial was held in 1816, and the
ruling was that the territorial legislature had exceeded its authority to grant
such monopoly rights. Later suits brought in the Federal District Court in
New Orleans in 1817 were dismissed on the grounds that the court lacked
jurisdiction. At this point both Fulton and Livingston were dead, and their
heirs apparently gave up the fight.

The failure of Fulton and Livingston to gain exclusive navigation rights
deprived them of any legal grounds to restrict others from entering the river
transportation market via steamboats. And since initial capital requirement
were so small, it was obviously impossible for the two men (or anyone else
to bar entry by effecting a control of all the diverse sources of capital. Had
their claim been upheld in the courts, Fulton, Livingston, and their heir
clearly might have been among the first financial giants of American industry
But as conditions stood, the steamboat business simply offered no opportuni
ties for huge monopoly profits.

The failures of Fulton and Livingston to achieve a monopoly did not stop
efforts by others to restrict competition. All subsequent attempts, however
involved voluntary agreements rather than legislative means and were ineffec
tive for lack of government backing and effective control.

Apparently, the first attempt at voluntary monopolization was by a group
of keelboat owners in Pittsburgh and came just as the impact of steamboa
competition was beginning to make itself felt. In 1819 the Western Naviga
tion and Insurance Company was formed, with the avowed purposes to
remedy the defects of individual keelboating enterprises by providing regula

---

[36] The Fulton and Livingston activities are described in some detail by Thompson
(1956): 28–40; also see, Hunter (1949): 8–14.

ervice at all stages of the river and to prevent the extreme fluctuations of freight rates that had marred previous seasons. However, when a number of independent boatmen refused to join the association and charged it with attempting to monopolize the entire carrying trade of the Ohio River and its tributaries, the enterprise ran aground within a few weeks.

All subsequent attempts to restrict competition were by steamboat owners and operators, beginning in 1825 when some thirty-odd owners at Louisville adopted a uniform method of charging freight on barreled goods. Somewhat later, in the fall of 1828, the owners of boats operating upstream from Cincinnati reached some form of organization. Unfortunately, little is known about these efforts except that they were short lived.

The first significant steamboat combination, called the Ohio and Mississippi Mail Line, was formed in 1832. As Hunter describes it:

The plan and purposes of this organization were announced in a long advertisement published in the newspapers. In the eagerness of the business community to exploit the new mode of transportation, ran this statement, more steamboats had been built than could at times find employment. Rates were forced to an unprofitable level, and in the effort to get business and to reduce costs many unfortunate practices grew up: overloading, running under unsafe conditions of navigation, racing and driving machinery beyond its strength. As a result many accidents occurred, attended by heavy loss of life and property. "Deeply sensible of these evils, growing out of the violence of competition, a number of principal steamboat proprietors suggested a union of these conflicting interests," continued the advertisement, "by which the public would be better served, and the owners of this property, at the same time, be more fitly remunerated." Among the advantages of this arrangement to the public, its promoters emphasized greater safety, prompt and regular departures and uniformity of rates. The names of officers, directors, business committee and agents were announced, a mail contract was secured and by the spring of 1833 the enterprise seems to have been fairly launched. . . . No further reference to the line appeared after June 1833. If the *Ohio and Mississippi Mail Line* . . . did not endure long it was the forerunner of many similar steamboat combinations in later years.[37]

In 1843 it was reported that the masters of steamboats running from New Orleans to Louisville and Cincinnati had agreed upon a rate tariff, and reports of combinations on the upper Mississippi and Missouri rivers to control rates are found as early as 1845.[38] Hunter observes that

rivalry between competing lines and packets became pronounced in many trades during the late 'forties and the evils of competition in the succeeding years were a subject of increasing comment. By the middle of the next

---

[37] Hunter (1933–34): 97–98.
[38] Ibid., footnote 127, p. 96.

decade, excessive competition had become a principal concern of steamboat men and combinations began to appear with great frequency and in a variety of forms. . . . Steamboats operating in a given trade established lines and alloted sailing days, made agreements to "load in turn" or adopted minimum rate tariffs. Lines competing in the same or overlapping trades reached understandings as to rates. There were "marine" and "captains" benevolent associations . . . designed to include all boats operating in the principal trades from a given port.[39]

The combinations operating within a single trade were the most numerous and effective, and the usual form of such combination was a "line," generally comprising the largest and fastest boats in a trade. Under the agreement the boats would sail on specified days and would share such services as wharf boats, agencies, and advertising; otherwise they operated independently. One of the famous and successful lines of this type, the Pittsburgh and Cincinnati Packet Line, was established in 1842 and survived for a decade. But even where a line existed it was frequently true that some of the regular packets were holdouts, and plenty of transients were always ready to enter the trade if a lucrative situation presented itself.

Another form of intratrade combination involved the practice of loading in turn. By this arrangement only one boat at a time was loaded at a given port, in the order of its arrival, and it remained at the dock until a paying cargo had been put aboard. Such agreements usually included minimum rate tariffs as well, but did not specify regular departure times nor, necessarily, sharing of services. One of the earliest instances of loading in turn occurred in the spring of 1855 when the owners of steamboats at Cincinnati running in the New Orleans trade practiced such an arrangement successfully for season.

The marine or captains' associations—more ambitious than the other groups—attempted to harmonize the interests of steamboatmen operating in all trades from a given port. Specifically, their goals were to establish minimum tariffs for all trades, to preclude the undercutting of freight rates and occasionally to act on other matters of common interest, such as wages and conditions of employment for crews. Such associations were first established in Pittsburgh, Cincinnati, and Louisville in 1853.

Attempts to form combinations are often observed in the wake of adverse market conditions, as viewed by industry participants, and agreements by the Lousiville owners in 1825 may well have been a response to the generally poor economic conditions of the period. No obvious external conditions explain the 1828 and 1832 attempts, but they do suggest that the industry had achieved a long-run competitive equilibrium by that time. A new rash of agreements crops up in the early forties, the next period of generally poor

economic conditions, and a further intensification in the early fifties probably resulted from poor navigation conditions and a growing competition
from railroads, at least in the Ohio valley.

In any case, such sporadic attempts to combine and restrict trade did not
alter the general characteristic of keen competition in the western river
freight business during the ante-bellum years.[40] Low capital requirements
minimized the financial difficulties of entering the business, and many individuals, either alone or in partnership with others, could readily launch their
ventures during the high tides of anticipated profits.

Although the history of western river transportation is thus replete with
attempts to establish monopolies or otherwise restrict competition, it was
fortunate for the general public that these attempts invariably failed. Such
failures epitomize the subtle interplay of market forces that takes place in
situations where ease of entry is not cut off by government regulations nor by
other considerations.

---

[40] It is interesting to contrast these atomistic market characteristics with the formation of marketing associations among contemporary boatmen on the Erie Canal; see Odle
1952), pt. V: 248–52. His descriptions reveal that these associations offered gains in
efficiency in marketing and handling cargos, but he gives no evidence of price manipula-
tion or attempts to block entry. It would be of interest to discover whether or not such
attempts were made and, if so, whether or not they were successful. In any case, similar
associations on the western rivers did not materialize in the ante-bellum years.

4

EXPANSION
ALONG THE TRIBUTARIES

"The steamboat *Atlas* started on Friday last from Ditto's landing
on her first trip to Knoxville, toward which place she is now
wending her way through the "Suck" and over the "Boiling Pot,"
a passage which has, heretofore, been deemed impossible to be
performed by any being or thing except the sturgeon and the cat-
fish."

A Huntsville newspaper, 1828

As settlers pouring over the trans-Appalachian barrier pushed the frontie
of settlement ever westward, they brought vast expanses of virgi
country into productive use. Commercial centers sprang up along th
path they followed, and originally the most successful of these entrepôts wer
located on the major rivers, mainly along the Ohio and Mississippi river
downstream from Pittsburgh and St. Louis.[1] Since these portions of the rive
system generated the greatest demand for river transportation services an
offered the best conditions for river navigation, they came to be know
commercially as the trunk river trades, and it was here that the steamboat
like its more primitive forebears, the flatboat and keelboat, was first intro
duced.

Steamboat entry on all the major trunk routes was accomplished by 1820
and scattered evidence on the number of arrivals at the major terminals show
that early in that decade steamboating had expanded notably throughout th
trunk river trades. For instance, steamboat arrivals at Pittsburgh were 41 i
1823 and 126 in 1824; in Cincinnati arrivals totaled 360 in 1825; a
Louisville, 196 in 1823 and 300 in 1824; at New Orleans, 198 in 1820 an

---

[1] This excludes the cities of the Great Lakes basin.

·02 in 1825; and at St. Louis, 57 for the nine months ending July 1, 1826.[2]

This rapid growth of steamboating on the trunk routes was spurred by the initial opportunities for bonanza profits, which (as we observed for the Louisville–New Orleans trade) was reduced by 1830 to normal levels because of rapid entry and competitive forces.

The evidence just cited on the early and parallel activity of steamboating on all the trunk routes suggests that overall levels of profits would have followed the same general pattern as in the Louisville–New Orleans trade. The market and navigational conditions were similar on all the major routes, as attested by the findings of our comparative analysis of the operating characteristics of steamboats on the various runs.[3] It would be inaccurate, however, to generalize these findings to the entire system of western river transportation. Significantly different problems of navigation and operation were encountered when the growth of population and the regional development finally demanded extension of the steamboat services up the backwater rivers.

EXTENSION OF STEAMBOATING

Steamboating on the tributaries was a slow starter in contrast to activity on the trunk routes, where the new technology had encountered instant welcome and fairly rapid growth almost from the beginning. There are several possible reasons why the tributary routes were established much later and grew more slowly. The pattern of settlement is one of these. The Mississippi valley was coming into its own during this period, and with plenty of good agricultural land along its major waterways settlement tended to lag further upstream.

This explanation is most valid for the western part of the region, linked together by the upper Mississippi and Missouri rivers and their tributaries. For instance, although St. Paul had first been reached by steamboat in 1823, "in the next twenty years the steamboats running in this part of the river were small in size, few in number, and irregular in operation."[4] What early steamboating activity did occur in these areas was in response to the fur trade and the government's need to transport troops and military supplies. Subsequently, the development of a lead trade from Galena greatly stimulated steamboat operation on the Mississippi above St. Louis. Not until the rapid settlement of the western part of the region in the 1850s did steamboats

---

[2] Hunter (1949), Table 2: 644.
[3] See Appendix F, Tables F–3 and F–4, and the related discussion. The analysis is based on 1850 census reports for forty-five steamboats that called at Louisville. Twenty-two of the boats were reported as being in the Louisville–New Orleans trade. Another nine were reported running in four trunk routes. The remaining fourteen boats were spread over five tributary trades. Together they represent roughly 7 percent of the number and 10 percent of the tonnage of all western river steamboats in that year.
[4] Hunter (1949): 45.

operate on many of those tributaries, or venture onto the Minnesota, Wiscon sin, St. Croix, Chippewa, Black Rock, and Des Moines rivers.

The evolution of steamboating along the network of the Missouri followed a similar pattern. Five boats were in operation along the lower reaches of the Missouri in 1831, and by 1842 this number had grown to 26.[5] However except for the requirements of trappers and the military, the activity was generally confined to the lower portions of the river, partly because of upstream turbulence. The Montana gold rush of the 1860s provided a rousing incentive to overcome these obstacles, and steamboating then expanded above Sioux City.

Presumably, the natural hazards of rapids, shoals, and other obstacles were also responsible for the slow arrival of steamboating along some of the tributaries in Ohio and Kentucky, where settlement had occurred at an early date. The impact of navigational dangers is highlighted by a comparison of the development of steamboating on two major tributaries of the Ohio River—the Cumberland and the Tennessee.

The first steamboat to travel up the safer Cumberland to Nashville was the *General Jackson,* a 142-ton vessel that arrived in 1818.[6] Within a few years arrivals were a common occurrence, and vessels regularly traveled between Nashville and New Orleans, Louisville, and elsewhere. The busiest section was from the Ohio to Nashville, a distance of about 200 miles, but the river was navigable for small steamboats for another 120 miles to Carthage, and during brief periods of high water small steamboats could reach Burnside, yet another 200 miles further upstream.

Quite different was the story for the crochety Tennessee River. Although steamboat had first ventured into its waters in 1817, a full year before the *General Jackson* steamed up the Cumberland, it was not until 1821 that vessel reached even 260 miles upstream on the Tennessee to Florence, the head of navigation for the lower river.[7] The principal peril to further navigation lay in treacherous Muscle Shoals. There passage was first accomplished in 1828 by the 162-ton *Atlas.* The indomitable little craft was welcomed in Knoxville with a lively celebration and a gift of $640 from elated citizens; but in spite of such encouragement it soon left and never returned.[8] Thereafter passage over the Shoals remained infrequent and was attempted only during periods of very high water. As a general custom, or small vessel was maintained in operation above the Shoals throughout the 1830s to make through-passage unnecessary; over the next two decades the number increased until seven or eight were in service by 1850.[9] These were

[5] Ibid.
[6] Wooldridge (1890): 303–4.
[7] Hunter (1949): 40.
[8] Campbell (1932): 13–17.
[9] Ibid., pp. 39–43.

essels of less than 100 tons, and the lengthy but obdurate Tennessee
emained only a minor avenue of steamboat commerce throughout the
period.[10]

Along other tributaries of the Ohio, the rate of steamboat expansion was
generally somewhere between these two extremes. The navigation of the
Wabash was hampered by the presence of rapids and other obstructions;[11]
the Green, Kentucky, Barren, Scioto, Miami, Licking, Big Sandy, and
Kanawha induced only minor and irregular steamboating activity until the
830s, and even then it was limited primarily to high-water periods.[12]

In most cases the effect of obstructions and navigational hazards was to
delay rather than to prevent the extension of steamboat services. Probably
the single most important factor in conquering the obstacles to navigation
was the change in design of steamboats, especially a reduction in draft. Wide
variations in draft for vessels of similar size are found during this ante-bellum
period, although it is difficult to find measures of the reductions undertaken.
For example, the *Magnet* (150 tons), built in 1822, had a light draft of 42
inches while the *Velocipede* (109 tons), built two years earlier, had a light
draft of only 24 inches.[13] Specific information is not available on these
changes in draft, but we do have a reasonable proxy in figures showing the
depth of hull. This represents the maximum loaded draft and may be taken as
broadly indicative of the light draft, which generally ranged between 0.35 and
0.45 of the hull depth.[14] The average depth of hull for steamboats measuring
between 150 and 175 tons in various years was as follows:

Year	Average tonnage	Average depth[15] of hull (ft.)
1818	157	7.68
1827	161	6.80
1835	159	5.53
1841	168	5.12
1847	168	4.78
1851	162	4.53
1860	166	4.35

The above figures indicate, then, a 43 percent reduction in draft during the
ante-bellum period of which almost two-thirds had been achieved by 1835.
The obstacles to navigation on the tributaries had thus become less serious

[10]Hunter, (1949): 41.
[11] Ibid.
[12] Ibid.
[13] Hunter (1949), Table 6: 647.
[14] Ibid.
[15] Ibid., Table 8: 652.

over time, leading to a gradual expansion of steamboat operations on the backwaters.

One more reason for the delay in steamship progress up the tributaries was undoubtedly the early profitability of trading along the trunk routes, where returns on investment remained high until the 1830s. Before giving up such a relatively easy harvest, any steamboat owner would have taken a long, hard second look at the natural and economic hazards of pushing into the far-back country. Whatever the reasons for the lag, its net effect was to extend the plodding and useful life of both keelboating and flatboating for many more years.

OPERATING CHARACTERISTICS OF TRIBUTARY STEAMBOATS

The natural differences between trunk and tributary rivers account for a logical diversity of operating characteristics once steamboats made their way up the new channels. We can only wish for a large body of data which would allow comparisons among tributary routes as well as between trunk and tributary operations. No such wealth of information is available, possibly due to the relatively small scale of most tributary routes, but we are fortunate in having data on a sample of steamboats which was compiled as part of the 1850 census and is given in Appendix F. The data cover 31 trunk vessels and 14 tributary steamboats; since the latter operated exclusively on five Ohio River tributaries in the Louisville area, the figures may not be fully representative of all steamboats plying the backwaters. However, as the best statistics available they constitute the basis for much of our analysis.

As indicated earlier, navigation on the tributaries was normally more hazardous than on the trunk routes. Moreover, climatic conditions badly curtailed the length of operation each year: certain points on the rivers were simply impassable except during flood stages, and in the northern reaches the first freeze could clamp the route shut for months. For instance, in the upper Mississippi trades the season typically closed from November until the spring thaw, which near St. Paul was usually in April. In addition, periods of low water in August and September made the larger boats unusable and subjected even smaller boats to delays on sandbars and reefs where the crews had to engage in lighting the cargo to get free. On the upper Mississippi:

The chief difficulties in navigating . . . low water were the cost of lighting the cargo over the rapids and time spent on sandbars in the river and the reefs on the rapids. "The river has risen 15 inches in the last 48 hours," noted an editor in the spring of 1847. "Several boats have been stuck fast on the rapids for a number of days. They will now be able to get off, likely." During low water the rapids at times became so treacherous that even the cost of lighting did not always save the steamboat from being grounded indefinitely or from being sunk by some hidden rock. In July, 1846, the *Saint Anthony* struck a rock on the Lower Rapids and was sunk. The *War Eagle* experienced the same misfortune on the Upper Rapids, but was raised after much difficulty and towed to Rock Island for repairs. When two such accidents occurred within the space of a week, the larger boats usually withdrew from the trade and awaited a more favorable stage of water.[16]

These conditions restricted steamboat operations to about six months or fewer on an average, and the level of freight rates fluctuated inversely to river conditions.[17] Similar cycles of freight rates and river conditions occurred on the trunk rivers as well, but there the navigation season was approximately nine months by 1830.[18]

Because of the comparative thinness of trade and more hazardous river conditions, especially during periods of low water, the average size of vessels operating on the tributaries was notably smaller than on the trunk routes. Most of the maiden ventures up the tributaries and backwaterways were made in vessels that were small even by the standards of the period, and the early regular boats on these waters were commonly less than 200 tons. The differential in size remained in the late ante-bellum period when, as shown in Table 12, the average size of vessels on the tributaries was less than half of that on the trunk routes.

Table 12. Average Steamboat Operating Characteristics by Route Type in 1850

	Trunks	Tributaries
Size of vessel (tons)	381	149
Size of crew (men)	46	30
Men per 100 tons	12.9	20.5
Service life of vessel (years)	6.3	5.4

Source and notes: These are means from a sample of 45 steamboats, 31 of which were trunk vessels and 14 tributary vessels. All operated from Louisville. For a more detailed analysis of the data, see Appendix F, Table F–5. As noted in Table F–5, the differences in each of these means are statistically significant, except for the difference in the service life.

---

[16] Petersen (1937): 231.

[17] For a discussion of freight rate fluctuations and changing river conditions on the upper Missouri, see Petersen (1937): 231–33. Of course, the actual number of days of steamboat operation varied geographically, being lowest in the far northern waters and on the smaller tributaries, which were more subject to freezing. See Petersen (1933): 453.

[18] See Appendix C, page 144, and Appendix F, Table F–5. On any particular route smaller vessels typically had longer-than-average periods of navigation, and the evidence in Appendix F, Table F–5, shows the "tributary boats" to have had a period of operation of 9.9 months in 1850, compared to 8.9 months for the larger vessels on the trunks. This difference, however, is explained by the tributary boats moving to the trunk routes to operate after the season closed on the tributaries.

The same table shows that vessels on the tributaries typically carried only two-thirds the crew of those on the trunks. Nevertheless, labor requirements per measured ton were considerably higher on the lesser rivers, and steam boating operations were significantly more labor intensive there.

The more perilous conditions of navigation on the tributaries are also vividly though statically portrayed in Table 12. The average service life of vessels on the trunk rivers in 1850 was 6.3 years, compared to 5.4 years for vessels plying the hazardous tributaries. Additionally, the evidence on insurance costs leaves little doubt regarding the incidence of losses: relative to their values per ton, vessels on major rivers paid less than one-half the insurance premiums levied on backwater boats.[19]

Were steamboats on the tributaries less efficient, then, than those on the trunk rivers? Comparisons of labor requirement per ton, length of service life and insurance costs per ton all favor the trunk boats. In addition, vessels generally could not sustain high speeds on the tributaries and could not operate at night, except along channels familiar to the pilots. Lastly, on many tributaries crews had to stop to gather their own fuel, whereas fuel stations were available for quick stopovers on the trunk routes. Of course, such evidence on input, or operation, is only suggestive, and we cannot properly assess differences in efficiency without additional evidence on output, or product; but it is unlikely that tributary vessels carried more passengers and freight per measured ton than did trunk river vessels, as we discuss below.

More decisive evidence, however, is obtained from data on freight rates per ton mile, which were distinctly higher on the tributaries than on the trunks. Table 13 shows that between 1840 and 1850 freight rates between Louisville and selected tributaries were three to four times higher than rates to New Orleans. These rate differences could not have resulted from higher wages or prices of other inputs, since these, taken together, were lower on an average on the tributaries. This leaves little doubt that trunk river vessels were more productive than those on the tributaries—a conclusion further supported by evidence from the 1850 manuscript census on freight revenues.[20] Though freight rates per ton mile on the tributaries were three or four times those on the trunk routes, freight revenues per measured ton were only twice as high. Thus tributary boats carried fewer ton miles of freight per measured ton than did trunk vessels. A similar picture, though based on more sketchy evidence, is found for passenger traffic.[21]

---

[19] Table 14 and Appendix F, Table F–5; also, see Serial set 619, Senate Exec. Doc. 42, 116–17, which gives steamboat freight insurance rates in 1849 for various major rivers and tributaries.

[20] Appendix F, Table F–5. Hunter concurs that steamboating on the tributaries was less efficient than on the trunks; see Hunter (1949): 377.

[21] Hunter (1949): 420.

Table 13. Typical Freight Rates between Louisville and Selected Trades, 1840–50

	River	Category	Cents/ton mile
Louisville to:			
Bowling Green	Barren	Tributary	1.943
Terre Haute	Wabash	Tributary	1.353
Florence	Tennessee	Tributary	1.733
Nashville	Cumberland	Tributary	1.382
New Orleans	Mississippi	Trunk	.444

Source: Hunter (1949): 659 and Appendix D, Table D–1.
Note: The Louisville–New Orleans rate is the downstream rate, which was typically higher than the upstream rate during that period.

It is also apparent that steamboats on the tributaries provided a less dramatic cost saving over the older technologies of keelboats and flatboats than happened on the trunk rivers. No quantitative evidence is available to determine the period of decline of flatboating on the tributaries, but it seems likely that the primitive flat-bottoms not only played a more important economic role but also persisted longer there than on the trunk rivers. As to keelboating, the evidence is still more persuasive; certainly it held its place longer on the tributaries than on the major rivers. Though keelboats had disappeared from the Louisville–New Orleans trade by the 1820s, they continued to work the rivers north of St. Louis until the mid-1840s, and their arrivals at St. Louis from the upper Mississippi were recorded as 108 in 1841, 88 in 1842, and 55 in 1843. After that date, arrivals were no longer categorized by type of craft.[22]

The tenacity of keelboating on the backwaters was due largely to the craft's functional advantages. We have already seen that the turbulent and obstacle-wracked tributaries presented risky challenges to steamboats, both economically and physically. But the spunky little keelboats, generally around 30 tons in size,[23] could much more easily navigate in periods of low water and in dangerous shallows. (On the other hand, they were probably less easy to handle and to power on the larger trunk rivers.) Another plus factor for keelboating in remote areas was that the typically scanty shipments could be accommodated without difficulty in smaller holds. For instance, Lass reports that on the upper Missouri: "As long as the fur trade was concentrated at Fort Union, there was no driving need to extend steamboating to the head of navigation. Most of the furs received at Fort Benton came in so late in the spring and in such meager quantities that it was much easier to ship them downstream to Fort Union by mackinaw than to try to navigate a

[22] Serial set 434, Senate Doc. 179, 29.
[23] See Table 1, chapter 2 for keelboat sizes.

steamboat between Fort Union and Fort Benton, the shallowest part of the Missouri."[24]

Paradoxically, the new technology of steamboating itself served to postpone the demise of the keelboat. On the upper Mississippi, the upper Missouri, and elsewhere it became a common practice for steamboats to tow keelboats on their upriver return. For instance, on the upper Mississippi "In 1841 the *Otter* . . . made fifteen trips from Galena to St. Louis, towing nine keelboats up the river during the season. . . . From 1841 to 1843 inclusive, the *Iowa* made a total of sixty-two trips, towed thirty-eight keelboats, and cleared $43,000 on freight and $28,000 on passengers."[25] Such services, of course, resulted in substantial savings in labor and capital to keelboat operators and increased their average number of yearly round trips.

The favor was returned when keelboats served to "light" steamboat cargo over shallow waters. The following advertisement in a Knoxville newspaper by Waller, French and Company illustrates this practice: "The steamboat *Harkaway* will commence regular trips between Knoxville and Decatur, Ala., early in next year and continue through the boating season. Having six keels (or lighters), some of which will at all times meet her at the principal obstructions, will enable her to ascend to this place on 30 inches of water, consequently goods shipped to this or intermediate points on our boat will not meet with the delay which has long interrupted our trade."[26] Such interdependence made the two technologies complementary to one another, as well as competitive, on the tributaries.

PROFITS ON THE TRIBUTARIES

The factors that put steamboating in a better position on major rivers than on tributaries in terms of costs and efficiency did not hold true in the case of profits. Quite the contrary! The legendary bonanza profits in western steamboating, which had ended in the 1830s on the main trunk routes, remained as a fact of life along the tributaries, even in the last decade of the ante-bellum period.

Table 14 puts the aspects of the case clearly. In each category, and for the total, costs on the tributaries were typically more than half of those on the trunk rivers, although the tributary boats were less than half the size. In general, then, costs on the tributaries were higher on a per ton basis, which is consistent with our preceding evidence on comparative levels of productivity. On the other hand, tributary boats earned relatively better revenues, especially on the carriage of freight, which almost matched that earned by the

---

[24] Lass (1962): 11.
[25] Petersen (1937): 236.
[26] Campbell (1932): 43.

Table 14. Average Annual Steamboating Revenues, Costs, and Profits by Route Type in 1850

	Trunk[b]	Tributaries[b]
Revenue:		
Freight	$29,980	$25,940
Passengers	30,020	15,950
Total Revenue	60,000	41,890
Costs:		
Depreciation	$ 5,506	$ 2,183
Wages	16,590	11,070
Insurance	3,366	2,690
Fuel	12,680	6,095
Provisions	10,620	5,923
General Expenses	5,213	2,730
Lockage	–	1,595
Total costs	53,970	32,290
Annual profits	$ 6,030	$ 9,600
Profit rate[a]	8.5%	23.6%

Source: See Appendix F.

[a]Annual profits divided by the sum of the original cost of the vessel and working capital for one round trip voyage.

[b]These values are means calculated, using data from the same sample of 45 steamboats used in Table 12.

much larger vessels on the trunk rivers. The average annual costs of tributary boats were 60 percent of those of trunk river boats, but owners received 70 percent as much revenue. What is more important, their annual profits were greater, despite the much smaller scale of operations and capital investment. In fact, vessels on the tributaries enjoyed a profit rate or return on investment approximately three times the "normal" level earned on an average on the trunk routes.

The significantly higher profit rate on the tributaries does not necessarily imply that competition was lacking. However, entry into steamboating was predictably slower on these rivers than on the trunk routes, primarily because of the much higher risks of operation and the irregularity of cargoes and trades, which made it difficult and costly to obtain information. The risks of operation on the tributaries are attested both by the higher insurance costs and by the higher salaries paid to pilots.[27] Consequently, the higher rates of

[27] According to Merrick (1909): 163, a pilot on the upper Mississippi earned $500 per month in 1857, more than three times the wage earned on the Louisville–New Orleans route (see Appendix C, Table C–2).

return which distinguished steamboat operation along the tributaries were in effect a bonus payment to entrepreneurship and to the taking of risks in small and irregular markets. Additional support is given by an 1855 contemporary steamboatman who alleged that under average conditions an annual profit of 30 percent on the original investment could be expected on the Missouri River, a figure which "cannot be considered . . . unreasonable or unproportioned to the risk incurred."[28]

[28] Hunter (1949): 386.

5

STEAMBOATS AND
THE GREAT PRODUCTIVITY SURGE

"At the time of its introduction in the West the steamboat was a
poorly coordinated combination of seagoing vessel and sta-
tionary engine, neither of which was suited to the use to which it
was put. Within twenty five years this makeshift affair had been
transformed into an instrument admirably adapted to the
requirements of Western river commerce."

Louis C. Hunter, 1949

Although the first steamboat on the Mississippi ended as a failure,[1] its
progeny established on western rivers a remarkable historical record
matched by few other transportation improvements. Chapter 3 told
how freight rates per hundred pounds from New Orleans to Louisville
plummeted from approximately $5.00 to 25 cents, between 1815 and 1860.
These upstream rates felt the greatest impact of the steamboat, but cost
reductions downstream were also highly significant, with rates declining from
$1.00 to just above 32 cents (per hundred pounds) over the same period.

Of course, the pioneering voyages had presaged this success when they
demonstrated, in however primitive a form, that steam power could one day
replace man's dependence on river currents for downstream passage and the
bruising efforts of hauling and rowing on the upstream return. Even more
important than the initial trial runs of the steamboat, however, were the
activities and efforts of widely separated individuals who were constantly
making improvements in the structure, handling, and operations of the new
craft. In combination, these efforts deserve a great share of credit for the cost
reductions in western river transportation. On the Louisville–New Orleans

[1] See Dayton (1925): 333–34.

59

route in a mere five years from 1815 to 1820 the rates per hundred pounds fell from approximately $5.00 upstream and $1.00 downstream to about $2.00 and 75 cents respectively.[2] However, because in terms of 1820 dollars the real rates in 1815 would have been only $3.12 and 62 cents respectively,[3] even that sharp reduction in the initial period was less drastic than the rate reductions that occurred during the era of improvements, from 1820 to 1860. This later decline (to 28 cents upstream and 39 cents downstream, in 1820 dollars) was a greater reduction both in absolute and relative terms.[4]

MEASURES OF THE PRODUCTIVITY ADVANCE

These cost reductions in real terms stemmed from a series of advances that boosted output relative to the combined inputs in the production of the new river services. To show this, we use two measures of change in total factor productivity.[5] The first compares the rate of growth of output (ton miles of freight and passengers carried, appropriately weighted) to a weighted index of the rate of growth of labor, capital, and other inputs. Our second measure compares the rate of growth of output prices (a weighted index of freight rates and passenger fares) to the rate of growth of a weighted index of prices paid to the factors of production, the labor, capital, and other inputs.

Fortunately, sufficiently good data are available to permit estimates of changes in steamboat productivity on the trunk rivers by both measures. Ideally, if the data were perfectly consistent, both measures should give identical results. Such precision in data is hard to come by, but the use of two measures does allow us to register a likely range of productivity advance.

Both measures are based on the assumption that the industry was competitive, and in effect we are tracing the movement from one long-run competitive equilibrium to another, in the years from 1815 to 1860. This assumption is consistent with the evidence given previously on the degree of competition among the various river craft before and after the arrival of the steamboat.

Lastly, our estimates, and the following analysis of the sources of change in productivity, are restricted to the route between Louisville and New Orleans. As we noted earlier, this not only was the main traffic artery in the trans-Appalachian West, but it offered the most complete data. Moreover, this route was typical of other trunk routes, and our interest here is to isolate the

---

[2] See Appendix D.

[3] The adjustments to real rates are made from the Warren-Pearson general price index, *U.S. Historical Statistics* (1960): 115.

[4] This finding is further supported below by the productivity estimates shown in Figure 3 (and Appendix G, Table G–1, Column 13, and G–2, column 15).

[5] See Appendix G for an algebraic statement of these two measures of productivity change.

effects of improvements on a "typical route," rather than to show differences among routes.

As shown in the previous chapter, despite the lower average price of labor and other inputs on the tributaries, the level of freight rates per ton mile was typically higher on the backwater ways and hazardous tributaries. Consequently, the level of total productivity was lower on these routes than on the trunk routes. In addition, the period of rate decline came later there. Nevertheless, despite differences in levels and periods of decline, the structure of rates on the rivers followed the same downward course throughout the ante-bellum years, and, except for the question of timing, there is little reason to suspect that the rates of change were atypical on the Ohio and Mississippi. Our estimates and the analysis of sources below are probably indicative of the history of productivity change on most of the western rivers in the ante-bellum period.[6]

Five-year moving averages of our two measures are given in Figure 3. Steamboat productivity from 1815 to 1860 advanced at an annual compounded rate of 4.9 percent or 4.1 percent, according to our two measures.[7] Either conclusion indicates an impressive rate of increase, especially in comparison with other important transportation media, such as canals, ocean shipping, and railroads. The available evidence suggests that the increase of steamboat productivity on western rivers between 1815 and 1860 exceeded that of any other major transportation medium over any equal time in the nineteenth century. For instance, the rate of advance of total factor productivity in U.S. railroads from 1839 to 1910 was approximately 3.5 percent (5.4 percent 1839–59).[8] Similarly, the rate of change in ocean shipping from 1814 to 1860 has been measured at 3.5 percent,[9] and the fall in real rates in

---

[6] Of course, certain particular findings for the Louisville–New Orleans route, such as the average ship size by decade, the average number of round trips per year per vessel by decade, and some other aspects are obviously not representative of all other routes, as noted in Chapter 4.

[7] It is important to note sources of possible bias. Government expenditures on river improvements between Louisville and New Orleans, though of modest size, did aid navigation, reduce accidents, and increase the output of steamboats. The resources used for these improvements should be included in our input index, but no appropriate way to include them is evident, and, in any case, when averaged over all steamboats, these costs, as shown in Chapter 7 below, were less than 2 percent of total costs. Consequently, this source of bias is insignificant. Of course, the selection of base-year weights inevitably adds other biases to the measures. In this case, however, the variations appear quite insignificant. Our choice of 1840–49 base-year weights is primarily because this was the period for which the data are the most complete, and it is near enough to the middle of the time period not to impose a large bias. To illustrate the sensitivity of the selection of weights, moving weights slightly change the above rates of 4.9 percent and 4.1 percent to 4.5 percent, and 4.6 percent, respectively, and 1815–19 base-year weights give rates of 3.8 percent and 5.2 percent, respectively.

[8] Fishlow (1966): 583–646.

[9] North (1968): 953–70; it should be noted that a comparison of deflated rates from

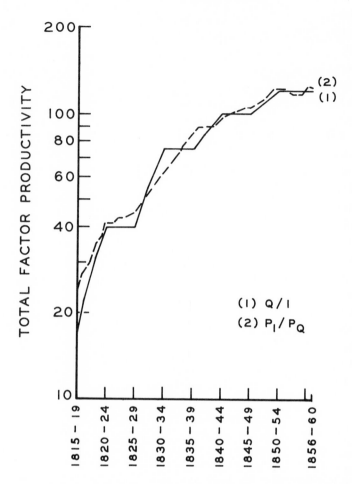

Fig. 3. Five-year moving averages of indexes of steamboat total productivity. *Source:* Appendix G.

the last half of the nineteenth century, when steam replaced sail, was less than during that earlier period.[10] We are unaware of any productivity studies for canals during the nineteenth century, but it is doubtful that canal productivity increased significantly and it may even have declined.[11]

The advance of steamboat productivity was not steady, however, and the great surge occurred before 1850. From the periods of 1815–19 to 1846–50

periods of war to peace probably overstates the true productivity increase, because ocean rates were unusually sensitive to international conflicts.

　[10] North (1966): 109–10.

　[11] The significance of these productivity increases or rate reductions, of course, also depends on the volumes shipped. Meaningful comparisons require an analysis of total cost savings.

these rates were, respectively, 6.0 percent and 5.0 percent, according to our two measures. From 1846–50 to 1856–60 they were 1.4 percent and 1.3 percent respectively. Despite the exceptionally high rate of productivity change, the steamboat industry did exhibit typical features of industry growth and retardation in that most of the productivity advance occurred early, and this gave way to a noticeable slowing up and apparent attainment of maturity by mid-century. Meantime, in the transportation sector as a whole, productivity was continuing to advance, most notably in the railroads.

THE SOURCES OF ADVANCING PRODUCTIVITY

To determine the sources of this advance in steamboat productivity we analyze in two parts the cost determinants of steamboating. The first investigation focuses on changes in the input requirements per payload ton of an average steamboat on a single voyage, to single out changes in the input requirements of an average steamboat. Second, we analyze changes in the time components per voyage to determine how the average number of voyages per steamboat each year could have risen so sharply.

The major inputs and payload tons (utilized ton-miles carried) for an average steamboat making one round-trip voyage are given by decade in Table 15.[12] As indicated, although average ship size and crew size less than doubled, the number of payload tons delivered per voyage increased more than threefold between 1815 and 1860, despite less complete utilization.

As displayed in Table 15, captial inputs per payload ton were only about one-half as large at the end of the ante-bellum period as at the initial stage of steamboat development. Similarly, the number of labor inputs per payload ton was about two-fifths as large in 1860 as in 1815–19, and fuel inputs per payload ton had shrunk by one-half. Insurance costs per round trip underwent a precipitous decline, and the decline in those costs measured per payload ton was even more pronounced.[13]

---

[12] All statements in this first section of the analysis are in terms of a single voyage, with the number of yearly round trips assumed unchanged.

[13] It is tempting, perhaps, to conclude from Table 15 that the sources of productivity advance were more labor-saving than capital-saving. Clearly, we do observe that an average steamboat in 1860 used more capital relative to labor than did its 1815 counterpart. However, changes in the relative prices of capital and labor affected the observed factor proportions as well as did technological change, or other sources of productivity advance. The average wages of steamboatmen rose 50 to 60 percent over the period, while average capital costs per measured ton fell by almost half. This change in relative prices probably led to some movement along the production function, and a portion of the rise in labor productivity is probably due to the substitution of capital for labor. The shift of the production function led to a fall in capital inputs per payload ton despite the relative price decline of capital. Therefore, capital inputs per payload ton clearly were reduced. Labor inputs per payload ton probably also were saved, but we cannot be certain without knowing the exact position of the production function isoquants before and after the productivity advance.

Table 15. Inputs of an Average Steamboat per Payload Ton for a Single Voyage in the Louisville–New Orleans Trade, 1815–60

Period	Ship size (measured tons)	Ratio of carrying capacity to measured tonnage		Average[a] utilization rate	Payload[b] tons per round trip	Crew size (Men)	
		Downstream	Upstream				i
(1)	(2)	(3)	(4)	(5)	(6)	(7)	
1815–19	220	0.50	0.25	0.75	288	26	
1820–29	290	0.80	0.40	0.75	532	35	
1830–39	310	1.00	0.50	0.75	704	37	
1840–49	310	1.60	0.80	0.61	815	37	
1850–60	360	1.75	0.88	0.53	934	43	

Source: Appendixes C and D.

[a]The average freight utilization rate per trip is the sum of upstream and downstream freight tons divided by the round trip carrying capacity.

[b]Payload tons per round trip are the sum of freight (in tons) carried upstream and downstream per round trip and the number of passengers in each category (upstream cabin, upstream deck, downstream cabin, downstream deck) carried per round trip, all converted to equivalent tons of downstream freight by taking ratios of 1840–49 rates/fares, using the 1840–49 downstream freight rate (per ton) as the numeraire.

[c]These inputs are equivalent deck hand units (see Appendix G, Table G–1, note[b]).

od	Fuel per round trip (cords of wood)	Insurance per round trip	Capital input per payload ton (tons/ton)	Labor input per payload ton (deck-hands/ton)	Fuel input per payload ton (cords/ton)	Insurance input per payload ton ($/ton)
)	(9)	(10)	(11) (2)/(6)	(12) = (8)/(6)	(13) = (9)/(6)	(14)= (10)/(6)
5–19	330	$1,650	.76	.17	1.15	5.73
)–29	483	957	.55	.11	.91	1.80
)–39	496	512	.44	.09	.70	.73
)–49	504	279	.38	.07	.62	.34
)–59	529	270	.39	.07	.57	.29

Chief credit for the reduction of input requirements per payload ton went to a remarkable increase in the ratio of carrying capacity to measured tonnage—more than a threefold improvement during the period. If utilization and carrying capacity per measured ton had remained unchanged over time, the input requirements of capital, labor, and fuel per payload ton would have remained almost static on the basis of a single voyage. Falling insurance costs did lower the expenses per round trip, but even that effect was magnified by the increase in capacity that reduced insurance costs per payload ton.

Two basic changes in the physical structure of the steamboat led to this all-important improvement in carrying capacity per measured ton. One was a pervasive change in the design and proportions of the hull, the other was the reduction in weight of the steamboat and its equipment.

From early descriptions we learn that the physical characteristics of the ancestral western steamboat were similar to those of a seagoing vessel. Hulls were heavily structured, with low breadth-to-length and high depth-to-length ratios. Sitting low in the water, they housed the cargo, machinery, and even passengers' quarters, below decks. Hunter notes how these lines, unsuitable to river travel, gradually accommodated themselves to the new conditions: "The model, proportions, and manner of construction of the hull underwent radical changes. The keel disappeared, the hull lost depth, and the superstructure mounted higher and higher. In stern-wheel boats the rudder was extended forward as well as aft of the stern post; the single rudder gave way to two, three, and even more rudders."[14]

The form and proportions of the hull were again subjected to problem-solving to meet the needs of western river commerce:

The more immediate problem facing the boatbuilders was to reduce the draft for boats of a given tonnage so that they might carry heavier loads and operate during longer seasons. The solution of this problem is shown in the steady increase in the water plane area, of which the product of "L by B" provides a rough index. An increase in the latter of nearly two-thirds for all classes of boats in the period 1818–1860 represents a very significant decrease in the depth of water associated with a given displacement and a corresponding increase in the load capacity of the hull. In this manner a major problem of adapting the ship's hull to use on the western rivers was solved.[15]

Although changes in hull dimensions varied by vessel size, the trends can be illustrated by the fact that a typical 200 to 225 ton vessel grew in length by 21 percent, increased in breadth by 34 percent, and declined in depth by 39 percent, between 1818 and 1860; this yielded an increase of 62 percent in the water plane area (length times breadth).[16]

---

[14] Hunter (1949): 66.
[15] Ibid., p. 75.
[16] Ibid.

The shift toward lighter construction and equipment was also functionally sound: "The reduction of the weight of the steamboat and its equipment was hardly less important in decreasing draft and enlarging cargo capacity than were the changes in proportions and design of the hull. . . . Reduction of the size and number of timbers and of the thickness and amount of planking was the simplest way of adapting such staunchly built vessels to shallow-river navigation."[17] The upper works, or superstructure, also came to be built of thinly planked light woods (white pine or poplar), and much of the main deck was left unenclosed. As the depth of the hull receded, new decks appeared on the superstructure to house cargo and passengers. This gave the steamboat its typical topheavy appearance, which was actually, however, countered by the placement of engines and cargo below the main deck.

Such changes in design, proportions, and weight not only increased carrying capacity per measured ton but, as shown in the following second section of the analysis, produced other important productivity effects as well.

Of course, Table 15 does not completely reveal all of the improvements, and the increased yearly number of voyages per steamboat also raised productivity. Although fuel and insurance costs varied directly with the number of voyages,[18] crews were not hired by the voyage, but instead for that portion of the year that was the navigation season.[19] Likewise, the yearly capital costs of the steamboat did not vary with the number of voyages made per year.[20] Therefore, the input requirements of labor and capital per payload ton were inversely related to the number of voyages per steamboat.

Table 16 shows, by decade, that the average number of round trips per steamboat increased quite significantly, from three to approximately twelve round trips per year.

As a means of raising productivity, this change was of comparable importance to the increase in the ratio of carrying capacity to measured tonnage. To illustrate this, suppose utilization and carrying capacity per measured ton had remained unchanged; even in that case, the fourfold increase in the number of voyages per year would have reduced capital requirements per payload ton in 1860 to one-quarter of those in 1815–19. Because part of the

---

[17] Ibid., pp. 79–80.

[18] Insurance coverage was typically for a specific time period rather than on a per-voyage basis. Coverage on steamboats was generally taken out by the month or the year, with three to six months the most frequently mentioned periods, Hunter (1949): 367. However, the insurance rates would reveal the rate of steamboat losses, which would have been a direct function of the running time or the number of trips taken each year.

[19] Except for the captain and first mate (who were hired on an annual basis), crews were paid monthly and were typically hired for the year's navigation season. See Appendix C, Table C–2.

[20] Depreciation and repairs may have varied with the number of trips per year, but the evidence, though somewhat inconclusive, suggests not. See Appendix C, Tables C–1 and C–3.

Table 16. Time Components and Yearly Number of Voyages per Average Steamboat in the Louisville–New Orleans Trade, 1815–60

Period	No. of round trips per year	Days per passage upstream	Days per passage downstream	Days per round trip passage	Days of running time per year	Days out of water per year	Days[a] in port	Days of[b] port time per round trip
(1)	(2)	(3)	(4)	(5) = (3) + (4)	(6) = (2) × (5)	(7)	(8)	(9) = (8)/(2)
1815–19	3	20.0	10.0	30.0	90	95	180	60.0
1820–29	5	12.5	7.5	20.0	100	95	170	34.0
1830–39	8	9.5	6.6	16.1	128	95	142	17.8
1840–49	10	7.5	5.5	13.0	130	95	140	14.0
1850–60	12	6.5	5.2	11.7	141	95	129	10.8

Source: Appendix C, Table C–3.

[a]Column (8) = 270–(6), since a steamboat averaged 270 days in water.
[b]These do not represent average port time in the usual sense of the term. See text for clarification.

increase in average voyages per year was due to a longer navigation season, as will be discussed later, labor inputs per payload ton would have fallen by something less than three-quarters, but probably by more than one-half. Yearly fuel and insurance costs increased with the number of voyages, but probably only in proportion to the increase in the days of running time per year, or something on the order of 50 to 60 percent. Consequently, these input requirements per payload ton were substantially reduced by the four-fold increase in round trip voyages; taken together, these savings would have matched those generated by increased carrying capacity.

As we see from Table 16, the average time from New Orleans to Louisville decreased during the period from approximately 20 days to 6 or 7 days, and the return downstream passage was shortened by almost half, from approximately 10 days on an average in 1815 to about 5 days in 1860. The overall passage time for a round trip voyage in 1860, exclusive of days in port, was less than two-fifths that required in 1815–19.

The shortened transit times, however, can account for only a fraction of the increased number of round trips each year. A sharp decline in the number of days a vessel was laid up in port was also an important factor. Vessels were typically out of the water for cleaning and repairs about three months of the year; then if we assume that an average steamboat was in operation[21] 270 days each year, the average number of days in port per round trip can be computed from the number of round trips times the number of running days per round trip. From these estimates it appears that days in port per round trip fell from approximately 60 to 10 or 11 (see column 9, Table 16).

Table 17 attempts to determine the relative importance of the declines in the various time components. Suppose the number of days in port per round trip had remained unchanged at the 1815–19 level. Then the actual decline that occurred in the number of days to complete an upstream and downstream passage would have raised the average number of round trips per year from 3 to approximately 4.3 in the period from 1815 to 1860 (see column 5, Table 17). By comparison, if the combined number of days per round trip passage had remained at the 1815–19 level of 30, then the estimated fall in days in port per round trip would have increased the average number of round trips from 3 to about 6.6 = (270 days/[30 days + 10.8 days]), in the same span.

The importance of increased speeds has been considerably over-emphasized in the past literature on steamboats. For example, consider Kirkland's stress: "They quickened their speeds. Whereas in 1815 it had taken twenty-five days for the voyage from New Orleans to Louisville, the pre-bellum record, made in 1853, was four days, nine hours, and thirty minutes.

---

[21] The term "in operation" refers to the period in which the vessel was not out of water, and this remained nearly constant at approximately nine months per year.

Table 17. The Relative Importance of the Declines of Various Time Components, 1815–60

Period	Days of port[a] time per round trip	Days in[b] port due to limited navigation season	Cargo[c] collection time (in days) per round trip	Round trips[d] per year if only passage times declined	Round trips[e] per year if only cargo collection times declined	Round trips[f] per year if only the navigation season was increased
(1)	(2)	(3)	(4)	(5)	(6)	(7)
1815–19	60.0	90.0	30.0	3.0	3.0	3.0
1850–60	10.8	0.0	10.8	4.3	4.4	4.5

Source: Table 16.

[a]See column 9, Table 16.
[b]The navigation season was increased from approximately six months to almost nine months, 1815–60. See Appendix D and footnote 24.
[c]Column 4 = column 2 minus (column 3, divided by the number of round trips per year [column 2, Table 16]).
[d]This assumes a six-month navigation season and a cargo collection time per round trip of 30 days, with passage time falling from 30 days to 11.7 days per round trip.
[e]This assumes a six-month navigation season and passage time per round trip of 30 days with cargo collection time falling from 30 days to 10.8 days per round trip.
[f]This assumes a cargo collection time and passage time of 30 days per round trip each and an extension of the navigation season from six to nine months.

These record breakers traveled day and night and averaged nearly fourteen miles an hour. More customary were trips of four and a half to six days. *While speed increased, fares decreased*" [our italics].[22] Clearly, from our earlier comparisons, the reduction in the number of days in port, not passage time, was primarily responsible for the increased number of annual round trips. Moreover, it should be remembered that speed is not the only determinant of travel time.

Changes in the physical characteristics of the steamboat did serve to increase speed, as in the transition to longer boats and from low-pressure condensing engines to high-pressure noncondensing ones.[23] Larger engines and greater pressures also hastened speeds. But even in the early period, before the mid-1820s, passage times had already been notably reduced by such expedients as operating the steamboat at night and by shortening the stoppage times to cut and gather fuel wood. In fact, Table 16 shows that since most of the fall in passage times occurred prior to 1830, these factors probably explain a substantial portion of the overall reduction of passage times.

The important decline of days in port per round trip was due primarily to two factors: (1) an extension of the navigation season and (2) a reduction of cargo collection times. The navigation season was extended from approximately six months before 1830 to about nine months during the last half of the ante-bellum period.[24] Because of the more limited navigation season before 1830, early steamboats were in port considerably longer than their later counterparts. If we assume that 90 days (equal to the change in the average navigation season) out of the 180 days of port time in 1815–19, were attributable to the more limited navigation season, then approximately 30 days were required, on an average, to collect cargoes and passengers for each round trip, 1815–19 (see column 4, Table 17). If passage times and cargo collection times (per round trip) had remained unchanged at 30 days each, the longer navigation season would have raised the average annual number of round trips per steamboat from 3 to 4.5. If only the cargo collection times had declined (from 30 days to almost 11 days), then the increase would have been from 3 to 4.4.[25]

---

[22] Kirkland (1969): 142. For another example, see Healy, in Williamson, *ed.* (1949): 172–88.

[23] See Hunter (1949), chap. 3, for descriptions of the mechanical improvements in steamboating.

[24] Hunter (1949): 222–23. The six-month navigation season before 1830 meant that three months of the period that the vessel was in operation was necessarily port time. The length of the navigation season, of course, varied according to river conditions and ship size, and the above estimates are only rough averages.

[25] Although the increase in the navigation season appears to have been more important than the reduction in cargo collection times or passage times, it was only capital-

Here again, changes and alterations in the steamboat's physical charac
teristics were important factors. As implied above by Hunter, the increase
buoyancy of the vessel, plus the reduction in the depth of the hull, plus suc
other alterations as the elimination of keels, increased the navigation season
But to complete the story, the longer season was also the result of rive
improvements and an increase in the skills and know-how of pilots an
captains. As to the shorter time needed to collect cargoes and passengers, it i
unlikely that this was much affected by changes in the structure of th
vessels, although the stowing of cargo on upper decks instead of in holds ma
have facilitated loading and handling. But we suggest that the decline in carg
collection time was mainly due to the growth of market trade and t
improvements in commercial organization.

A SUMMARY OF STEAMBOAT PRODUCTIVITY ADVANCE

In summary, the steamboat brought an impressive surge of productivity t
inland water transportation, although this early vitality, which occurre
before the mid-1840s, was followed (as in so many other industries) by
slackening and eventual stagnation.

The major improvements in steamboating were an increase in the carryin
capacity per measured ton, a lengthening of the navigation season, and a fa
in time required for cargo collection and passage. Alterations in the physica
characteristics of steamboats primarily accounted for the increase of th
carrying capacity per measured ton and for a substantial portion of th
increased navigation season and lower passage times. But other factors con
tributed as well. For instance, river improvements both lengthened th
navigation season and, together with the development of a steamboat inspec
tion system and the improved skills of captains and crews, increased safet
and lowered insurance rates. Improved labor skills, plus the establishment o
fuel stations, helped lower passage times. Finally, the significant and impo
tant reduction of cargo collection times probably was determined primaril
by the growth of the market and by improvements in commercial organiza
tion resulting from economies of scale.

---

saving, not labor-saving. Labor costs rose almost in proportion to the increase in th
navigation season, because the payroll for the entire crew, except the mate and captain
grew with the extension of the season. However, the increase in the number of roun
trips per year, caused by the decline in passage times and cargo collection times (whicl
were approximately of equal importance), was both labor-saving and capital-saving, anc
the relative importance of the longer navigation season suggested in Table 17 is over
stated in terms of the combined savings of labor and capital. When both input savings ar
considered, it appears that the fall in passage times was about equal in importance to th
reduction of cargo collection times, and the increase in the navigation season was slightl
less important.

Clearly, the story of improved steamboat productivity on inland waters was not simply one of technical advances in knowledge that lowered inputs per unit of output. The introduction of steam power in itself was obviously of great importance, but most of the reduction of costs came from subsequent improvements after the introduction of steam. Moreover, these later improvements, primarily alterations in the physical characteristics of steamboats, might be better described as the result of learning by doing. They came gradually, by trial and error, and for the most part they comprised a whole accumulation of minor alterations, instead of any few major changes.[26] More specifically, once steam had been introduced, progress depended on adapting the structural design and mechanical equipment of seagoing vessels to the special requirements of shallow water transportation.[27] Many men shared in these efforts. In general, they were not the result of new knowledge about basic principles, but a restructuring of known principles of design and energy. As stated so ably by Hunter:

The story is not, for the most part, one enlivened by great feats of creative genius, by startling inventions or revolutionary ideas. Rather it is one of plodding progress in which invention in the formal sense counted far less than a multitude of minor improvements, adjustments, and adaptations. The heroes of the piece were not so much such men as Watt, Nasmyth, and Maudslay, Fulton, Evans, and Shreve—although the role of such men was important—but the anonymous and unheroic craftsmen, shop foremen, and master mechanics in whose hands rested the daily job of making things go and making them go a little better.[28]

[26] It should be noted that although changes in the physical characteristics came gradually, most of them occurred fairly early, and "by 1840 the western steamboat had reached the form which in essentials it was to keep to the end of its day." Hunter (1949): 64.

[27] It is important that the period of technical diffusion, or the time between the development and adoption of new improvements, was apparently quite short. The average stock of tonnage was completely renewed every five to six years. This relatively short lifespan of the average steamboat (which changed little over the period) meant that new improvements were rapidly introduced into the fleets.

[28] Hunter (1949): 121.

6

THE PERSISTENCE AND
DEMISE OF OLD TECHNOLOGIES

"Keelboats and barges, . . . could not begin to compete in speed
or rates with even the first crude and inefficient steamboats. The
larger of these boats, the barge, went out of use rapidly."

Louis C. Hunter, 1949

"Yet the flatboat trade was as important because of its
continuing economic role, down to 1860, as it was because of the
colorful rivermen and folklore for which it is best remembered."

Harry N. Scheiber, 1969

The impressive rise in steamboat productivity and its consequent reduction in shipment costs dominate the story of western river transportation during the ante-bellum period. But what was happening meanwhile to the older technologies of keelboating and flatboating? Did they devise some productivity advances of their own to counter the competition? Or did the new craft completely shoulder aside the lumbering old behemoths of western river commerce?

As we have seen, the advent of the steamboat did quickly eclipse the keelboat from operations on major trunk routes. Prior to 1817, all upriver commerce had been carried by large keelboats,[1] whereas by 1821 it is reported that steamboats "have almost entirely superseded the use of Barges, which were formerly the largest boats in use."[2]

In contrast, flatboating not only survived on the trunk routes but even expanded in the face of the stiff competition generated by the newer technology. For instance, as shown in Table 4, some 1,287 flatboats had arrived at New Orleans in 1816, the year before the first successful steamboat

[1] Hall (1848a): 13.
[2] Serial set 78, House Doc. 35, 22.

navigation of the western rivers. Thirty years later the number of arrivals increased to a peak of 2,794.

The contrasting fate of the two older craft is explained in part by the differential impact of the steamboat on upstream and on downstream rates. Earlier we pointed out that successful keelboat operations depended primarily on upstream revenues and that approximately five-sixths of their total revenues were earned on that passage. As we have observed, it was on the upstream rates that the steamboat had its most dramatic effects, and the estimates in Chapter 3 indicate that revenues earned by keelboats on the Mississippi route had actually fallen below average variable costs by the decade of the 1820s. Keelboating now made economic sense only on the shallower waters off the main trunk routes, and it predictably retreated to those remote areas as steamboating services spread throughout the Mississippi river system.

Keelboating probably experienced some productivity-raising improvements and, as noted previously, input savings resulted from the practice on the tributaries of towing keelboats by steamboat. Nevertheless, because of the paucity of data and the brevity and irregularity of service on any particular route, such advances would be difficult to measure. In any case, given the limited role of keelboating compared to total river transport services, such advances would have been of minor importance for the western river system as a whole, and for the trunk river routes they would have been nil.

A quite different conclusion attends the case of flatboating, however, and the remarkably persistent survival and expansion of this older technology occurred despite the fact that flatboats retained all their simple crude physical characteristics, nor apparently were there any technical advances in their handling or navigation.

To explain such persistence we must again analyze productivity change, first measuring the amount of advance that was achieved by flatboating and then seeking its sources. As this productivity analysis will show, competition was not the only important link between steamboating and flatboating.

The next step is then to analyze the influence of the flatboat on the market for river transportation services, and here we discover that one of the major roles of the flat was the flexible and rapid expansion and contraction of freight services over short periods. The seasonality of freight rates for the western rivers mirrors this function, providing a very different schedule than for ocean shipping, or for shipping on the Great Lakes. The flatboat obviously offered no mere stubborn persistence, but a genuine economic service.

MEASURES OF THE PRODUCTIVITY ADVANCE

The same measures used in the previous chapter to estimate the total factor productivity of steamboats are employed here. The first estimates changes in output per unit of inputs, each appropriately weighted by its share of total costs; the second compares changes in output price relative to input prices, again appropriately weighted. As noted, given consistent data and a competitive market for flatboat services, the two measures should give identical results; but, again, severe data limitations preclude any but a range of estimates achieved by the use of the two measures. We hope that this range reflects the approximate degree of improvement. The required data on output, inputs, output prices, input prices, and weights are derived from evidence in the Louisville–New Orleans trade, and our indexes are given in Appendix G, Tables G–3 and G–4.

From 1815 to 1860, total factor productivity increased at an annual compound rate of 4.4 percent or 3.8 percent, depending on the measure.[3] As shown in Figure 4, however, these figures obscure the fact that most of the productivity advance occurred before the mid-1840s, with only modest changes after that time. For instance, by the two measures, flatboat productivity grew at an annual rate of 7.4 percent or 5.1 percent between 1815–19 and 1835–39, and at 1.6 percent or 2.6 percent thereafter. The earlier rates which were more than twice as high as in the later periods, are impressive especially when it is recalled that neither a significant change in the physical characteristics of the boats nor any breakthrough in the techniques of their navigation occurred during this period. Indeed, over the entire period 1815–60 the rate of productivity advance for flatboats was only slightly less than that for steamboats.

THE SOURCES OF ADVANCING PRODUCTIVITY

Although technological change had no direct effects on flatboating productivity, certain positive externalities arose from the introduction and improvements of steamboats. Similar to the effects of keelboat towing on the tributaries, the steamboat saved flatboatmen the arduous return journey by land, and historians generally agree that this labor-saving externality was an important stimulus.[4] Prior to the steamboat, the return voyage had taken

[3] The selection of base-year weights inevitably adds some bias to our measures. To illustrate the sensitivity of the selection of weights, moving weights change the above rates of 4.4 percent and 3.8 percent to 4.9 percent and 4.3 percent respectively; 1815–19 base-year weights give rates of 4.9 percent and 4.4 percent respectively; and 1850–60 weights give rates of 4.6 percent and 3.8 percent respectively. On the basis of these small differences we feel fairly confident that the rate of change was near or slightly above 4 percent. In addition, our failure to appropriately include the expenditures on river improvements in our input indexes may add some bias. As previously discussed in footnote 7 of Chapter 5, however, we conclude that the bias, if any, is quite small. When the average annual expenditures from improvements on the trunk Mississippi route (see Table 20) are averaged over all the vessels in operation there, they form an insignificant percentage of the average annual total costs per vessel.

[4] See, for example, Taylor (1951): 64–65; Scheiber, in Ellis, ed. (1969): 286–87, Berry (1943): 25; and Baldwin (1941): 180–82. Conceptually, the above measures view

several months.[5] By adding some waiting time for the vessel to depart to our estimates of upriver steamboat passage times, we find that by the early 1820s the return time by steamboat would, on average, have approximated one month and by 1840 would have been reduced to one or two weeks. Moreover, upstream deck passenger fares were steadily declining.

These savings, particularly in time, were highly important to the many flatboatmen who were principally farmers and who could now be back home in time for such critical tasks as planting. In short, one vital externality of the steamboat was a significant reduction in the opportunity costs of labor in flatboating.[6]

The speedier return, by making more journeys possible, also spurred the development of a specialized class of flatboatmen. According to Scheiber, in contrast to the earlier "dealer boatmen" or "peddler boatmen," there emerged in the 1830s and 1840s a class of "agent boatmen."[7] These were professional transportation agents who improved safety, reduced passage time, and had the know-how to handle larger flats. Thus the technological change embodied in the steamboat further provided several spillover advantages for flatboating.

One additional link between the two techniques was the development of towing services upriver, which increased the service lives of some flatboats. This was not a common practice however, and the capital savings that resulted were only a small part of total costs. When averaged over all flatboats, the significance of these exceptional operations was very minor.

Further information on the sources of productivity advance is gained by viewing changes in the capital and labor requirements per payload ton. As Table 18 clearly indicates, while capital inputs per payload ton remained unchanged, labor inputs per payload ton fell to about one-tenth the 1815

---

the labor input component in terms of man-days per round trip, and account is taken of the decline in labor inputs resulting from the arrival of the steamboat and the safer and faster upriver journey after 1820. One problem with taking this view is how to determine the actual number of men who returned upriver. We have assumed that all of the men returned; consequently, the above measures contain an upward bias if a portion of the men did not return upriver. To take the other polar extreme, where it assumed that no men returned upsteam (that is, where the labor inputs are expressed only for a one-way voyage), then the comparable rates of productivity advance are 2.4 percent or 1.6 percent by the two measures. However, since most of the men did return upriver, the round trip view seems conceptually superior. In any case, the two extreme views should allow us to bracket the true historical productivity advance.

[5] For a discussion of the return routes, see Baldwin (1941): 124–25.

[6] It is noteworthy that between 1815 and 1860, while money wages for steamboat deckhands rose by 25 percent, money wages for flatboat crewmen remained unchanged (see Appendixes C and E). Although the average supply price of steamboat labor (an average of 19 crewmen and 7 officers) increase by more than one-half (see Appendix G., Table G–2) when the opportunity costs of labor are included in flatboat labor costs, these *fall* by more than one-third over the period (see Appendix G., Table G–4, note b).

[7] See Scheiber, in Ellis, ed. (1969): 290–96.

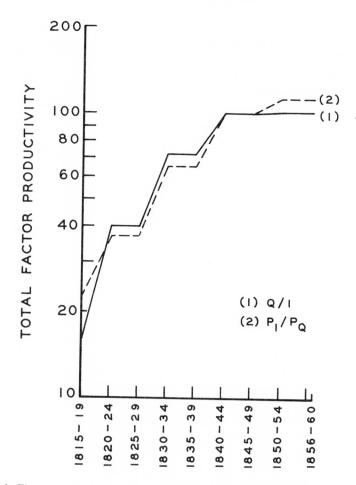

Fig. 4. Five-year moving averages of indexes of flatboat total productivity. *Source:* Appendix G.

counterpart. From a comparison of columns (2) and (3) in Table 18 it would appear that the reduction in input requirements resulted partially from economies of scale; that is, larger flatboats required more men, but not in proportion to tonnage. The use of larger flatboats was itself a function of labor skills and of river improvements,[8] however, and, as viewed by flatboat owners and operators, the latter were economies external to the industry.

_____

[8] It should be emphasized that the sharp increase in vessel size after 1830 closely followed the period of greatest expenditures for river improvements, 1825–38 (see Table 20, Chap. 7). We suggest that the reduction of river hazards, coupled with the increased skills of flatboatmen, explains the shift to larger flats. Consequently, the labor savings apparently due to economies of scale are largely the effect of externalities.

Moreover, as emphasized above, most of the reduction in labor inputs per payload ton were due to the reduction in the time component. If the vessels had remained unchanged in size and only the time component had changed, then the rate of measured productivity advance from 1815 to 1860 would have been 2.8 percent (Q/I, 1840–49 weights). In other words, nearly two-thirds of the productivity advance was due to the change in the time component; and most of this—about seven-eights—was due to the reduction in time expended returning up river (see Table 18, note c); the remainder was due to the faster downstream journey. In contrast, if only the size of the vessel and crew changed as they did, and the time component had remained unchanged, then the rate of advance (of Q/I) would have been only 1.5 percent in 1815–60.

Judging from contemporary sources, river improvements appear to have been an important source of productivity advance. Flatboating was always considered a hazardous business—so hazardous, in fact, that insurance companies generally refused to insure these vessels. Snags cost the life of many a flatboat (and steamboat) during the ante-bellum period. Early attempts to remove snags began in the late 1820s, and by 1831, techniques were perfected with notable results.[9] According to William F. Switzler:

From 1822 to 1827 the loss in the Ohio and Mississippi Rivers by snags alone, including steam and flat-boats and their cargoes, amounted to $1,362,500. From 1827 to 1832, when quite a number of snags were removed, these losses were greatly reduced, and did not exceed $381,000. In the latter year, 1832, in consequence of the successful working of the snag-boats, not a single boat was lost.[10]

In addition to increasing safety, river improvements reduced passage times by enabling flatboats to operate at night. On the Louisville–New Orleans route, passage time declined by approximately one-third to one-half,[11] and a government report (1831) on river improvements noted similar reductions elsewhere: "Flat-boats navigating the Mississippi river from the mouth of the Missouri to New Orleans, now float at night with as much safety as they do in the Ohio River, by which means their passage is now made in one-half the time it was three years ago."[12]

Although river improvements had an immediate and impressive effect on flatboat passage times, their effect on total labor time, as noted above, was

[9] Hunter (1949): 192–200.
[10] Serial set 2552, Exec. Doc. 6, pt. II, 198. Of course, 1832 was an exceptional year; accidents continued and were fairly numerous in the 1840s.
[11] From notes graciously supplied to us by Thomas Berry, and according to Hunter 1949): 56, and Baldwin (1941): 67, the decline was from 30 to 35 days during the early 800s to 18 to 24 days in the 1840s.
[12] Serial set 216, House Doc. No. 2, 92.

Table 18. Input Requirements per Payload Ton of an Average Flatboat in the Louisville–New Orleans Trade, 1815–1860

Period	Ship size[a] and payload tons per trip	Crew size (Men)	Adjusted[b] crew size	Days per[c] round trip	Labor days per round trip	Capital input per payload ton	Labor input per payload ton
(1)	(2)	(3)	(4)	(5)	(6) (5)×(4)	(7) (2)/(2)	(8) (6)/(2)
1815–19	30	5	5.9	120	708	1.0	23.6
1820–29	41	5	5.9	60	354	1.0	8.6
1830–39	56	5	5.9	40	236	1.0	4.2
1840–49	93	7	8.5	30	255	1.0	2.7
1850–59	146	10	13.0	30	390	1.0	2.0

Source: Appendix G, Table G–3.

[a]A flatboat typically carried a capacity load. The average carrying capacity of a flatboat therefore equaled its tonnage.

[b]These labor inputs are expressed in equivalent crewman units, using money wage rates as weights.

[c]Days downstream were approximately 30 before 1830 and 20 thereafter. Days upstream were about 90 before 1820, falling to 30 in 1820–29, were 20 in 1830–39, and were around 10 thereafter.

small by comparison with the savings in time afforded by steamboating for the return trip. The shortening of flatboat passage time due to river improvements and increased labor skills did contribute to the lowering of the real costs of flatboat labor; but in the absence of any reduction in passage times on the return voyage, total round trip passage between Louisville and New Orleans would have been reduced by only 10 to 12.5 percent. In contrast, steamboating lowered the round trip passage time of flatboat labor by approximately 70 to 75 percent.[13]

In summary, the remarkable survival and expansion of flatboating on the western rivers is largely explained by externalities. Flatboating reaped a bountiful, if indirect, harvest from the new steamboat technology, abetted by subsequent improvements in steamboating and by river improvements. Because the steamboat reduced the opportunity costs of labor by shortening return passage times and by lessening the hardships of the upriver trek, it created an inducement for the acquiring of new flatboat skills and, in conjunction with river improvements, thus led to the use of larger flatboats, which further economized on labor. Because of these improvements, flatboats were enabled to maintain an active role on the western rivers until the very brink of the Civil War.

The persistence of old technologies is often explained, at least in part, by the fixity and durability of capital. As long as total earnings exceed the costs of operations, some rents accrue to the old capital, thus justifying its continued use;[14] consequently, new technologies do not always immediately replace old techniques. Often, a great deal of time passes before an innovation asserts its full productivity-increasing effects throughout the industry.

It is apparent, however, that this explanation does not apply in the case of flatboating because of the extremely short life span of the vessels. Each voyage typically required a new flatboat, and investments would certainly have dried up unless revenue earnings of that one voyage were sufficient to cover all costs for the crew, for other variable expenses, and for the new vessel itself. A more likely thesis, and one which we feel has been neglected, is that old technologies may often hold on stubbornly, either because they continue to improve independently or, as in this case, because they benefit from external improvements.[15] The frequent practice of scholars to concen-

---

[13] See note c, Table 18, and also footnote 11 above. The percentage reduction is calculated by holding flatboat passage time constant.

[14] This explanation assumes that the technology is embodied in the old capital equipment, either in its design or construction. Such was the case for the craft on the western rivers.

[15] For an excellent discussion of these and other reasons for the persistence of old technologies (with illustrations) see Rosenberg (1972): 3–34. A classic example of this point is sail vs. steam in nineteenth-century ocean shipping, a topic which has been the subject of recent debate. See, for example, Graham (1956): 74–88; North (1958): 537–55; Knauerhase (1968): 390–403; and Walton (1970): 435–41.

trate on the new and to ignore the old reenforces the traditional, and often inaccurate, view of technological progress as a series of discontinuities in the historical record.

FLATBOATING AND THE PATTERN OF FREIGHT RATES

The productivity analysis that emphasizes the influence of the steamboat on the productivity and costs of flatboating highlights one important link between the two technologies. Another was the impact of the steamboat on the long-term level of freight rates. But another link that deserves considera- tion is the effect of flatboating on short-term freight rates.

Although competition among the many steamboats was probably suffi- cient to maintain a generally competitive market for freight services, flatboat- ing served to heighten the competition and also exerted real pressure on the *short-run* supply of downriver freight services.

A typical feature of many transportation systems is that, in the short run, the capacity, or supply, of the service is relatively fixed.[16] Consequently when the demand for such services tends to fluctuate, shortages and surpluses of capacity develop, leading to high freight rates during periods of peak activity and low rates during slack periods of excess capacity.

This rather common phenomenon is illustrated in the case of ocean transport by the ante-bellum seasonal pattern of coastal traffic and freight rates. As noted by Robert Albion: "The freight rates showed a seasonal fluctuation. *During the peak of the rush in late winter and early spring* [our italics], the rate on a bale of cotton from New Orleans or Mobile to New York was about $3, from Charleston and Savannah, $1. By June, the Gulf rate had dropped to $1 and the Charleston–Savannah rate to 50 cents."[17] A similar pattern prevailed on the Great Lakes during the ante-bellum period. "Lowest in the summer, freights advanced in the fall of the year when the new crops were harvested."[18]

In contrast, the seasonal pattern of downriver freight rates and river use shows an inverse relationship. As indicated in Figures 5, 6, and 7, during the low water months of the summer, when the rivers were a hazard to navigation, freight rates were extremely high and river use was minimized for both steamboats and flatboats. By the fall months the rates had fallen, and activity was greatly increased. The peak shipping season for both craft, but especially for flatboats, was in the high-water spring period, when the hazard

[16] To the economist this is known as an inelastic supply. Generally, supply is relatively inelastic in the short run but quite elastic in the long run, after sufficient time is allowed for capacity increases.

[17] Albion (1938): 73. This description is confirmed by Berry (1943): 64–65, "It appears that ocean rates, in marked contrast to river freights, were uniformly higher in winter than in summer."

[18] Odle (1952), pt. IV: 187.

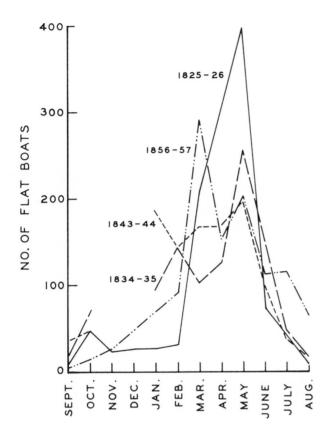

Fig. 5. Indexes of monthly flatboat arrivals at New Orleans for selected years. *ource:* Calculated from the New Orleans Prices Current, 1825–26; 1834–35; 1843–44; 856–57.

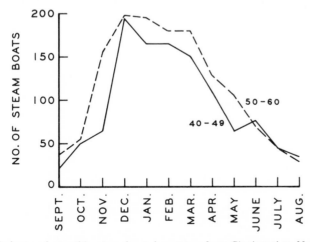

Fig. 6. Indexes of monthly steamboat departures from Cincinnati to New Orleans, 840–49 and 1850–60. *Source:* Calculated from Haites (1969), Table C–2, p. 232. Also ee Appendix D, footnote 9.

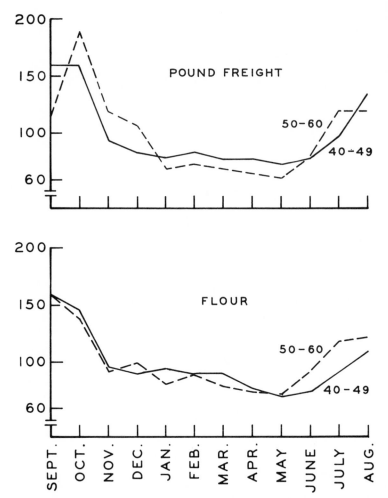

Fig. 7. Indexes of monthly steamboat freight rates from Cincinnati to New Orleans, 1840–49 and 1850–60. *Source:* Calculated from Haites (1969), Tables C–1 and C–5, pp. 229 and 238. Also see Appendix D, text and footnote 8.

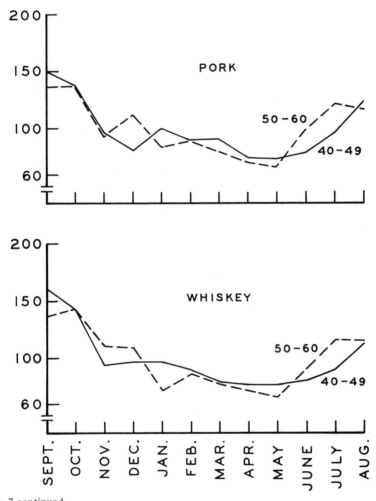

Fig. 7 continued.

of navigation were comparatively slight and rates typically reached thei lowest level.[19]

Thus, the seasonal characteristics of the rivers bore heavily on the patter of rates. Many boats simply laid up for cleaning and repairs during th summer months, and smaller steamboats were generally the only ones willin to risk low water navigation. As the waters rose, so did the supply of carg capacity. The larger steamboats now came out of drydocks. In additior however, the high water brought forth a tremendous hatch of flatboat ready and able to expand the total supply of freight services during thes periods of peak demand. Their one-voyage life span assured that the suppl would diminish equally fast when the demand for transport subsided.

To the flatboat, therefore, goes credit for making the supply of rive freight services unusually responsive to fluctuations in demand. Of course, th

[19] "The two seasons of trade were opened by the spring rise and the fall rise in th rivers. Of these the spring rise was the more dependable and lasting, having its origin i the combined product of melting snow and ice and spring rains. In the Ohio River th spring rise arrived ordinarily sometime between the beginning of February and th middle of March, high water continuing usually until the middle or latter part o June. . . . The fall rise was based upon the rains alone and was briefer in duration an much less reliable than that of the spring. It did not often make its appearance befor the middle of September and was regarded as late if delayed beyond the first week o October." Hunter (1933–34): 7. Serial set 542, House Exec. Doc. 59, 646–59, report the harvest periods for the major western crops of the ante-bellum period as follows:

Crop	State	Time of Harvest
Wheat	Tennessee	June 15
	Kentucky	July
	Ohio	June 28 to July 20
	Indiana	June 15 to July 20
	Illinois	May to July 1
	Michigan	June to July 30
Corn	Tennessee	Oct. and November
	Kentucky	Oct. and November
	Ohio	Oct. and November
	Indiana	Oct. 1 to Nov. 30
	Illinois	Oct. to December
	Michigan	Sept. 20 to Oct. 15
Tobacco	Tennessee	Aug. 1 to Sept. 20
	Indiana	September
	Ohio	August
	Illinois	September

This suggests that the ante-bellum farmer harvested his wheat first, then his tobacco (i any), and then his corn. Hogs and cattle were fattened during and after the corn harvest Cist (1851): 279. The pork-packing season "begins in November and ends in March" Cis (1851): 278. In prerefrigeration days the pork-packing plants "tended to locate alon; the Ohio River and its tributaries where winter temperatures continued near freezing bu did not go below frequently enough to interfere with meatcutting," Leavitt (1934): 23 Thus the crops tended to be shipped during the fall and the products during the spring.

everage effect of flatboat tonnage on total tonnage was lessening by the end of the period. In 1840, flatboat tonnage was about 20 percent of the total volume of tonnage arriving at New Orleans, as against about 5 percent in 1860 (see Chap. 2, footnotes 32 and 33). The leverage effect on the total tonnage within a few months of high water would have been much greater, however, and it was this significant marginal addition (or contraction) on short-run supply that was critical to the seasonal pattern of rates. In general, where flats held a larger share of the total tonnage in operation, as on nontrunk routes, we would expect this effect to be even more impressive. The sizable increase or contraction in tonnage that could take place almost overnight[20] both influenced the structure of freight rates and furthered the interdependence of steamboating and flatboating.

Finally, this effect on the structure of freight rates was, of course, highly advantageous to the western farmer and to consumers. Farmers enjoyed low-cost shipping when they most needed freight services. In turn, consumers enjoyed lower prices for western produce than could otherwise have been possible. Stated in economic terms, over a year or a decade the *weighted average* of downriver rates was minimized because of the elastic characteristic of the short-run supply of downriver freight services.

---

[20] This explanation is also consistent with the observation that flatboat activity was renewed shortly after the Civil War, when steamboat tonnage was low because of war damage. See the New Orleans, *Register of Flatboats.*

7

GOVERNMENT IN WESTERN
RIVER TRANSPORTATION BEFORE 1860

"Prompted by these actual observations, I could not help taking a
more contemplative and extensive view of the vast inland
navigation of these United States, and could not but be struck
with the immense diffusion and importance of it; and with the
goodness of that Providence which has dealt his favours to us
with so profuse a hand. Would to God we may have wisdom
enough to improve them."

George Washington, 1783

Recent investigations of the role of government in the ante-bellum
American economy have led to a reevaluation of several key features
of early U.S. development.[1] The prevailing view had been that ante-
bellum capital formation and business activity were largely the result of
private initiative and enterprise. Now that general theme of laissez-faire, even
if properly qualified, has passed out of vogue, giving way to the current
orthodoxy labeled "the American System," which emphasizes government
involvement in the economy in partnership with private enterprise.

The scholarly investigations leading to this reassessment have concentrated
overwhelmingly on the government promotion of canals and railroads,[2] and
in that area the evidence is convincing that, taken together, federal, state, and
local aid played a central role in their development.

Nevertheless, as we have been stressing here, not canals nor railroads, but
the river system was actually the major transportation medium in the West. It
was the dominant medium until 1845 and was an integral part of the
transportation network throughout the entire ante-bellum period. Furthermore, in that connection our evidence in the following pages will suggest that

---

[1] For a survey of these reassessments, see Lively (1955): 81–96; Goodrich (1970):
289–311; Soltow (1971): 87–105; Broude (1959): 4–25; and, for the initial challenge to
the older view, see Callender (1902): 111–62.

[2] See, for instance, Goodrich (1960, 1961, and 1967) and Scheiber (1969).

it would be wise to heed the caution by Albert Fishlow, that "the recent useful destruction of the myth of ideological laissez-faire in the United States must not give rise to the equally erroneous impression of all-embracing, and essential, public promotion."[3]

Of course, various river improvements by government were important to steamboating and flatboating, and we have emphasized the effects of these improvements in the analysis of productivity change. Nevertheless, by comparison with government promotion of canals and railroads, the western rivers received very little support, either direct or indirect. In addition, as will be shown in our following analysis, government expenditures on river improvements were a pittance in terms of the total costs of river operations.

As with other types of internal improvements, the issue of constitutional interpretation proved troublesome at the national level. Although many of the early presidents actually favored internal improvements, including work on rivers, their sense of duty to the Constitution, as they interpreted it, often restricted their action. Federal government activity was particularly limited in the last two decades of the ante-bellum period when strict constructionists generally prevailed. As a clamor for improvements arose, paralleling the rise of western commerce and the consequent loss of life and property on the rivers, the "broad school" intensified its arguments, but governmental activity remained limited, and little was resolved until the Civil War.

Similarly, on state and local levels government involvement was impeded by various problems, including financing and, more particularly, questions of cooperation among the western states.

FEDERAL GOVERNMENT AND WESTERN RIVER IMPROVEMENTS

The earliest federal involvement in "western waters" was by way of general exploration and surveys. Soon after the War of 1812, topographical engineers undertook several fairly intensive studies of these waters, with expeditions in 1817, 1819, and 1823, under the leadership of Major Stephen Long. Congress granted appropriations totaling $6,500 for his 1819–20 explorations and, in April of 1820, a further grant of $5,000 for a detailed study of the western rivers from Louisville to Balize was approved.[4] To undertake this study, the Board of Engineers for Fortifications was transferred from its work on coastal defenses in 1821.

The survey report from this study, by General Bernard and Colonel Totten, excellently summarizes the problems of navigation on the Ohio and Mississippi during the ante-bellum period. On the Ohio River, the major obstacle to navigation was the falls. In addition:

---

[3] Fishlow (1965): 307; and, for further challenges on these reassessments, see North (1966): 98–107.
[4] Hill (1957): 157.

there are many minor ones [obstacles], which, however, completely inter-
cept the navigation of the Ohio in its low stage, except to boats with very
little draught. These are shoals of gravel or sand, extending quite across the
river. The deepest water over these, is confined to very narrow channels,
generally: and great attention and experience, on the part of the pilots, are
necessary to hit these channels, and to avoid being drawn, by the lateral
currents, upon the shoals. Though these bars have water enough for "keel and
flat bottom boats," which draw but about 18 inches, to descend the Ohio,
from Shipping-Port to the mouth, at almost any season of low water; they
have so little, as to prevent the navigation by steam boats, (which draw from
four to seven feet) for five or six months every year.[5]

We now pass to the difficulties which the Mississippi presents, in its actual
state, to navigation. Those which result from the continual changes in the
course of its channel, can . . . only be remedied by time. Those which are
wrought by the current acting upon the shores and islands, are accompanied
by earthfalls of even acres of forests. Of the trees which are in this way
precipitated into the river, some are borne off by the stream, some are lodged
upon the shores, where they form "rafts," obstructing the navigation of
certain "branches," and require to be avoided with great care. . . . Others of
these trees become fixed in the bed of the river. When so fixed as to preserve
an immoveable position, they are called "planters"; but when, being inclined
from the vertical, and pressed upon by the current, they move in regular or
rather in uninterrupted oscillations, they are called "sawyers"; "snags" is a
term applied to either.[6]

As Bernard and Totten emphasized, the physical conditions of the rivers
were significant impediments to the expansion of western river transportation. Alterations in the physical characteristics of the various river craft and
improved skills of the operators partially overcame these limiting conditions,
but a pressing need remained for river improvements. Nevertheless, not until
1824 did Congress make its first appropriations for river improvements.
Although occasional enabling acts had been passed earlier to allow individual
states to assess tonnage duties to pay for river and harbor improvements, the
federal government had not appropriated any funds for western river improvements during the first three and one-half decades of its existence.[7] This
more decisive involvement came more than a decade after the introduction of
the steamboat on the western rivers.

When the federal government's river improvement work finally began, it
focused on two kinds of activities: (1) the removal of natural or permanent
obstructions, such as falls and rapids, which were bottlenecks at strategic

[5] Serial set 78, House Doc. 35, 11.
[6] Ibid., 21.
[7] Hill (1957): 154.

points on the river system, and (2) the removal of general obstructions such as snags, rocks, sand bars, and sunken boats.

Of the falls and rapids that impeded navigation, the government focused on three of special importance: the falls of the Ohio (Louisville), the Muscle Shoals on the Tennessee, and the Des Moines and Rock Island rapids on the upper Mississippi. Only one of three efforts produced any measure of success, the other two were resounding failures.

In the initial year, 1824, Congress gave Alabama 400,000 acres of land, the proceeds of which, totaling $1.4 million, were to be applied to the improvement of the Muscle Shoals. A survey in 1828 concluded that a canal was the only practical solution to this obstacle, but after an expenditure of $700,000, less than one-half of its planned length was actually completed, and this was rendered useless within a few months of its opening when a freshet opened great breaches in its banks. Nearly forty years passed before work in the area was resumed.[8]

The improvement of the Des Moines rapids which began in the 1830s was eventually suspended for want of financial support. Additional appropriations were not made until the 1850s and 1860s and even then the project was not completed until 1890.[9]

Bernard and Totten had regarded the falls of the Ohio as one of the principal barriers to navigation on the western rivers. This series of rock ledges extending across the Ohio River at Louisville presented a bottleneck to navigation throughout most of the year; passage over them was extremely risky except at near-flood levels and usually lay-over or transshipment was required.[10]

Two companies had been incorporated in Kentucky, in 1804 and 1818, for the purpose of building a canal around the falls at Louisville, and another, the Jeffersonville Ohio Canal Company, had been incorporated in Indiana in 1818 with the same objective, but all had failed.

Efforts were renewed in 1825 with the incorporation in Kentucky of the Louisville and Portland Canal Company with a total capitalization of $600,000 (6,000 shares with a par value of $100). On July 3, 1826, Congress authorized the purchase of 1,000 shares of this stock, and on May 6, 1829 voted to purchase the remaining unsold 1,335 shares for a total investment of

---

[8] Hunter (1949): 187–89; W. E. Martin (1902): 162–63.

[9] Hunter (1949): 189 reports that ante-bellum attempts to improve the channel were abandoned and that in 1866 work was begun on a 7.6 mile canal, which was opened for public use in 1877 but not completed until 1890.

[10] Serial set 78, House Doc. 35, 9. A similar observation was made by a contemporary traveler: "For upwards of two months, the Ohio has been low; steamboats cannot now pass from the falls at this place to the Mississippi, nor can boats, descending with produce, get down the same rapids without unloading the greater part of their cargoes. The trade of the country is of consequence much interrupted." J. Flint (1904): 286.

$233,500. The rest of the 6,000 shares were held by some seventy individuals from five eastern and three western states, and neither the state of Kentucky nor the city of Louisville subscribed to any of the company stock.[11] The still uncompleted canal was finally opened for use in December of 1830, having cost close to $750,000.[12]

Steamboats, whether loaded or not, were initially charged a toll of sixty cents per measured ton to pass through the canal. As indicated in Table 19,

Table 19. The Number of Steamboats and Other River Craft[a], and their Total Tonnage Passing through the Louisville and Portland Canal, 1831 to 1860

Year	No. of steamboats	No. of other craft	Tonnage of river craft
1831	406	421	76,323
1832	453	179	70,109
1833	875	710	169,855
1834	938	623	162,000
1835	1,256	355	200,413
1836	1,182	260	182,220
1837	1,501	165	242,374
1838	1,058	438	201,750
1839	1,666	578	300,406
1840	1,231	392	224,841
1841	1,031	309	189,907
1842	983	183	172,755
1843	1,206	88	232,264
1844	1,476	168	304,384
1845	1,585	394	318,741
1846	1,626	283	341,695
1847	1,432	226	307,879
1848	1,523	248	341,501
1849	1,272	216	285,011
1850	1,170	200	253,034
1851	1,456	478	374,522
1852	1,194	404	318,555
1853	1,429	487	375,362
1854	998	312	254,199
1855	1,380	750	407,634
1856	1,002	506	232,780
1857	1,419	740	338,669
1858	1,079	529	249,360
1859	1,281	592	285,305
1860	1,520	1,299	340,898

Sources: Serial set 1349, House Misc. Doc. 83,
[a]Other river craft were predominantly flatboats, but a few keelboats and rafts were probably included.

---

[11] Hunter (1949): fn. 9, 183; also, see Trescott (1957–58) for the corporate history of the canal.
[12] Hunter (1949): 183.

annual steamboat traffic through the canal increased from 406 passages in 1831 to 1,256 passages in 1835 and from 1836 through 1839 averaged 1,352 steamboat passages per year. This declined to an average of 1,336 per year during the 1840–49 decade and to an average of 1,266 per year during the 1850–60 period. By the mid-1840s, the average aggregate tonnage of river craft using the canal had reached its peak.

The somewhat perplexing decline in the utilization of the canal after that date occured despite a reduction of the toll to fifty cents per measured ton in 1844 and the fact that the number of steamboats in operation on the western rivers doubled between 1836 and 1860.[13] In addition, as noted in Chapter 5, the average steamboat was making more round trips during these years. However, the canal's locks had been designed for boats of the late 1820s, and the subsequent growth in their size, according to an 1853 War Department report, indicated that 43 percent of the steamboat tonnage on the Ohio River was too large for the canal.[14] Even vessels small enough to use the canal faced delays and inconvenience because of the inadequate size of the locks:

Because only one passing chamber was provided it was necessary when business was brisk to establish one-way traffic moving first in one and then in the other direction. Descending boats were seldom allowed to enter the canal at night. These restrictions meant vexations and expensive delays. . . . The average time required to pass through the canal, including detentions at the entrances, was estimated at five hours; the larger boats often required ten, and at rush periods boats might be detained from one to two or three days.[15]

As a consequence, many steamboat operators chose the risky alternative of passing over the falls during periods of very high water. Unfortunately, no data exist to compare the numbers of vessels that used the two routes.

Complaints about the inadequacy of the Louisville and Portland Canal reached Congress rather steadily after 1840, supported by suggestions for enlarging the canal, for building a new canal parallel to the existing one or on the Indiana side, or for improving the river channel.[16] In 1842 the Kentucky legislature responded by authorizing the Louisville and Portland Canal Company to use some of its earnings to purchase, at $150 per share, shares of its stock held by individuals.[17] When all but five shares had been repurchased in 1857, ownership of the canal was transferred to the federal government, but

[13] See Appendix B, Table B–1.

[14] Hunter (1949): 185.

[15] Ibid., p. 184.

[16] Serial set 359, Senate Doc. 284; Serial set 421, House Doc. 126; Serial set 434, Senate Doc. 179; Serial set 434, Senate Doc. 185; Serial set 442, House Doc. 154; Serial set 490, House Report 661; Serial set 631, Senate Report 328; Serial set 656, House Report 166; Serial set 1309, Senate Misc. Doc. 5.

[17] Serial set 1349, House Misc. Doc. 83, 4; Serial set 1992, Senate Exec. Doc. 196, 193–268.

the project of its enlargement was not begun until 1860 and not completed until 1872.

Despite its shortcomings, the canal had proved a financial success from the beginning. Of the original $233,500 invested in the stock of the canal by the federal government, all and more was paid back in dividends within a decade. The government first received a stock dividend of 567 shares, valued at $56,700, in June 1833; between that date and January 1840 it received cash dividends of $196,836, averaging approximately 10 percent per year.[18]

Meantime, the federal government was also undertaking to cope with the more temporary hazards to river navigation. Indeed, the central purpose of the 1824 appropriation of $75,000, under the first act for river improvement, was earmarked for the removal of trees fixed in the river beds. Originally assigned to the War Department, the project was later transferred to Henry Shreve, a former steamboat captain.[19]

The initial efforts at removing snags were carried on using a "machine boat" designed by John Bruce of Kentucky.[20] Essentially it consisted of

two substantial flatboats placed side by side about eight to twelve feet apart and joined by cross timbers which supported a long and strong wooden lever. From the "short" end of the lever hung an iron claw: from the "long" end a heavy rope passed through blocks to a windlass operated by four men. The double boat was brought into position over the sunken tree trunk which formed the snag, the claw was made fast, and through the powerful leverage obtained by lever and windlass the snag was broken off, torn loose from the river bed, or raised sufficiently to permit its being sawed off and rendered harmless. This floating crane likewise proved very effective in raising and removing boulders, stumps, and other sunken objects.[21]

Although it took a man of Shreve's mechanical skills very little time to master the use of the machine boat, he found its use both laborious and hazardous, and in 1827 he reported: "In the event of funds being appropriated for the further prosecution of the work, I would recommend the application of steam power for the removal of the obstructions from the bed of the Mississippi river."[22]

---

[18] Hunter (1949): 184 and Serial set 434, Senate Doc. 179, 25–26.

[19] Succeeding Major S. H. Long, Shreve became the superintendent of western river improvements and held that position until he was forced to resign in a political dispute in 1841.

[20] For his plan he was awarded $1,000 and the first contract to construct the vessel. Hunter (1949): 193.

[21] Ibid.

[22] Serial set 170, House Doc. 11, 3. In the same report 4–5, Shreve also recommended "cutting down all the timber from off the banks of the river, at all places where they are liable to fall in, from three to four hundred feet from the margin of the river; in doing this, the first cause of the obstructions would be removed, and the banks of the rivers will be preserved." He did note that: "The value of the timber may be made an

A year later, the first steam snagboat, the *Heliopolis*,[23] designed by Shreve, was under construction; in 1829, it went into its first season of operation:

The snag boat was similar to the machine boat in having a double hull, but it was much larger and heavier; its lifting machinery was geared to the engine and was of course far more powerful than the hand-operated equipment of the machine boat, and it moved under its own power instead of being towed or maneuvered by hand. A central feature of the snag boat not found in its predecessor was the heavy *snag beam* which joined the two hulls at the bow. In going into action the snag boat was run full tilt at the projecting snag in such a manner as to catch it on the snag beam and force it up out of the water. This powerful blow was often enough either to break off the snag or loosen it from the river bed. Then the snag was brought under the snag beam, raised by the engine-power machinery, and cut up. The heavy portions such as the stump and roots were either dropped into a deep pool or carried ashore for disposal while the remaining pieces were allowed to float harmlessly off. Snags weighing as much as seventy-five tons and embedded in the river for many feet were removed without difficulty by the snag boats, which were nicknamed "Uncle Sam's Toothpullers."[24]

The success of the snag boat was quickly recognized, and between 1827 and 1838 Congress made annual appropriations for general river improvements, as shown in Table 20. In total, however, appropriations for western river improvements amounted to only about $3.3 million before the Civil War.[25] Of this amount, about $1.9 million, or nearly 58 percent, was allocated before 1839 and subsequent appropriations were made only irregularly. Except for the years 1841–44, no major appropriations in the ante-bellum period were made again until 1852, and no expenditures for general river improvements were made after 1855.[26]

The irregular pattern in federal appropriations after 1838 meant that on three separate occasions river improvements were suspended: in 1840–41,

---

objection; but that being almost entirely cotton wood and sycamore, it cannot be a consideration either to individuals or to the Government." He estimated that to complete this work from the mouth of the Missouri River to New Orleans would cost $400,000. The recommendation was not implemented.

[23] For the record of the operations of the *Heliopolis,* see Serial set 204, Sen. Doc. 72.

[24] Hunter (1949): 194.

[25] Table 19 does not include small amounts appropriated for surveys, subscription to the stock of the Louisville and Portland Canal, and another $690,000 allocated for the improvement of the mouth of the Mississippi River; the last was intended to aid the navigation of ocean-going vessels (see serial set 1992, Senate Exec. Doc. 196, 237). Federal monetary outlays for both western and non-western river improvements over the period 1815–60 totaled nearly $6,000,000 according to Taylor (1951): 68.

[26] The appropriation for 1856 was not for general river improvements, but specifically for the continuation of work on the Des Moines Rapids.

Table 20. Federal Government Appropriations and Expenditures for Ante-bellum
Western River Improvements

Year	Amount of appropriation	Amount of expenditure
1824	$ 75,000	$ 2,842
1825	0	11,244
1826	0	16,002
1827	74,911	35,716
1828	75,000	54,430
1829	50,000	62,961
1830	50,000	71,738
1831	200,000	156,867
1832	117,628	97,939
1833	50,000	124,825
1834	130,000	110,500
1835	190,000	151,951
1836	243,600	194,821
1837	363,000	315,098
1838	270,000	282,786
1839	0	121,034
1840	0	18,922
1841	75,000	22,500
1842	100,000	30,237
1843	150,000	77,742
1844	280,000	195,756
1845	0	236,761
1846	0	41,941
1847	13,629	12,628
1848	0	0
1849	0	0
1850	0	0
1851	0	0
1852	600,00	1,000
1853	0	194,757
1854	0	176,133
1855	0	227,238
1856	200,000	0
1857	0	0
1858	0	41,101
1859	0	30,272
1860	1,350	88,028
Total	$3,309,119	$3,205,771

Source: Serial set 1992, Sen. Exec. Doc. 196, 193–268.

under President Van Buren; in 1846–51, under Polk's administration; and again in 1856–60, under Pierce and Buchanan.[27] During these periods some of the snag boats were sold and others were either laid up or loaned to local agencies. In addition, experienced workers were discharged and perishable properties were sold. In some cases, additional appropriations were necessary to phase out operations in progress.[28]

The river improvements had been yielding ever greater economic dividends as western commerce grew; yet the efforts to maintain the rivers after 1838 were only sporadic. Appendix C shows how the life span of steamboats on the Louisville–New Orleans route was shortened, partly as a consequence of this inaction, falling from an average of 6.5 years in the 1830s to 5.3 in the years 1840–50 decade. Later, it rose to 6.1 years as a consequence, we believe, of the federal safety regulations enacted in 1852.[29]

Despite emphatic public demands for river improvements, ultimately expressed through great conventions, two major factors limited the size of appropriations and affected the timing of specific projects. Not only did presidential interpretations differ as to what they were empowered to do, constitutionally, in the domain of internal improvements, but they often lacked available funds to carry out such projects.

One of the first basic guidelines to the limits of federal involvement was laid down by Andrew Jackson in his Maysville veto of May 27, 1830, and his Wabash River veto of December 1, 1834. The first vetoed bill was to authorize the subscription of stock in a road company; Jackson argued that because the entire road was contained within a single state, Kentucky, he was unable to "view it in any other light than as a measure of purely local character."[30] In the Wabash River veto he elaborated on the differences between local measures and

another class of appropriations for what may be called, without impropriety, internal improvements, which have always been regarded as standing upon different grounds from those to which I have referred. I allude to such as have for their object the improvement of our harbors, the removal of partial and temporary obstructions in our navigable rivers, for the facility and security of our foreign commerce. I have prescribed a limitation . . . to places below the port of entry or delivery established by law.[31]

---

[27] Hill (1957): 196.

[28] Serial set 413, Senate Doc. 1, 285; Hill (1957): 182–98.

[29] The effects of the federal safety legislation are discussed below.

[30] Richardson (1908), vol. II: 487. Jackson continued, "If it be the wish of the people that the construction of roads and canals should be conducted by the Federal Government, it is not only highly expedient, but indispensably necessary, that a previous amendment of the Constitution, delegating the necessary power and defining and restricting its exercises with reference to the sovereignty of the State, should be made" (ibid., pp. 491–92).

[31] Ibid., vol. III: 121–22.

It is difficult to measure the impact of these guidelines, but some evidence suggests that in their absence the total requests and appropriations for internal improvement would have been larger.[32] It is true that Jackson's appropriations were larger than appropriations by other presidents before the Civil War. Nevertheless, Jackson's appropriations, and those of subsequent ante-bellum presidents, were limited to the Ohio and Mississippi rivers and a few of their major tributaries.[33] Moreover, only two presidents departed significantly from Jackson's guidelines in the prewar period. These were Polk and Pierce, who entirely suspended appropriations and expenditures for western river improvements.

In his August 3, 1846, veto of a bill for harbor and river improvements, Polk addressed Jackson's guidelines directly: "If the restriction is a sound one, it can only apply to the bays, inlets, and rivers connected with or leading to such ports as actually have foreign commerce—ports at which foreign importations arrive in bulk, paying the duties charged by law, and from which exports are made to foreign countries."[34] In line with this reasoning, no federal appropriations of any importance were made for western river improvements during his term.

Pierce's constitutional interpretation was even more strict than Polk's. In a veto message of December 30, 1856, he said: "From whatever point of view, therefore, the subject is regarded, whether as a question of expressed or implied power, the conclusion is the same, that Congress has no constitutional authority to carry on a system of internal improvements."[35] According to Pierce, the only power expressedly delegated to the federal government is "to provide for the common defense and to maintain an army and navy."[36]

The constitutional issue, therefore, chiefly explains the cessation of western river improvements during two of the three periods of their suspension before the Civil War, and the general importance of this issue has received considerable attention.[37]

In contrast, financial factors which have been largely ignored appear to have had a bearing, especially in the third period, during Van Buren's administration.[38] Earlier, Jackson did have finances in mind when he recom-

---

[32] For substantiating evidence, see, for examples, Richardson (1908), vol. II: 513; vol. III: 120; and vol. IV: 460 and 612.

[33] Serial set 1992, Senate Exec. Doc. 196.

[34] Richardson (1908), vol. IV: 463.

[35] Ibid., vol. V: 263.

[36] Ibid., p. 387.

[37] The suspension of river improvements began during Pierce's term of office and was continued by Buchanan, who did not specify his reasons. However, we surmise that his failure to resume improvements can be attributed largely to the recession of 1857–60, which made rigid economy imperative. See ibid., p. 524.

[38] See, for examples, Hunter (1949): 181–215; Hill (1957): 153–98; and Lippincott (1914): 630–60. Despite this oversight, the whole question of internal improvements

mended that "appropriations for such as were of a national character . . . be deferred until the national debt is paid,"[39] and Polk also argued for restraint during a time of financial stringency occasioned by the war with Mexico (1846–47).[40] Nevertheless, it was during Van Buren's term of office that financial considerations appear to have dominated the determination of federal appropriations for internal improvements in general. In 1838, the first year in which Van Buren exercised any considerable influence over the federal budget, western river improvements received $270,000, but a major economic recession during subsequent years reduced federal revenues sharply and his response was outlined in 1839 in his Third Annual Message:

To avoid the necessity of a permanent debt and its inevitable consequences I have advocated and endeavored to carry into effect the policy of confining the appropriations for the public service to such objects only as are clearly within the constitutional authority of the Federal Government; of excluding from its expenses those improvident and unauthorized grants of public money for works of internal improvement which were so wisely arrested by the constitutional interposition of my predecessor, and which, if they had not been so checked, would long before this time have involved the finances of the General Government in embarrassments far greater than those which are now experienced by any of the States.[41]

Table 21. Federal Government Receipts and Expenditures, 1834–41 (in millions $)

Year	Receipts[a]	Expenditures[b]
1834	21.8	18.6
1835	35.4	17.6
1836	50.8	30.9
1837	25.0	37.2
1838	26.3	33.9
1839	31.5	26.9
1840	19.5	24.3
1841	16.9	26.6

Source: U.S. Historical Statistics (1964):711.
[a]Excludes receipts from borrowing.
[b]Excludes debt repayment.

first stemmed from economic considerations. The first, and clearly the most comprehensive, plan for internal improvements by the federal government before the Civil War is contained in Albert Gallatin's "Report on Roads and Canals" (1808). Gallatin's report contains detailed proposals to construct a system of roads and canals and other improvements along the seaboard and between the seaboard and the interior. The financial feasibility of these proposals rested on an expected federal revenue surplus that never materialized, however, because of the Embargo and the War of 1812. See Goodrich (1967): 3–42.
[39] Richardson (1908), vol. II: 511, 488–89.
[40] Ibid., vol. IV: 465–66, 611.
[41] Ibid., vol. III: 612.

Prior to this, it should be remembered, expenditures by the federal government had been booming, partly due to the largesse that became available after the public debt was paid off in 1835.[42] Now Van Buren's economy move to balance the budget reversed the trend, as shown in Table 21, and allotments for western rivers dried up completely for the duration of that administration.

In summary, the extent of federal government involvement in western river improvements was determined partly by how each president viewed the legitimate role of the federal government under the Constitution, and partly by economic and other considerations.[43] For instance, an additional factor was that responsibility for the size and timing of appropriations was shared by Congress, which, with a predictable eye for regional or local benefits, sometimes included items of strictly local interest and thereby subjected entire bills to veto, although other more general items might well have been approved by the Executive Branch.[44] Federal involvement in western river projects therefore was picayune until the wake of the Civil War brought large appropriations for improvements.[45]

STATE GOVERNMENTS AND WESTERN RIVER IMPROVEMENTS

Prior to the federal government's 1824 initiation of its program for western river improvements, various individual states had struggled to im-

---

[42] Ibid., pp. 160–61, 609.

[43] A simple regression shows that variations in the annual federal government appropriations (A_t) for western river improvements were correlated with the availability of funds (i.e., total federal government revenue receipts of the preceding year (TR_{t-1}). The lagged variable (TR_{t-1}) should be interpreted as a behavioral variable serving as a proxy for expected revenue receipts in year t, the hypothesis under test being: Federal government appropriations for western river improvements in the year t are a function of the amount of expected total revenue receipts in year t. The results in the period 1824–40 are as follows:

$$A_t = -121,790 + .00843 \ TR_{t-1} \qquad \text{Adjusted}$$
$$(-1.4440) \ (2.8577) \qquad\qquad R^2 = .31$$

The values in parentheses are t-values.

However, the results are not statistically significant for the longer 1824–60 period due to insignificant results for the subperiod 1841–60.

Consequently, these findings are consistent with our conclusion that the extent of federal government involvement in western river improvements was determined not only by financial considerations but also by differences in the constitutional interpretation of the presidents and for other reasons. Finances were clearly important through Van Buren's administration, but over the whole period of 1824–60 it appears that the question of constitutionality and other matters were dominant.

[44] See, for examples, Richardson (1908), vol. IV: 330–33; and Hill (1957): 195–96.

[45] For instance, from 1866 to 1882 Congress appropriated about $25,000,000 for the improvement of the Ohio, Mississippi, Missouri, and Arkansas rivers. From 1882 to 1910, Congress appropriated $61,704,000 for the Mississippi alone; $4,587,000 for the Ohio, 1882–1909; and $9,259,000 for the Missouri, 1882–1905. See Lippincott (1914): 655–60; and Hunter (1949): 192.

prove harbor and river navigation on their own, but for the most part these limited efforts were restricted to river improvements within their own state borders.[46] One cooperative venture was attempted in January 1817 when an Ohio legislative resolution invited cooperation from the states of Virginia, Pennsylvania, Kentucky, and Indiana in considering measures to improve the Ohio River. The first three states responded favorably, and a survey was made in 1819, but instead of decisive cooperative action,[47] the states merely undertook improvements on rivers internal to their borders: Kentucky on the Green, Licking, and Kentucky rivers; Ohio on the Muskingum; and Indiana and Illinois on the Wabash.[48]

Most westerners, feeling that improvements, at least on the major trunk waterways such as the Ohio and Mississippi rivers, were the business of the federal government, repeatedly emphasized their convictions in memorials to Congress:

> If it be asked why the improvement of the Ohio and Mississippi has not been undertaken by the States whose borders are washed by these streams, it might be inquired, in return, why a few states, of which these rivers form the boundaries, should assume a work of such magnitude, and of so obviously a national character. As well might the States on the seaboard be required to erect lighthouses, and to improve the harbors of the sea coast, as the Western States be left to open the navigation of those great rivers, which separate States, that are declared by the supreme law of the Union to be public highways for all the States, and upon which no single State nor combination of States can place an obstruction or collect a toll, and not lying within the territory or civil jurisdiction of any one member of the Confederacy, the navigation belongs to the whole American people, and is a proper subject of national legislation.
>
> But there are obvious difficulties in the way of any joint or several action by the States in relation to this work. If undertaken by the States singly, it would be difficult to assign the limits within which the labor of each should be expended; if by all, jointly, the diversity of population, wealth, and interest, would embarrass and probably defeat any attempt to apportion the expenditure. . . .
>
> The financial resoures of the Western States are limited, and have already been taxed to the full extent of their ability. . . .
>
> The magnitude of the undertaking, and the wide extent of territory through which it must be conducted, require that there should be unity in the

---

[46] Most early river and harbor improvements were undertaken by states on the eastern seaboard. For instance, as early as 1790 the state of Rhode Island, with Congressional consent, passed a law levying tonnage duties on vessels arriving in the port of Providence. The revenues were intended "for the purpose of clearing and deepening the channel of Providence River and making the same more navigable." Also, in 1805 Pennsylvania passed a similar law to finance the removal of "obstructions to the navigation of the river Delaware below the city of Philadelphia," Richardson (1908), vol. V. 616.

[47] Serial set 434, Senate Doc. 179, 21.

[48] Ibid.

plan, skill in the execution, and rigid economy in the expenditures, to give it the full efficiency of which it is susceptible. The Government has the command, in its able corps of engineers, of all the talent, experience, and scientific knowledge requisite for the work.[49]

In short, westerners argued that: (1) Congress was constitutionally empowered to improve the rivers; (2) formidable difficulties hindered cooperation among the states, even for essential projects;[50] (3) the individual states were financially ill-equipped to undertake major projects;[51] and (4) the federal government had expertise to conduct the work most efficiently. These same reasons suggest why western states failed to initiate improvements after the federal government suspended improvements on major western rivers in 1838. Instead, each suspension was followed by the calling of massive conventions to formulate memorials to Congress pleading for the resumption of funding.[52] Perhaps the most indignant outburst greeted Polk's veto of the general river and harbor bill in 1846. That action, reported the *Cincinnati Gazette*, "can never be forgotten by the western people. Every boat that is snagged, every one that gets fast on a sand bar, every article that is lost, and every life that is sacrificed in consequence will forcibly remind us of the destructive blow aimed by a Locofoco President against our prosperity."[53]

Such western attitudes, however, cannot fully explain the reluctance of state and local governments in river improvements, remembering how actively they participated in the promotion of canals and railroads—even outpacing the federal government in pre-Civil War days. Capital shortages impeding any of these developments were impressive; but in the case of river improvements the main difficulty appears to have been that the wide distribution of gains generally made intergovernmental cooperation imperative.

As the declaration in the *Cincinnati Gazette* suggests, snags were one of the major persisting problems on the rivers, and our evidence confirms that they caused by all odds the major part of the property loss,[54] although gravel, rock, and sandbars also posed dangers. Clearly, any particular state or

[49] Ibid., pp. 21–22. For similar statements elsewhere, see Serial set 434, Senate Doc. 185; Serial set 477, Senate Doc. 410; Serial set 656, House Report 166; Serial set 775, House Report 545, 23.

[50] For example, it took nearly twelve years of off-and-on negotiations before Indiana and Illinois came to terms to jointly improve the Wabash River. Krenkel (1958): 12–15.

[51] Many of the western states, including Michigan and Illinois, did not embark on major internal improvement programs until 1837, after the federal government began to distribute Treasury surpluses to individual states. Uncertainty about federal intentions further delayed decisions to commit state resources until Jackson's Wabash River veto partly clarified the issue.

[52] Hunter (1949): 191; Lippincott (1914): 638, 644–45; and also footnote 49 above.

[53] Cincinnati Gazette, October 2, 1846.

[54] The annual loss of property from snags was estimated in 1824 at "from five to ten percent upon the whole amount which is hazarded upon the river." Serial set 105, House

local government stood to benefit if others would finance the removal of snags and other miscellaneous hazards on the major trunk routes. But precisely because the advantages of such improvements were extremely dispersed and largely independent of financial contributions by any specific state or locality, it was unlikely that their financial gains would accrue to the investing area or to individual investors.[55] In contrast, local support could be rallied for canals and railroads because these investments so obviously vitalized the areas through which they were built.

"Local mercantilism" of the type noted in Ohio by Scheiber for the canal era and later for railroads by Fishlow was therefore less to be expected for river improvements;[56] nevertheless, as we have seen, individual western states did initiate improvements on rivers flowing within their borders, and levees, docks, and wharves were also built with municipal aid. The approach to these efforts differed considerably from place to place. For example, some states, such as Iowa and Wisconsin, chartered private companies to make river improvements and authorized tolls to cover their expenses.[57] Others, like Ohio and Kentucky, appropriated funds for river improvements and then imposed tolls to partially recover these expenditures.[58] Yet other states simply appropriated funds and instead of charging user fees, elected to make payments from their so-called 3 percent funds[59] or from surplus revenues distributed by the federal government after 1835.

Report 75, 3. A government report in 1870 estimated the causes of steamboat losses on the western rivers, 1811–49, at:

Lost by collision	50
Lost by burning	150
Lost by explosion	184
Lost by snags	446
Total	830

Serial set 1418, House Exec. Doc. 175, 23. These losses represented about 35 percent of all steamboats constructed on the western rivers before 1850 (see Appendix B, Table B–1). Of these losses, 54 percent were caused by snags for a total monetary loss (for boats and cargo) of approximately $23.5 million. These estimates do not include lives lost, steamboats damaged, nor losses on flatboats.

[55] In some cases, even when a local area was likely to receive most of the benefits from clearing log jams, snags, and the like, requests for state funding went unheeded. See, for example, the case for aid on the Osage River around 1840, in James N. Primm (1954): 88–89.

[56] Scheiber (1969a), chap. 1; Fishlow (1965): 309–10.

[57] Wisconsin chartered the Fox and Wisconsin River Improvement Company and Iowa chartered the Des Moines River Improvement and Navigation Company. *Hunt's Merchants' Magazine*, vol. 36: 546–47.

[58] Ohio did this on the Muskingum Improvement, and Kentucky did so on the Kentucky, Green, and Barren rivers. Morris (1889): 107–36; *Hunt's Merchants' Magazine*, vol. 21: 398; vol. 22: 229.

[59] This fund was so called because it represented 3 percent of the proceeds from the sale of public lands within the states.

Although it is difficult to obtain a precise estimate of the totals spent by the various state and local governments on the western rivers between 1810 and 1860, its aggregate would probably be little more than the amount spent by the federal government on such projects. For instance, Alabama appropriated only $135,000 for river improvements during the ante-bellum period,[60] and Tennessee about $450,000.[61] Michigan appropriated $76,834 in the years from 1837 to 1841 but spent only $61,945,[62] and Ohio put $1,628,028 into the Muskingum River improvement.[63]

Evidence gathered by Charles Holt indicates that Kentucky allocated $676,000 for river improvements from 1839 to 1859, but Indiana allocated only $19,000 between 1837 and 1852,[64] after appropriating $12,000 (1834) for the improvement of the Wabash River, jointly carried out with Illinois.[65] In that effort, Illinois had embarked on its first river improvement program (1833) by matching the Indiana appropriation of $12,000 for the joint endeavor.[66] In 1837 the Illinois legislature passed a bill providing for a general system of projects, including river improvements, and between 1837 and 1839 it appropriated $902,000 for work on the rivers. However, only $524,082 of that sum had been spent by 1840, when construction was halted on all public works because of financial difficulties.[67]

---

[60] The amounts and specific uses were $55,000 in 1837 for the improvement of the Coosa and Tombigbee rivers and $80,000 in 1839 for the Coosa, the Paint Rock, the Choctawhatsee, the Elk, and the Black Warrior rivers. W. E. Martin (1902): 159.

[61] Folmsbee (1939). The $60,000 appropriated to the eastern section funded improvements on the Tennessee River, which allowed the first steamboat to reach Knoxville. Goodrich (1960): 154.

[62] Michigan's legislature in 1837 authorized a Board of Internal Improvements to implement 321 miles of river improvements. The appropriations and expenditures for the period 1837–47 were:

Project	Appropriated	Spent
Grand and Maple rivers	$30,000	$26,498
Kalamazoo River	8,000	6,572
Flint River	6,250	6,249
St. Joseph River	32,584	22,625

Source: *Hunt's Merchants' Magazine*, vol. 22: 134.

[63] Morris (1889): 135; and *Hunt's Merchants' Magazine*, vol. 21: 398.
[64] Holt (1970), Appendix: 56–58 and 75–76.
[65] Krenkel (1958): 15.
[66] Ibid., 14–15.
[67] Ibid., 101–2. The expenditures and their amounts were:

Rock River	$123,991
Illinois River	82,781
Little Wabash River	46,531
Kaskaskia River	13,061
Great Wabash River	12,977
Embarrass River	193
Great Western Mail Route	244,547

Despite years of political efforts by local merchants on the Osage River, Missouri made no expenditures on river improvements until 1855, when a trivial sum was granted.[68] We have no evidence of any significant action, either appropriations or expenditures, taken by Louisiana or Mississippi, but given the generally good conditions of the rivers there, we would expect only limited state involvement. The sums stipulated above give a lower bound estimate of state expenditures of a little under $2 million over the entire period. Allowing for possible incomplete coverage might raise the total state expenditure on western river improvements to about $3 million. Admittedly, the estimate is crude; but it does suggest that state expenditures were roughly similar to but probably not more than the total of the $235,000 in stock subscriptions and $3.2 million in improvements spent by the federal government from 1824 to 1860.[69]

Unfortunately, very little systematic evidence exists with respect to local government expenditures on river improvements and related facilities. Our investigations have unearthed only a few scattered accounts of municipal expenditures. The evidence for Pittsburgh is the most complete, and the ante-bellum expenditures there on wharves totaled approximately $60,000.[70] There is no indication of other river-related expenditures at Pittsburgh. The records for New Orleans for the years 1852 through 1860 show substantial expenditures on levees as well as wharves. Apparently, several of these years were ones of extensive levee repairs or construction, because four of them account for almost the entire $831,000.[71] The expenditures in other years were on the order of the wharf expenditures at Pittsburgh. It is likely that much of the expenditure on levees was required for flood protection and is not attributable to the river traffic.

Although the *Wharfmaster's Records* for Cincinnati have been destroyed, the records of the city's finances for 1861 indicate that the total wharfage fees collected were less than $20,000.[72] Expenditures were probably less

---

[68] Primm (1954): 88–89.

[69] It should be noted that in addition to the $3.2 million outlay, an additional $700,000 spent by Alabama was funded by a federal land grant, for the Muscle Shoals project.

[70] Thompson (1948): 216, reports the total municipal expenditures on wharves at Pittsburgh (rounded to the nearest $1,000) as:

1824–29	$2,000
1830–39	$29,000
1840–49	$10,000
1850–60	$19,000
Total	$60,000

[71] Provided in private correspondence dated Nov. 5, 1973, by C. B. Hamer, Jr., New Orleans Public Library.

[72] From the Eighth Annual Report of the City Auditor, provided in private correspondence dated Nov. 28, 1973, by J. R. Hunt, Librarian, The Public Library of Cincinnati and Hamilton County.

than receipts. Another piece of evidence, for Louisville in 1840, records the expenditure of $2,000 for wharves and the wharfmaster's salary.[73]

Given this fragmentary evidence, it is difficult to generalize about river-related spending by all municipalities for the entire ante-bellum period. Nevertheless, they do suggest only a modest involvement where costly levees were not needed, and we hazard the conjecture that total municipal expenditures for river-related improvements and facilities did not exceed the amount spent either by the states or by the federal government. Consequently, if we purposely exaggerate the amount spent by all levels of government, the total would not be more than $10 to $12 million.

This sum is miniscule compared to the massive government outlays for canals and railroads before the Civil War. Goodrich reports:

In the case of the canals, it is clear that public authorities provided the greater part of the initiative and of the resources. Total expenditure for canal construction from 1815 to 1860 has been estimated at about $195,000,000. Of this amount, 62 percent represents public works, including the major programs of New York, Pennsylvania, and Ohio; and allowance for government participation in mixed enterprises like the Cheasapeake and Ohio and Louisville and Portland Canals would bring the total of public investment to about 70 percent of the whole. . . .

For the nation as a whole . . . in railroads . . . the total of public commitments in cash or credit amounted to somewhat more than $280,000,000 in addition to the value of the federal land grants. The capitalization of the railroads in operation in 1861, according to the figure commonly used, was $1,143,000,000. Though this is far from a perfect measure of the cost of construction, it would appear that up to this time government agencies had provided at least 25 percent and more probably some 30 percent of the entire investment in railroad building.[74]

Clearly, government expenditures for canals, railroads, and other internal improvements in that period towered far above those for the rivers. Though the evidence is fragmentary, it appears that improvements to the natural waterways received even less state and local support than did turnpikes, plank roads, and bridges, before 1860.[75]

While such comparisons of total amounts by transportation type are interesting, the more pertinent question is government involvement in percentage terms. However, at this point it is important to stress two limitations. First, there is a problem of measurement. The expenditures and costs under-

[73] From the Report of the Finance Committee of the City of Louisville (1841) provided in private correspondence dated Oct. 29, 1973, by N. L. Dawson, The Filson Club, Louisville.

[74] Goodrich (1960): 270–71.

[75] Taylor (1951): 25–26.

lying the percentage calculations were made in different years. Ideally, these should be discounted to make expenditures in different years comparable. However, in our calculations below, as in Goodrich's above, they are not. The direction of the bias introduced by not doing so is unclear, so the effect is to add a degree of crudeness to the estimates.

Second, there is a problem of definition. For railroads, Goodrich measures the government share of investment in the basic facility (right-of-way, track, etc.) and in the equipment and ancillary facilities (engines, cars, terminals, etc.). But with canals he measures only the share of government investment in the basic facility. Since canal boats, warehouses, horses and the like were largely privately owned, this introduces an upward bias into his measure of government involvement in canal promotion.

With these caveats in mind, we construct percentage estimates comparable to those by Goodrich by dividing our $10 to $12 million aggregate estimate for western river improvements by the total construction costs of steamboats and flatboats.[76] This produces a result between 11 and 13 percent. These percentages boldly overstate the government involvement in terms of total resources employed. It cannot be stressed too strongly that both Goodrich's and our calculations have been limited to construction costs and other capital costs. Perhaps this serves as a reasonable measure of government promotion,[77] but as a measure of government involvement it is inadequate and greatly exaggerates the direct role of government in these enterprises.

Since we are concerned with the overall mix of public and private enterprise the total resource is the proper standard by which to measure the direct commitment by government. If Goodrich had included labor and other operating costs in his measure his percentages would have been considerably lower. For instance, in terms of total resources employed, the government commitment in total river operations amounted to only about 2 percent of the total costs of steamboat operations and even less when the costs of flat operations are included. It would fall still further if only completed and operational government projects were included, because many investments were abandoned, like the $700,000 for the uncompleted Muscle Shoals

---

[76] Total steamboat construction costs over the period are simply the sum of the total tonnage constructed in each decade (Appendix B, Table B–1) times the average construction costs per decade (Appendix C, Table C–1). Flatboat construction costs are based on the assumption that there were an average of 4,000 flats on the rivers each year, averaging 40 tons each before 1840 and 60 tons each thereafter (see Chap. 3). Construction costs per ton were about $1.50 (Appendix E).

[77] Because the construction of canals and railroads typically required very large initial financial outlays that were difficult to accumulate without some government intervention, government investment as a percentage of construction costs is suggestive of government promotion. Goodrich viewed the situation in this way, and his use of this measure should be interpreted in that context.

project. In brief, river transportation in the ante-bellum West owed its very life primarily to private initiative and private enterprise.

SAFETY REGULATION BY GOVERNMENT

There was another dimension to the role played by government in western river transportation. By the last two decades of the ante-bellum period, the imposition and regulation of steamboat safety standards was burgeoning as one of the earliest forms of government regulation.[78]

In effect, the steamboat that brought such economic benefits had also been exposing the West to its first view of the hazards of industrialization. The horrors of the occasional boiler explosion, which wrought indiscriminate slaughter among crew and passengers, had aroused violent emotional reaction among the public.

Actually, as we have shown, accidents by snags were by far the more common source of property damage and loss on the western rivers during the ante-bellum period, and contemporary investigations indicate that steamboat passage was no more dangerous than other forms of travel.[79] Nevertheless, to cut down the spectacular terrors of boiler explosions, both state and federal governments legislated safety regulations.

The first official inquiry into the causes of steamboat explosions, undertaken by Philadelphia in 1817, produced no legislation.[80] In the West Alabama became the first to pass legislation (1826) for steamboat inspections.[81] Louisiana (1834), Kentucky (1836), and Illinois and Wisconsin (1837–38) soon took similar action,[82] but these state laws failed to provide adequate means of enforcement and applied only to intrastate trips. As a result, state jurisdiction was extremely limited and almost totally ineffective.

The federal government became involved in the regulation of steamboat

---

[78] Of course, government regulation of some industries was not unknown, but it was rare. In the interest of public health and safety, Congress also had regulated ocean passenger transport after 1819. Unlike internal improvements, however, such regulation was based on the commerce clause and thereby hurdled the troublesome Constitutional issue; see Hunter (1949): 526. Short (1922) gives a history of the steamboat inspection service.

[79] Hunter (1949): 520–21. Between 1807 and 1853, when the steamboat inspection act of 1852 went into effect, 7,013 lives were lost in steamboat accidents for the entire United States; Serial set 2137, House Misc. Doc. 42, vol. 4, 4. The annual loss of lives averaged 150 for 1807–52 and about 340 for 1832–52. Captian Embree estimated in 1848 that only one out of every 2,506 persons traveling by steamboat was injured or killed in accidents and concluded: "Can any other mode of conveyance compare with this in safety?" Embree (1848–49): 319.

[80] Hunter (1949): 522. Also, see Burke (1966): 1–23, for an overview of safety legislation on inland commerce.

[81] Hunter (1949): 523.

[82] Ibid.

n 1838, fourteen years after it had first considered such action. The Act of 1838 was also futile, however, because its provisions were vaguely and loosely worded, and the important provision for the inspection of steamboat boilers was "emasculated by the elimination from the bill of the requirement of proof by hydraulic test, long recognized as the only adequate means of determining the strength of the boiler."[83]

The 1838 act was considerably strengthened by a new law in August 1852, but its provisions applied only to steamboats carrying passengers; others continued to operate under the Act of 1838. The 1852 enactment was long and elaborate. Among other things,

The hydrostatic test of boilers was established, and the maximum steam pressure allowed was fixed. Inspection was extended from the boilers to the manufacture of boiler plate. Provision was made for the formulation and publication of rules of passing in order to prevent collisions. Precautions were ordered to be taken to prevent the communication of fire from heated metal in and about the furnaces and boilers to wood or other combustible materials on the boat. Fire engines and hose as well as life preservers and lifeboats were mandatory equipment on river boats as well as on lake and seagoing vessels, and rules were established for the carriage of highly combustible and explosive materials. Special attention was given to deck passengers in a section requiring the provision of adequate means of escape to the upper deck in case of accidents.

Two other changes of special importance were introduced by the act of 1852: first, provisions for the examination and licensing of both engineers and pilots; and second, the adoption of administrative machinery vastly superior to that provided for in the act of 1838.[84]

The Board of Supervising Inspectors created by the Act of 1852 estimated that during the five years prior to the passage of the act 1,571 lives were lost in steamboat accidents on the western rivers, 1,155 of them as a result of explosions.[85] During the subsequent five years, they reported, despite a substantial increase in the number of steamboats and passenger miles traveled, only 345 lives were lost in steamboat accidents on the western rivers, 131 of them as a result of explosions.[86] The report concluded: "With these facts before us, we conceive that the beneficial effect of the law can no longer be a matter of doubt."[87]

---

[83] Ibid.

[84] Ibid., pp. 537–38.

[85] Serial set 941, Senate Exec. Doc. 1, 213.

[86] Ibid. The totals given are 131 lives lost due to explosions and 345 lives lost in all steamboat accidents. However, if the components of these totals are summed the results are 132 and 346 respectively. We have assumed that the totals, rather than the components, are correct.

[87] Ibid.

Certainly its humanitarian advantages could not be disputed. But an economist would also have to count in the appraisal the costs of operating the inspection system, including the extra pay and facilities of the inspectors, the costs of stronger boiler plate, and the extra costs of safety equipment and vessel specifications. In any case, such regulation was widely supported and continued long after the Civil War. It was probably a factor in raising the average lifespan of steamboats in the 1850s. In the ante-bellum period as a whole, however, the significance of this involvement was modest, and western river transportation remained predominantly in the hands of private enterprise.

8

SUMMARY AND
NEW INTERPRETATIONS

"In the past twenty years, American economic history has been undergoing profound change. . . . While this revolution is just beginning, its consequences are already of sufficient magnitude to suggest a basic overhauling of much of our understanding of the past. Some results serve primarily to challange existing interpretations and to point the way toward further research. . . . Other implications are that traditional major problems or issues are not really problems or issues at all. And still other new findings suggest alternative answers widely at variance with existing interpretations."

Douglass C. North, 1966

Settlement of the vast empty spaces of the New World has always piqued the interest of historians. Nowhere was this process more successful than on the North American continent, particularly in the marked transitions of the ante-bellum period. As indicated in Table 22, on the eve of the second war with Great Britain most of the population still clung to the eastern seaboard, and less than 15 percent of the population lived west of the Great Appalachian barrier. Within half a century, however, the nation had spread out over a substantial portion of North America, and the population center had shifted westward to somewhere near Chillicothe, Ohio. By 1860 over 40 percent of all Americans lived in the trans-Appalachian West.

Although population also grew rapidly in other regions, the rate of growth in the West outstripped all others and thus accounted for the impressive geographical shift. Between 1810 and 1860 the total population in the United States grew from 7.2 million to 31.4 million, while the West was busily expanding from just over one million to almost thirteen million. In terms of annual rates of change, the West boasted an increase of 5.1 percent between 1810 and 1860, or well over double the 2.2 percent growth rate in the rest of

Table 22. Population of Various Sections of the Trans-Appalachian West, 1810–60 (000s)

Region/year	1810	1820	1830	1840	1850	1860
Ohio	230.8	581.3	937.9	1,519.5	1,980.3	2,339.5
Indiana	24.5	147.2	343.0	685.9	988.4	1,350.4
Illinois	12.3	55.2	157.4	476.2	851.5	1,712.0
Michigan	4.8	8.8	31.6	212.3	397.7	749.1
Wisconsin				30.9	305.4	775.9
Iowa				43.1	192.2	674.9
Missiouri	20.8	66.6	140.5	383.7	682.0	1,182.0
Kentucky	406.5	564.1	687.9	779.8	982.4	1,155.7
Tennessee	261.7	422.8	681.9	829.2	1,002.7	1,109.8
Arkansas		14.3	30.4	97.6	209.9	435.5
Mississippi	40.4	75.4	136.6	375.7	606.5	791.3
Louisiana	76.6	152.9	215.7	352.4	517.8	708.0
Trans-Appalachian West	1,078.3	2,088.5	3,363.0	5,786.2	8,716.8	12,984.1
United States	7,239.9	9,633.8	12,866.0	17,069.5	23,191.9	31,443.3
West as % of United States	14.9%	21.7%	26.1%	33.9%	37.6%	41.4%

Sources: Serial set 2030, House Exec. Doc. 133, 50–152.

the country. The fastest rate of expansion of all occurred in the grain belt of the Northwest, but the cotton states were also gaining a fair share of the burgeoning population.

As suggested by these comparative rates of population increase, migration into the West was substantial over the period.[1] By our calculations, over 70 percent of the western population in 1860 was composed of post-1810 migrants and their descendants.[2] The majority of these new westerners hailed from the eastern seaboard, and domestic migration accounted for over one-

[1] For the five decades, respectively, these percentage rates are 2.0, 2.3, 1.8, 2.5, and 2.4 for the non-West, and 6.9, 4.9, 5.6, 4.2, and 4.1 for the West.

[2] To get an approximate estimate of the significance of migration, we must compare the rate of natural increase to the rate of total population growth. The evidence on the rate of natural increase for the entire United States in the first half of the nineteenth century suggests that it was around 25 per thousand in the population. See Bruchey (1965): 75; and Davis, Easterlin, and Parker, et al. (1972): 123–24. If we may assume that the natural rate of population increase in the West was similar to that for the country as a whole, then the western population by 1860 would have been about 3.7 million if there had been no migration into the West (1810–60). Consequently, the bulk of the western population, some 9.3 million people, apparently either migrated into the area after 1810 or were direct descendents of such immigrants. The findings by Yasuba suggest that over this period the trans-Appalachian West experienced fertility rates slightly above the national average and mortality rates not far from the national average.

half of the total increase in western population from 1810 to 1860.[3] By comparison, foreign migration, including descendants, roughly equaled the natural rate of increase of those westerners resident in 1810, each accounting for a little less than one-quarter of the increase.

Many factors contributed to the lure of the West, and Douglass North has emphasized the importance of economic opportunities in that connection.[4] Specifically, he shows a strong correlation between the timing of high cotton prices and large volumes of land sales in the Southwest and a similar coincidence of wheat prices and land sales in the Northwest.[5] The evidence points to boom decades in 1810–20, in the 1830s, and in the 1850s.

Some critics argue that land sales during these periods were caused by pervasive speculation.[6] But much of the land was actually being put to use; Table 23 shows that the periods of highest rates of change in the acreage of tilled land coincided with the boom decades for both staple prices and land sales. The percentage rates of change in improved acres were 9.0, 4.9, 5.3, 4.6, and 6.4 respectively for each decade from 1810 to 1860. In the Northwest region, for which the data are most reliable, the differences are even more striking: 23.5 percent, 6.5 percent, 7.1 percent, 5.4 percent, and 7.8 percent in each decade respectively from 1810 to 1860.[7] Consequently, the supply response to high staple prices is observed in terms both of population and of improved land in the West.[8]

---

see Yasuba (1962): 55, 80, for regional comparisons. Our assumption, then, that the natural rate of increase in the West was the same as for the nation gives a slight upward bias to the importance of migration in western population growth.

[3] The geographic origin of these new settlers cannot be determined with precision, but it is possible to construct a crude estimate of the approximate relative importance of domestic vis-à-vis foreign immigration into the West. Between 1820 and 1860 approximately 5.1 million foreigners arrived and stayed in the United States. See *U.S. Historical Statistics* (1960): 57. According to Thomas Page, 55.5 percent of the immigrants were located in the Northeast in 1850; Page (1912): 676–94. Although a few immigrants went south, the great mass of European settlers generally preferred the Northeast and the West. By assuming that most of the remaining immigrants went West, say about 40 percent, and that their natural rate of increase approximated that of the domestic population, then their number, including their descendants, would have been around 2.7 million in 1860. The remaining 6.6 million (9.3–2.7) were domestic migrants (including descendants) and 2.6 million resulted from the natural rate of increase of the 1810 westerners. The total increase was 11.9 million.

[4] North (1961), chaps. x and xi.

[5] North (1966): 124, 137.

[6] See, for instance, Albro Martin's review of David H. Fischer's *Historians' Fallacies. Toward a Logic of Historical Thought* (New York: Harper & Row, 1971), in *Journal of Economic History*, 32, no. 4 (December 1972): 968–70, and Temin (1969): 93–112.

[7] For an extremely useful account of developments in the Northwest, see Clark (1966). It should be noted that the coincidence of these rates is clear for the Northwest. For the Southwest the picture is somewhat more cloudy because of the necessary aggregation and crudeness of our estimates of improved acres in Table 22.

[8] The only variable slightly out of step with this general sequence is the rate of western population growth, 1850–60. A general slowing of population growth would be

Moreover, such supply responses did not occur coincidentally in an iso lated market. As transportation developments more solidly linked its region: to the seaboard and abroad, the West evolved into an important segment of the national and international economy. Although economic unification on a national scale was far from complete in the early nineteenth century, consid erable progress had been achieved fairly early in the commodity markets. As Thomas Berry's analysis of regional price movements graphically shows, a strong linkage was forged between the East and West during the period:

It is difficult to point to any consistent lag of the West behind the East during this early period (1788—1817) because of such diversity in general behavior; i is safe to state, however, that in such first-magnitude movements as those o 1793—1797 and 1810—1817 there was a lag measuring somewhat more than a year in length. . . . Taking a later interval (1816—1860) weighted genera indices of monthly prices in New York, New Orleans, and Cincinnati show agreement with each other to a surprising degree. . . . Cincinnati prices lagged the greater part of a year in their decline in 1819—1820, but they were only three or four months behind the seaboard markets in the turning-point o 1839 and reacted simultaneously at the time of the panic of 1857.[9]

As we have repeatedly emphasized, a viable transportation system was the *sine qua non* for the perfecting of a market for commodities between the West and other regions. In combination, the rivers, canals, and in later decades the rails, linked the West to the seaboard and between 1810 and 1860 brought about a tremendous reduction in the costs of internal trans port, which vastly improved the economic returns to western farmers engaged in crop production for market.

Table 24, which shows estimates of Cincinnati prices as a percentage o New York, Philadelphia, and New Orleans prices for selected western goods indicates that over time and without exception the farmers were obtaining a larger share of the selling price of their crops. As a corollary, consumers were paying an ever decreasing share of the purchase price for transportation and other marketing costs.

---

expected in the West, however, as the region's growing population lessened the effect o migration on its overall growth rate. In addition, we would expect the link betweer population growth and agricultural expansion to lessen as various improvements i agriculture raised output relative to the number of workers, equipment, and othe inputs. And that is what happened. According to Robert Gallman's estimates, produc tivity in agriculture rose at an annual rate of almost 0.5 percent (1810—60), and as note in Table 21 (note 2) the number of acres of improved land per person took a shar jump in the 1850s (Gallman [1972]).

The supply response to the jump in staple prices in the 1850s was apparently more i terms of improved acres and productivity advances than in terms of population. See, fo instance, David, in Fogel and Engerman, *eds.* (1971): 214—27.

[9] Berry (1943): 97—99.

Table 23. Acres of Improved Land[a] in the Trans-Appalachian West, 1810–60

State/year	1810	1820	1830	1840	1850	1860
Ohio	225,675	2,892,456	4,665,000	7,558,750	9,851,493	12,665,587
Michigan					1,929,110	3,419,861
Indiana	125,530	751,445	1,751,409	3,485,729	5,046,543	8,161,717
Illinois	72,692	325,272	931,860	2,818,373	5,039,545	13,251,473
Missouri	89,805	286,870	605,117	1,653,001	2,938,425	6,246,871
Iowa				184,969	824,682	3,780,253
Wisconsin				105,930	1,045,499	8,746,036
Kentucky					5,968,270	7,644,217
Tennessee					5,175,173	6,897,974
Arkansas	3,847,200[b]	6,024,700	8,587,600	11,929,900	781,530	1,933,036
Mississippi					3,444,358	5,150,008
Louisiana					1,590,025	2,734,901
Total	4,360,902	10,280,743	16,540,986	27,736,652	43,634,653	80,631,934

[a]Serial set 1476, House Misc. Doc. (unnumbered), vol. 4, 689, states that "by 'Improved Land' is meant cleared land used for grazing, grass, or tillage, or lying fallow."
[b]Data on the number of acres of improved land in the states of Kentucky, Tennessee, Arkansas, Mississippi, and Louisiana were not available for the decades prior to 1850. To estimate these data a relationship between the population and the number of acres of improved land has been sought for the remaining states for which data are available. The results were as follows:

Decade	Population	Improved land (acres)	Improved land (acres person)
1810	293,169	513,702	1.75
1820	858,957	4,265,043	4.94
1830	1,610,473	7,953,386	4.94
1840	3,351,542	15,806,752	4.72
1850	5,397,485	26,675,297	4.94
1860	8,783,809	56,271,798	6.41

The acreage of improved land per person in the states of Kentucky, Tennessee, Arkansas, Mississippi, and Louisiana was 5.11 in 1850 and 5.80 in 1860. On the basis of these results and the consideration that those five states were relatively much more settled and developed than the other states of the trans-Appalachian west in 1810, we have assumed that these states had an average of 4.9 acres of improved land per person from 1810 through 1840. Thus, for the states of Kentucky, Tennessee, Arkansas, Mississippi, and Louisiana we had:

Decade	Population	Improved land (acres)
1810	785,146	3,847,200
1820	1,229,532	6,024,700
1830	1,752,569	8,587,600
1840	2,434,674	11,929,900

Sources: National Ship–Canal Convention. Serial set 1476, vol. 4, House Misc. Doc. (unnumbered), 688.

Table 24. Cincinnati Wholesale Prices as a Percentage of Philadelphia, New York, and New Orleans Wholesale Prices, 1816–60

	Commodity																	
	Flour (bbl.)			Wheat (bu.)			Corn (bu.)			Mess Pork (bbl.)			Lard (lb.)			Whiskey (gal.)		
Period	Phil.	N.Y.	N.O.	Phil.	N.Y.	N.O.	Phil.	N.Y.	N.O.	Phil.	N.Y.	N.O.	Phil.	N.Y.	N.O.	Phil.	N.Y.	N.O.
1816–20	63	66	72	45	48	—	51	48	—	56	58	63	65	69	68	—	—	—
1821–25	52	52	56	39	38	—	38	32	30	63	67	76	59	65	68	68	70	67
1826–30	68	67	67	50	48	—	49	41	29	67	68	78	56	65	66	80	79	75
1831–35	73	74	76	57	56	—	55	49	36	77	77	85	69	71	78	89	89	83
1836–40	73	73	77	59	61	—	56	51	47	87	85	86	83	82	87	91	91	79
1841–45	77	73	86	68	65	90	53	47	65	82	79	84	79	83	91	80	77	87
1846–50	78	71	87	68	63	88	51	48	62	81	90	88	80	86	93	74	73	90
1851–55	82	79	90	73	61	90	61	59	74	85	90	92	82	93	94	78	78	88
1856–60	88	95	89	79	70	86	70	66	72	91	94	93	86	96	94	85	83	87

Sources: Cole (1938) Statistical Supplement, pp. 174–356.

Note: These computations were made from worksheets kindly provided by Thomas A. Berry.

To the farmers, therefore, reductions in transportation costs and other transaction costs served to increase the demand for western products and thereby exerted a buoyant influence on the prices of their goods. To consumers, on the other hand, cost reductions appeared as an increase in supply, which thus pressed downward on prices.[10]

It is generally conceded that the overcoming of distance was such a critical problem in the development of the early West that the limits of feasible commercial agriculture were determined by the costs of moving goods. As freight costs were reduced, new areas could be profitably cleared and cultivated.[11] Increased specialization of production, therefore, was highly dependent on improvements in western transportation.[12]

[10] For a formal model indicating the effects of such price adjustments due to falling transportation costs, see Shepherd and Walton (1972): 13–23.

[11] For a formal representation of these effects see Shepherd and Walton (1972): 13–23.

[12] It should be noted, of course, that in addition to developments in agriculture, manufacturing output also rose substantially in the West during this period, principally in the processing of agricultural products and in activities associated with the extractive industries of lead, copper, iron, and lumber. Unfortunately, the early census data, before 1840, are "so poor that they are almost worthless" (a statement made by Douglass C. North and supported by Raymond W. Goldsmith, as reported in Bruchey [1965]: 84). Therefore, any quantification of manufacturing output must be limited to the 1840–60 period. Our estimates below give the values of manufactures produced in the trans-Appalachian West, in 1840, 1850, and 1860. Though below the national average in per capita terms it is evident that a substantial amount of manufacturing development had taken place by 1840. In aggregate terms, manufacturing output in the West grew faster than that of the rest of the country (1840–60). However, in per capita terms, it did not keep pace—a reflection of the growing regional specialization of manufacturing in the Northeast. Though manufacturing added considerable economic diversification to the region, agriculture remained the principal sector during the ante-bellum period.

Value of Manufactured Products for the States of the
Trans-Appalachian West, by Decade, 1840–60

State/Year	1840[a]	1850[a]	1860
Ohio	$ 27,681,578	$ 62,692,279	$ 121,691,148
Michigan	3,327,671	11,169,002	32,658,356
Indiana	8,138,274	18,725,423	42,803,469
Illinois	5,956,327	16,534,272	57,580,886
Missouri	4,505,186	24,324,418	41,782,731
Iowa	347,713	3,551,783	13,971,325
Wisconsin	1,468,723	9,293,068	27,849,467
Kentucky	12,182,786	21,710,212	37,931,240
Tennessee	8,089,992	9,725,608	17,987,225
Arkansas	1,473,715	537,908	2,880,578
Mississippi	2,386,857	2,912,068	6,590,687
Louisiana	8,641,439	6,779,417	15,587,473
Total	84,200,261	187,955,458	419,314,585
United States	$441,360,814	$1,019,106,616	$1,885,861,676

Western river developments, of course, were only one link in the overall improvement in transportation; but it should be stressed that the cost reductions resulting from the changeover to water transportation instead of wagon and other early land transport were greater per unit, both absolutely and relatively, than the subsequent savings from the railroad.[13] By far the most impressive decline in costs was on the upriver run, but significant saving were also achieved downstream.

The full impact of the steamboat and other craft on western development probably can never be determined precisely, and it is doubtful that a mean ingful estimate of social savings, similar to those made for railroads, could be calculated for river craft.[14] Conceptional difficulties and specification prob lems abound. What alternatives were there—wagons and canals? Or should the railroad also be considered? Any calculations would also be highly sensitive to the year selected because of yearly climatic variations. For such a calculation of social savings, one would need to know the volume of ton miles carried on the western rivers, the comparative costs of alternative media that might have substituted for the steamboat and other craft, and the elasticity of demand for such transport services. Further research along these lines could prove extremely interesting and useful.[15]

In any case, the history of the early West was inseparable from the economic flow of the rivers, and despite any attempts of counterfactual history to explain away their importance it is evident that much of the development of that area swept through the watery gateways of the river system.

Sources: Serial set 814, Senate Exec. Doc. 2, 98, and 99; Serial set 1476, House Misc. Doc. (unnumbered), vol. 4, 798, 799.

[a]Serial set 814, Senate Exec. Doc. 2, 96, 97, 100, and 101 gave somewhat different figures for the values of goods manufactured in 1840 and 1850. The total values of manufactures in the trans-Appalachian west for 1840 and 1850 according to those figures were respectively $100,164,506 and $218,169,324.

[13] North (1966): 11.

[14] See, for examples, Fishlow (1965), and Fogel (1964).

[15] Despite the above difficulties one study has attempted some tentative estimates of the social returns to western steamboats from the carriage of freight (see Davis, Easterlin Parker et al. [1972]: 518–19). Comparing steamboat rates to rates that would have likely prevailed without the steamboat shows that significant social gains were accruing to steamboat investments, but because the resource commitment to steamboating was limited (by comparison to railroads) social savings in the aggregate were also limited by comparison. Alternatively, by lumping all river craft together the social savings of using the rivers would take on significant proportions, and the size of the resource commit ment would be beside the point. Indeed, one of the low-cost aspects of river transporta tion was precisely that no large capital outlay was required for a canal ditch or rail bed

INDUSTRY CHARACTERISTICS IN HISTORICAL PERSPECTIVE[16]

This study has touched on a number of essential features of early western river transportation, especially those on the trunk river routes. Perhaps the one most deserving emphasis is competition as a general market characteristic. Repeated efforts failed to alter the competitive structure of the market for western river transportation services during the ante-bellum years. The initial attempt by Fulton and Livingston to secure a government-sanctioned monopoly was as unsuccessful as the later voluntary associations formed to restrain trade. The modest capital requirements needed to enter the business assured a competitive market, devoid of any significant barriers to entry in the absence of governmental interference.

As a consequence, the series of productivity-raising improvements which generated a remarkable record of cost reductions over the period were completely passed on to western transport users and to consumers generally. As reduced costs temporarily raised short-term profits, new investors added to the stock of tonnage. This in turn depressed river freight rates and, as our analysis has shown costs and freight rates followed a parallel downward course per unit. In short, the combination of keen market competition and an impressive record of productivity advance exerted a strong favorable downward influence on the costs of river transport.

A major cause of the decline was, of course, the application of steam power. Even more important, however, was the stream of modifications and improvements that followed the maiden voyage of the *New Orleans* and which—in combination with the initial impact of steam power on the rivers—generated a rate of productivity advance far greater than occurred in any other transportation medium of the nineteenth century.

Apart from this distinction, steamboating followed a path of expansion much like that in other industries. Although we lack strictly comparable output series, our evidence on total tonnage and productivity change indicates that the industry did exhibit the normal features of industrial growth as set forth, for instance, in the classic study by Simon Kuznets, where it is declared that industries commonly grow very fast in the early decades following their formation and then expand at slower rates as they mature. [17] Our findings are similar to these more general observations.

---

[16] It should be emphasized that the following summary of key industry characteristics is based primarily on our analyses of quantitative information derived from the trunk route between Louisville and New Orleans. From the analysis in Appendix F, we are confident that these findings reveal the typical and major forces of change in the industry on the trunk river routes. Appropriate qualifications of these findings for the tributaries are made below.

[17] Kuznets (1967): 325.

In contrast to the earlier findings by Hunter (see Appendix B, Table B–2), however, our findings show that steamboating had not entered a period of absolute decline prior to the Civil War. Undoubtedly, the railroad was making inroads during the 1850s, first in passenger service and later in freight, but by our estimates total steamboat tonnage continued to expand right up to the outbreak of hostilities.

Like the persistence of flatboating on the western rivers, the continuance of steamboating after the advent of the railroad was not merely the result of keeping durable capital in use. New steamboat construction continued, and for a variety of services the railroad in the 1850s had not clearly demonstrated any superiority over shipment by water. Furthermore, in some respects the railroad was actually complementary to the river traffic: the establishment of short-haul feeder lines from the major ports was an expansionary force for shipping. Though modest by comparison with earlier decades, the advances in steamboat productivity continued into the final decades of the ante-bellum period, transfusing new life into the moribund technology. Of course, the railroad did erode steamboating business in many areas, especially in the provision of passenger services, but steamboating continued to spread westward with the population, and the loss of activity in the older regions was offset by the creation of new business in newly settled areas.

The major improvements which kept the steamboat competitively afloat were the increase in carrying capacity per measured ton, the lengthened navigation season, and the shortened times of passage and of cargo collection. Previous studies have noted such improvements, but for want of systematic inquiry into the sources of steamboat productivity, certain influences, such as the importance of increased speeds, have been misrepresented.[18] As we have shown, the significant increase in the average number of yearly round trips stemmed more from a prolonged navigation season and from reduced cargo collection times than from more rapid passage.

Adaptation of the steamboat's physical characteristics to shallow-water use—which stands out as the most important improvement—illustrates the process of learning-by-doing and is a tribute to the skills and the ingenuity of early craftsmen and mechanics. Except for the initial introduction of steam power on the rivers, the progress of steamboating owed less to new knowledge about basic principles than to the imaginative restructuring of known principles of design and energy to fit shallow-water conditions. Such improvements increased the carrying capacity per measured ton, stretched the navigation season, and contracted the passage times. River improvements were also

[18] See, for instance, Kirkland (1969): 142; and Williamson (1949): 124.

a factor in lengthening the navigation season as well as in lowering insurance costs. Improved labor skills similarly influenced insurance costs and, in conjunction with the establishment of fuel stations, lowered passage times. Although there is little direct evidence, we suggest that the fall in cargo collection times resulted primarily from economies of scale and from organizational improvements due to overall market growth.

Improvements in flatboating also added a chapter to the story of progress on the western rivers. The persistence of flatboating stands in sharp contrast to the quick surrender of keelboating from the major trunk routes and its continuing retreat throughout the river system before the chugging advance of the steam vessels. To understand the contrast between the fates of the two older vessels we recall that keelboats earned most of their revenues on the upriver passage, and that upriver rates plummeted with the coming of steam. The current-floated flat was threatened less drastically, since reductions in downstream rates were minor by comparison. More importantly, flatboating enjoyed positive spillover effects because the steamboat saved much time and hardship on the upriver trek for returning flatboat crews. The quick returns also permitted more journeys per year, which heightened skills and (in conjunction with river improvements) resulted in the use of larger flatboats, which in turn economized labor per ton mile carried.

The competition engineered by flatboats had an important bearing on the seasonal pattern of downriver freight rates. Unlike ocean rates and rates on the Great Lakes, which soared during periods of peak activity and dropped during underutilized periods, the river rates were pressed downward during peak river use because this coincided with periods of high water, when the thousands of flats descending the rivers greatly expanded the supply of services. Since flats just as quickly departed the rivers when low water (and low demand for shipping) occurred, the old technology provided an important short-run supply of downriver services and, coincidentally, was responsive to demand fluctuations.

Several of these findings for the trunk river routes, especially with regard to steamboating and keelboating, were not characteristic of the tributaries. The main differences between steamboating on the tributaries as compared to steamboating on the trunk rivers was the later arrival of the new technology, the later period of bonanza profits that continued into the 1850s, the greater risks and hazards of service on the tributaries and the lower levels of steamboat productivity there. Keelboats, which quickly disappeared from the trunk after the advent of steamboats, were able to operate on the tributaries and back waterways until the mid-1840s, partially because the thinness of trade and more hazardous river conditions on the tributaries made the small keelboats relatively more efficient there. In addition, keelboats and steamboats were both complementary and competitive to each other. Steamboats often towed the lumbering keelboats upriver, while keelboats were frequently used as lighters to assist steamboats in dangerous shallow waters.

Finally, the development of the western river transportation system as a whole stemmed primarily from private initiative. Investments made by the various levels of government to improve the rivers were miniscule compared to the total resources deployed there. Government involvement undoubtedly generated many benefits, but constitutional difficulties at the federal level and problems of cooperation at the state level limited involvement by the public sector. One major constraint at the state and local levels was the nature of river improvements, especially on the trunk routes where benefits were extremely dispersed and for the most part disassociated from financial contributions by any particular state or locality.

To the degree that public and private enterprise did cooperate in the development of the western river transportation system, the uneasy partnership was on a scale totally unlike that for canals and railroads during the era of internal improvements, though here too we feel that the degree of involvement has been exaggerated.

These findings strongly suggest that we reconsider the current orthodoxy that emphasizes significant public involvement in nineteenth-century internal transportation developments which appears to have resulted from preoccupation with canals and railroads. The development of the natural waterways on which the West so greatly depended in the ante-bellum years owed its very existence to private initiative and enterprise.

EPILOGUE

Although our story ends with the outbreak of hostilities, it is important to stress that the Civil War did not precipitate a long-run decline of steamboating on the western rivers. Despite heavy losses, which led to a fall in total tonnage in the early years of conflict, new construction more than made up for these losses. As displayed in Table 25, 1864 was a year of tremendous construction of steamboats, which raised the total tonnage to prewar levels. By 1865, the total stock of steamboat tonnage on the western rivers was at an all time high. Again, this evidence stands in contrast to the belief that steamboating had entered a period of decline in the 1850s. In fact, this period did not arrive until the 1880s.[1]

Table 25. Tonnage of Steamboats in Operation on the Western Rivers, 1860–68 (000s)

Year	Total tonnage lost	New tonnage constructed	Total tonnage
1860	33.4	35.6	195.0
1861	42.8	12.9	165.1
1862	24.9	17.1	157.3
1863	38.8	41.7	160.2
1864	28.2	61.2	193.2
1865	19.4	54.8	228.7
1866	31.3	41.0	238.4
1867	31.0	24.9	232.3
1868	28.2	7.9	212.2

Source: Appendix B, Table B–1.

[1] U.S. *Historical Statistics,* Series Q–174.

APPENDIX A

The Western Commercial Gateways
1810-1860

Table A–1. Freight Shipments from the Trans-Appalachian West Received by the Southern Gateway, 1810–60 (tons)

Year	Receipts at New Orleans*	Year	Receipts at New Orleans*	Year	Receipts at New Orleans*
1810	60,000	1827	235,200	1844	652,000
1811	60,000	1828	257,300	1845	868,000
1812	60,000	1829	245,700	1846	971,700
1813	60,000	1830	260,900	1847	937,600
1814	67,600	1831	307,300	1848	1,025,900
1815	77,200	1832	244,600	1849	1,009,900
1816	94,600	1833	291,700	1850	886,000
1817	80,800	1834	327,800	1851	1,058,200
1818	100,900	1835	399,900	1852	1,160,500
1819	136,300	1836	437,100	1853	1,328,800
1820	106,700	1837	401,500	1854	1,286,300
1821	99,300	1838	449,600	1855	1,247,200
1822	136,400	1839	399,500	1856	1,500,200
1823	129,500	1840	537,400	1857	1,431,800
1824	136,200	1841	542,500	1858	1,572,700
1825	176,400	1842	566,500	1859	1,803,400
1826	193,300	1843	782,600	1860	2,187,600

Sources: For 1814–60, Callender (1909): 315. Serial set 2552, House Exec. Doc. 6, pt. II, 184–85 reports the downstream commerce of the Mississippi River as follows:

Year	Volume (tons)	Value (dollars)
1801	38,325	3,649,322
1802	45,906	4,475,364
1803	49,960	4,720,015
1804		4,275,000
1805		4,371,545
1806		4,937,323
1807		5,370,555

On the basis of this information, the downstream shipments from 1810 through 1813 are estimated at 60,000 tons annually.

Note: These figures are the receipts of produce at New Orleans by river. The figures do not include articles rafted downstream, of which no records were kept. The figures do include articles floated downstream by flatboats and barges. They also include a small amount of produce received via Lake Pontchartrain, from 1 to 6 percent of the total. The data for the years 1810 through 1841 are for the twelve months ending September 30 of the year shown. The data for the years 1842 through 1860 are for the twelve months ending August 31 of the year shown.

*Rounded.

124

Table A–2. Freight Shipments from the Trans-Appalachian West by the Northern Gateway, 1810–60 (tons)

Year	Domestic exports	Erie Canal	New York Central R.R.	New York and Erie R.R.	Total*
1810	280				280
1811	400				400
1812	100				100
1813	–				–
1814	–				–
1815	740				740
1816	1,170				1,170
1817	2,320				2,320
1818	1,710				1,710
1819	560				560
1820	1,510				1,510
1821	1,070				1,070
1822	20				20
1823	20				20
1824	–				–
1825	–				–
1826	40				40
1827	30				30
1828	–				–
1829	40				40
1830	30				30
1831	500				500
1832	1,300				1,300
1833	4,700				4,700
1834	5,500				5,500
1835	3,200				3,200
1836	1,200	54,219			55,400
1837	4,100	56,255			60,400
1838	5,300	83,233			88,500
1839	4,600	121,761			126,400
1840	23,100	158,148			181,200
1841	17,600	224,176			241,800
1842	23,200	221,477			244,700
1843	7,700	256,376			264,100
1844	16,800	308,025			324,800
1845	11,400	304,551			316,000
1846	12,100	506,830			518,900
1847	18,500	812,840			831,300
1848	5,400	650,154			655,600
1849	7,300	768,659			776,000
1850	7,300	841,501			848,800
1851	13,100	1,045,820			1,058,900
1852	10,700	1,151,978	48,000	48,000	1,258,700
1853	10,700	1,213,690	70,000	70,000	1,364,400
1854	29,500	1,094,391	117,000	77,161	1,318,100
1855	43,100	1,092,876	147,500	113,331	1,396,800
1856	72,600	1,212,550	172,781	202,682	1,660,600
1857	90,600	1,019,998	179,647	157,820	1,448,100
1858	155,300	1,273,099	229,275	224,886	1,882,600
1859	117,100	1,036,634	234,241	171,206	1,559,200
1860	109,300	1,896,975	293,520	300,000	2,599,800

Table A–2 cont.

Sources: Domestic Exports: These represent exports from Ohio, Michigan, Illinois, Indiana, and Wisconsin to Canada or to the seaboard via the St. Lawrence seaway thus by-passing the Erie Canal. The estimates, as presented in the sources (cited below) are in terms of dollar values. These values are converted to tonnage equivalents by assuming that these exports had an average value of $50 per ton throughout the period, a figure roughly equal to the average value per ton of goods moved on the Erie Canal between 1837 and 1860. The tonnage estimates are rounded to the nearest 10 tons prior to 1831 and to the nearest 100 tons thereafter.

Poor (1881): xvii and Callender (1909): 315 gave both the amount of freight and the value of produce received at New Orleans by river for each year from 1816 through 1860. These data indicate that the value of goods shipped into New Orleans averaged approximately $100 per ton. In the calculation of tonnage estimates of domestic exports the average value of $50 per ton was used because it appeared that the Erie Canal data were more relevant than the New Orleans data.

The statistics on the value of exports of domestic products to Canada from customs ports west of Buffalo given in Serial set 1176, Senate Exec. Doc. 55, 113 indicate that at least for the period 1856–60 almost all of these exports were destined for Canada. The substantial increase in exports, starting in 1854 when the Reciprocity Treaty came into effect, supports this notion. It also raises the possibility that the exports for earlier years may be understated due to smuggling. The data for the years 1810 through 1842 are for the twelve months ending September 30 of the year shown. The figure for 1843 is for the nine months ending June 30, 1843. The remaining data are for the twelve months ending June 30 of the year shown. Serial set 330, House Doc. 330, 7–16; Serial set 349, House Doc. 253, 284; Serial set 361, Senate Doc. 577, 286; Serial set 379, Senate Doc. 238, 280; Serial set 399, Senate Doc. 356, 320; Serial set 425, House Doc. 220, 330; Serial set 435, Senate Doc. 289, 384; Serial set 456, Senate Doc. 125, 232; Serial set 482, House Doc. 13, 228; Serial set 494, Senate Doc. 7, 226; Serial set 504, Senate Exec. Doc. 5, 358–59; Serial set 541, House Exec. Doc. 42, 294–95; Serial set 553, Senate Exec. Doc. 3, 304–05; Serial set 604, House Exec. Doc. (unnumbered), 310–11; Serial set 628, Senate Exec. Doc. (unnumbered), 322–23; Serial set 622, Senate Exec. Doc. (unnumbered), 304; Serial set 703, Senate Exec. Doc. (unnumbered), 304; Serial set 750, Senate Exec. Doc. (unnumbered), 312; Serial set 825, Senate Exec. Doc. (unnumbered), 330; Serial set 886, Senate Exec. Doc. (unnumbered), 548; Serial set 931, Senate Exec. Doc. (unnumbered), 514; Serial set 989, Senate Exec. Doc. (unnumbered), 552; Serial set 1034, Senate Exec. Doc. (unnumbered), 544; Serial set 1087, Senate Exec. Doc. (unnumbered), 552. Erie Canal: North (1961): 251. New York Central and New York and Erie railroads: Callendar (1909): 342. Serial set 1176, Senate Exec. Doc. 55, 140, reports the following eastbound movements on the New York Central (in tons):

	1858	1859	1860
Through freight	229,275	234,241	293,529
Way freight	349,775	336,686	436,729
Total	579,050	570,927	730,258

(footnotes to Table A–2)

No figures are given for earlier years or for the New York and Erie.

*Rounded.

Table A–3. Freight Shipments from the Trans-Appalachian West by the Northeastern Gateway, 1835–60 (tons)

Year	Pennsylvania canals*	Pennsylvania R.R.	Baltimore and Ohio R.R.	Total*
1835	17,000			17,000
1836	17,200			17,200
1837	20,200			20,200
1838	25,100			25,100
1839	18,700			18,700
1840	27,900			27,900
1841	26,900			26,900
1842	32,900			32,900
1843	46,600			46,600
1844	39,600			39,600
1845	41,300			41,300
1846	52,100			52,100
1847	82,800			82,800
1848	60,200			60,200
1849	57,000			57,000
1850	82,800			82,800
1851	97,000			97,000
1852	111,800			111,800
1853		38,837	21,014	59,900
1854		53,825	90,368	144,200
1855		106,407	72,779	179,200
1856		88,707	145,598	234,300
1857		94,905	126,323	221,200
1858		141,268	171,084	312,400
1859		129,767	135,127	264,900
1860		150,000	149,651	299,700

Sources: Pennsylvania Canals: Reiser (1951): 213–24, gives a detailed breakdown of the shipments eastward from Pittsburgh from 1835 through 1850. To convert these data to tons, the following conversions were used: boards, 1,000 ft. = 3,333 lbs.; coal, 1 ton = 2,000 lbs.; fish, 1 bbl. = 280 lbs.; gypsum, 1 ton = 2,000 lbs.; oil, 1 gal. = 8.5 lbs.; salt, 1 bu. = 70 lbs.; stone, 1 perch = 4,000 lbs.; timber, 1,000 ft. = 3,333 lbs.; wood, 1 cord = 6,000 lbs.; posts and rails, 100 lbs. each; bricks, 4.5 lbs. each; flour, 1 bbl. = 200 lbs.; lime, 1 bu. = 80 lbs.; shingles, 1,000 = 250 lbs.; staves, hoops, etc., 2.2 lbs. each; whiskey, 1 gal. = 9 lbs.; window glass, 1 box = 80 lbs.; clover and grass seeds, 1 bu. = 60 lbs.; corn and other grain, 1 bu. = 56 lbs.; potatoes, 1 bu. = 60 lbs.; beef, 1 bbl. = 220 lbs.; pork, 1 bbl. = 220 lbs.; and wheat, 1 bu. = 60 lbs. Even substantial changes in most of the factors would have caused only small changes in the calculated shipments eastward by canal. The change in the total shipments out of the region would have been even smaller. This source contained a number of typographical errors, which became obvious in the process of conversion. It was possible to correct most of them by referring to other sources presenting the same information. In the remaining few cases assumptions had to be made.

Serial set 622, Senate Exec. Doc. 112, 721 listed exports from Pittsburgh by canal during 1852. To compute the total weight of these shipments the following additional conversion factors were required: barley, 1 bu. = 48 lbs.; bran and shipstuffs, 1 bu. = 20 lbs.; rye, 1 bu. = 56 lbs.; oats, 1 bu. = 32 lbs.; bark, 1 cord = 6,000 lbs.; hoop-poles and laths, less than 5 feet, 4 lbs. each; and liquors, foreign, 1 gal. = 9 lbs.

The shipments for 1851 were taken to be approximately equal to the average of those for 1850 and 1852. The shipments were made during the navigation season of the year shown.

Table A–3 cont.

The Pennsylvania and Baltimore and Ohio railroads: Callender (1909): 342; Serial set 1176, Senate Exec. Doc. 55, 138–40, reports the tonnages of goods shipped eastward from Pittsburgh on the Pennsylvania Railroad as follows:

	1859	1860	1861	1862
Through freight	129,767	176,007	386,439	502,884
Way freight	n.a.	n.a.	69,877	64,238
Total			456,316	567,122

No figures are given in this source for the Baltimore and Ohio Railroad.

Note: These estimates do not include freight shipped via the National Road or the Pennsylvania Turnpike, both opened in 1817. It is unlikely that these could have exceeded 10,000 tons annually.

*Rounded.

APPENDIX B

Estimates of Annual Steamboat Construction (Gross and Net) and Tonnage in Operation on Western Rivers, 1811 — 1868

Previous efforts have generated two sets of estimates on the aggregate operating tonnage of western river steamboats during the ante-bellum period. One set, the official one, was compiled by the Treasury Department, but is alleged to "give a greatly exaggerated picture of the extent of the western steamboat interest, the result evidently of a failure to strike from the enrollment lists many steamboats that had worn out or were lost through accident."[1] The second set was compiled by Louis C. Hunter from the Lytle List.[2] It, however, is deficient because (1) it is not adjusted for significant revisions made in the List since Hunter originally made his calculations; (2) it is incomplete and covers only a select number of years; and (3) Hunter's assumption about the average life span of ante-bellum western steamboats used in calculating his estimates of operating tonnage is not consistent with the evidence, and, consequently, he understates the operating tonnage for the last decade of the ante-bellum period.

Given the deficiencies of the estimates by the Treasury Department and by Hunter, we have derived a new series based on the revised Lytle List.[3] The Lytle List is an alphabetical (by name) listing of steamboats, based on the

[1] Hunter (1949): 32.
[2] Ibid. The exact citation being William M. Lytle, *Steam Vessels Built in the United States 1807 to 1856,* United States Department of Commerce, Bureau of Navigation (Washington, 1931).
[3] Lytle (1952, 1954, 1958).

original enrollment records of merchant steam vessels of the United States constructed between 1807 and 1868. The entry for each steamboat includes its measured tonnage, the year of construction, the port of construction, the first home port, and the year it went out of service. Since steamboats operating in the antebellum era on the western rivers were of special design, and boats not constructed at points on the river system were generally not designed to operate there,[4] we have isolated the western river steamboats on the basis of where they were constructed and the location of their first home port. Our estimated annual gross and net steamboat construction and the annual tonnage in operation on western rivers are presented in Table B–1.

Table B–1. Annual Construction (Gross and Net) and Tonnage of Steamboats in Operation on Western Rivers, 1811–68

Year	Gross ships constructed		Ships out of service		Net ships constructed		Ships in operation	
	No.	Tonnage	No.	Tonnage	No.	Tonnage	No.	Tonnage
(1)	(2)	(3)	(4)	(5)	(6)	(7)	(8)	(9)
1811	1	371			1	371	1	371
1812	0				0	0	1	371
1813	1	25			1	25	2	396
1814	3	689	2	396	1	293	3	689
1815	4	827			4	827	7	1516
1816	4	758			4	758	11	2274
1817	5	701			5	701	16	2975
1818	16	3201	2	355	14	2846	30	5821
1819	30	7266	1	131	29	7135	59	12956
1820	13	1840	3	588	10	1252	69	14208
1821	7	685	3	403	4	282	73	14490
1822	12	1216	14	2263	−2	−1047	71	13443
1823	16	1905	13	2806	3	−955	74	12488
1824	13	2037	20	4048	−7	−2011	67	10477
1825	27	4094	14	2044	13	2050	80	12527
1826	39	6513	12	1756	27	4757	107	17284
1827	36	5912	23	3508	13	2404	120	19688
1828	25	3518	27	4260	−2	−742	118	18946
1829	45	6945	23	3581	22	3364	140	22310
1830	35	5504	24	3240	11	2264	151	24574
1831	60	8417	28	4298	32	4119	183	28693
1832	89	12856	45	6358	44	6498	227	35191
1833	52	7482	40	5841	12	1641	239	36832
1834	70	8569	39	4379	31	4190	270	41022
1835	88	12650	34	3549	54	9101	324	50123
1836	124	18320	74	11076	50	7244	374	57367
1837	105	18059	80	11826	25	6233	399	63600

[4] See Chapter 2, and Hunter (1949), Chapter 2.

Table B–1 cont.

1838	65	10292	73	8579	−8	1713	391	65313
1839	129	18952	40	6062	89	12890	480	78203
1840	76	13183	62	8760	14	4423	494	82626
1841	112	18396	102	15863	10	2533	504	85159
1842	99	16167	145	24849	−46	−8672	458	76477
1843	103	18978	112	15544	−9	3434	449	79911
1844	123	21794	63	11389	60	10405	509	90316
1845	135	23037	106	17198	29	5839	538	96155
1846	147	25882	107	15700	40	10182	578	106337
1847	158	31868	98	15776	60	16092	638	122429
1848	155	31338	127	20411	28	10927	666	133356
1849	122	23701	140	26937	−18	−3236	648	130120
1850	113	25877	123	21431	−10	4446	638	134566
1851	132	28668	110	20306	22	8362	660	142928
1852	155	37203	139	27246	16	9957	676	152885
1853	135	37829	100	21461	35	16368	711	169253
1854	120	28336	135	28573	15	−237	696	169016
1855	133	33934	133	30255	0	3679	696	172695
1856	163	38768	98	23323	65	15445	761	188140
1857	163	39325	124	27895	39	11430	800	199570
1858	96	22360	117	25556	−21	−3196	779	196374
1859	137	27407	137	30964	0	−3557	779	192817
1860	183	35627	145	33422	38	2205	817	195022
1861	57	12874	209	42768	−152	−29894	665	165128
1862	113	17122	112	24948	1	−7826	666	157302
1863	238	41709	126	38845	112	2864	778	160166
1864	265	61248	124	28177	141	33071	919	193237
1865	191	54856	104	19379	87	35477	1006	228714
1866	137	40998	115	31277	22	9721	1028	238435
1867	81	24869	133	31028	−52	−6159	976	232276
1868	29	7919	131	28151	−102	−20232	874	212203

Source: Calculated from Lytle List.

Table B–2 compares our estimates (H-M-W) on the tonnage of steamboats in operation on western rivers for selected years with the official estimates and Hunter's estimates. Except for one year (1825), our estimates are significantly smaller than the official estimates, ranging from 53.6 percent of the official estimate to 83.6 percent. Compared to Hunter's estimates, ours are lower in 7 out of 11 years, the relative differences, however, being much smaller than between ours and the official estimates.

The most important difference between our estimates and Hunter's is for 1860. While Hunter's estimates show a substantial *drop* in the operating tonnage between 1855 and 1860 (Table B–2), our estimates show a substantial *rise* over the same period. It is impossible to determine exactly the sources of discrepancy between our estimates of operating tonnage and Hunter's. Any comparison of the two estimates is hampered by Hunter's

Table B–2. Estimates of Steamboat Tonnage in Operation on Western Rivers for Selected
Years: 1817–60

Year	H-M-W (tons)	Official (tons)	Hunter (tons)
(1)	(2)	(3)	(4)
1817	2,975		3,290
1820	14,208		13,890
1823	12,488	15,478	12,501
1825	12,527	9,140	9,992
1830	24,574	30,124	29,481
1836	57,367	79,981	57,090
1840	82,626	98,851	83,592
1845	96,155	156,739	98,246
1850	134,566	251,019	141,834
1855	172,695	268,799	173,068
1860	195,022	292,470	162,735

Sources: H-M-W estimates are calculated from the Lytle List and supplements. The
official estimates are adapted by Hunter from the Treasury Department's annual reports
of commerce and navigation. Both the official estimates and Hunter's estimates are from
Hunter (1949): 33.

failure to specify from the Lytle List his criteria for selecting western river
steamboats from all the steamboats built in the United States before the Civil
War. Even if we assume that the criteria used were the same, two differences
remain.

One difference is that Hunter used an earlier and different "Lytle List."
The Lytle List we used was published by the Steamship Historical Society of
America in 1952, with supplements being published in 1954 and again in
1958.[5] Hunter's book was published in 1949, and his estimates are based on a
"preliminary" list compiled under Lytle's supervision in 1931 and entitled
"Steam Vessels Built in the United States, 1807–1856," United States Department of Commerce, Bureau of Navigation (Washington, 1931). This list
not only was much revised in the final 1952 publication and in the subsequent supplements, it fails to cover the period, 1857–60. (Note that the 1952
publication which we used in our study covers the period 1807–68.)

The second source of discrepancy is in the different ways we used the Lists
to calculate the operating tonnage estimates of western river steamboats.
Hunter used the annual gross construction estimates compiled by Lytle and
obtained his operating tonnage estimates by assuming an annual life span of
five years per steamboat.[6] Hence, as an example, his estimate of the 1825
operating tonnage would be the sum of the gross construction estimates for

[5] See footnote 3.
[6] See footnote 2.

the years 1820–25, and so forth. In contrast, we obtained our annual operating tonnage estimates by actually compiling data using both the construction date and the date of demise of each boat, boat by boat. Since not all boats had an average life span of five years, as Hunter assumed, it was expected that some discrepancy between our estimates and Hunter's would arise. By decade, our calculations show that the average life span of a western river steamboat during the ante-bellum period was 5.7 years between 1811 and 1819, 4.8 years during the 1820 decade, 5.0 years during the 1830 decade, 4.9 years during the 1840 decade, and 5.9 years between 1850 and 1860.

As it turns out, it is Hunter's assumption regarding the average life span of western river steamboats that largely explains why he obtained a smaller operating tonnage figure for 1860 than for 1855. Using his method, the 1860 estimate would be the sum of the annual gross construction estimates for the years 1856–60. Summing up the gross construction estimates for the years 1856–60 in Table B–1 yields a total of 163,487 tons, a figure not too different from Hunter's estimate of 162,735 tons for the year 1860. However, this leads to the false conclusion that there was an absolute decline in western river steamboat operating tonnage between 1855 and 1860. In fact, the lengthening of the average life span by approximately 20 percent during the last decade of the ante-bellum period resulted in an actual operating tonnage figure for 1860 of 195,022 tons.

APPENDIX C

The Cost Determinants of Steamboating in the Louisville-New Orleans Trade, 1810-1860

SOURCES OF COST DATA AND ESTIMATION PROCEDURES

Our estimates of steamboat costs are based on data from a wide variety of sources, cited at the appropriate points. There is, however, one set of cost data that plays a very important role in our estimates. This is the data obtained from the manuscript "Census of Manufactures for 1850."

The census data provides summaries of the accounts of forty-five steamboats that called at Louisville during the census year 1850.[1] Included in the data are:

- the name of the steamboat;
- the route on which it operated;
- the construction cost of the vessel;
- the number of crewmembers;
- the monthly wage bill;
- the annual expenditures for provisions, fuel, insurance, general expenses,[2] and lockage;[3]
- the number and horsepower of the engines;[4]
- the annual freight and passenger revenues;[5] and
- the number of months per year during which the boat operated.

---

[1] The existence of these data stems from the failure of R. Dawson, assistant marshall of Louisville, to complete Schedule 5 of the Census in accordance with the instructions. Not all of the vessels were registered at Louisville, so it must be assumed that these vessels happened to be in Louisville on census day. The date is not known, since Dawson did not date his census declaration.

[2] General expenses are presumed to include repair costs and wharfage charges.

[3] The steamboats *Logan, Mammoth Cave,* and *Major Barbour* reported lockage charges and insurance costs together, while the *Blue Wing No. 2* and the *Sea Gull* reported them separately.

[4] No horsepower was reported for the *General Lafayette.*

[5] Passenger and freight revenues are reported separately. All of the vessels, except the *Uncle Sam* which carried only freight, carried both passengers and freight.

These data were uncovered in the course of work being done by Bateman, Foust, and Weiss on nineteenth-century industrial development.[6]

The census data is supplemented by information on the registered tonnage, the date of construction, and the date of cesessation of service obtained from the "Lytle List."[7]

This body of cross-sectional data is analyzed in considerable detail in Appendix F. At this point it suffices to note that twenty-two of the vessels operated in the Louisville– New Orleans trade. The data pertaining to these vessels is used as an important check on the cost estimates.

The census data on the Louisville–New Orleans vessels serve another important purpose as well. They have been analyzed to determine whether or not the various cost items varied directly with vessel size. The analyses indicated that all of the cost components were approximately linear functions of vessel size over the range of 150 tons to 450 tons. This means that costs can be prorated on a tonnage basis without serious distortion. This procedure is used extensively in the development of our cost estimates.

AVERAGE SIZE

Estimates of the average size of steamboats have been derived from the "Lytle List." From the selection of western river steamboats, discussed in Appendix B, we have further isolated the vessel types in the Louisville–New Orleans trade by basing the estimates on only those vessels exceeding two hundred tons. The reason for excluding the smaller steamboats listed by Lytle is that the trunk Mississippi route predominantly engaged the larger and more luxurious boats.[8] Rounding to the nearest ten tons gives decade averages of 210, 290, 310, 310, and 360 tons, respectively, 1810–60, and evidence from other sources support these estimates of average size.[9]

The average size of the vessels reported in the 1850 census as operating in the Louisville–New Orleans trade was 411 tons. However an analysis of all the vessels arriving in New Orleans from Louisville during the period August 25, 1848 to August 30, 1849 gives an average of 310 tons.[10]

---

[6] Fred Bateman, James D. Foust, and Thomas J. Weiss, recipients of National Science Foundation grants 2450 and 2456, *Collaborative Research in United States Manufacturing, 1850–1870.*

[7] Lytle (1952, 1954, 1958). See also Appendix B.

[8] Serial set 345, House Doc. 21, 319, suggests that only boats over 200 tons operated in the Louisville–New Orleans trade. Other sources suggest that only "larger" steamboats operated in this trade but give no indication of the tonnages of such boats.

[9] Chevalier (1961): 210; Hall (1848a): 132; Morrison (1958): 234; Robertson (1855): 120; Serial set 359, Senate Doc. 284, 13, 14, 33, and 35; Serial set 442, House Doc. 154, 8.

[10] The *New Orleans Prices Current* give the name, date of arrival, and origin of all

AVERAGE LIFE SPAN

Calculations of a steamboat's average lifespan are also derived from the Lytle List, and our estimates are for those vessels used in the calculations of the average steamboat size. The results show an average lifespan of 5.7 years prior to 1820, 6.0 years during the 1820–29 decade, 6.5 years 1830–39, 5.3 years 1840–49, and 6.1 years during the 1850–60 decade. After rounding, the estimates of the average lifespan of steamboats in the Louisville–New Orleans trade are 5 years during the 1840–49 decade and 6 years for the remainder of the 1810–60 period.[11]

Most sources indicate that the average life span of all steamboats on the western rivers was 5 years throughout most of the ante-bellum period,[12] but this discrepancy is easily explained. We have calculated the average lifespan of all western river steamboats for each period, using data from the Lytle List. The results are 5.7, 4.8, 5.0, 4.9, and 5.9 years for the respective decades 1810–60, thus attesting to the accuracy of these sources. However, as shown, the average life span of the larger steamboats operating in the Louisville–New Orleans trade was about 6 years for most of this period. These results imply that the operation of smaller steamboats on the tributaries was even more dangerous than the operation of larger steamboats on the major trunk routes. The comparison of trunk and tributary vessels from the 1850 census in Appendix F supports this.

CONSTRUCTION COSTS PER TON, INITIAL COST, AND ANNUAL DEPRECIATION AND REPAIRS

Steamboat construction costs varied widely. A plain boat fitted with used machinery could be constructed for as little as $60 per ton. By comparison, a boat devoted primarily to passenger traffic and finished in the finest steamboat gothic could cost as much as $250 per ton. The steamboats in the Louisville–New Orleans trade were among the larger, more luxurious steamboats, hence, their costs were higher than average.

Sources giving steamboat construction costs are plentiful, particularly for the period after 1830, and we have used a variety of sources. These are given

---

vessels arriving at New Orleans. The vessels arriving from Louisville were isolated and the tonnages were obtained from the Lytle List.

[11] The decline in the average lifespan of steamboats over 200 tons during the 1840–49 was probably the result of the suspension, in 1838, of the federal government's river improvement work, and we suggest that the increase in the average lifespan of such steamboats during the 1850–60 period resulted from the strict inspection and safety regulations required by the act of 1852.

[12] Chevalier (1961): 211; Embree (1848–49): 115; Gould (1951): 432; Hall (1848a): 129, 168; *Western Monthly Magazine* (vol. 4): 411; *Hunt's Merchants' Magazine* (vol. 1): 457; Hunter (1949): 100, 101; Lippincott (1916): 107; Serial set 359, Senate Doc. 284, 33 and 35; Serial set 434, Senate Doc. 185, 28; Serial set 656, House Report 185, 24.

Table C–1. Average Measured Tonnage, Life Span, Initial Cost, Annual Depreciation, and Annual Repair Cost of Steamboats in the Louisville–New Orleans Trade, 1810–60

Period	Average measured tonnage (tons)	Average life span (years)	Average cost per measured ton	Average initial cost (1) X (3)	Average annual depreciation (4)÷(2)	Average annual repairs
	(1)	(2)	(3)	(4)	(5)	(6)
1810–19	220	6	$125	$27,500	$4,583	$3,300
1820–29	290	6	110	31,900	5,317	3,828
1830–39	310	6	110	34,100	5,683	4,092
1840–49	310	5	90	27,900	5,580	3,348
1850–60	360	6	100	36,000	6,000	4,320

Sources: Columns 1, 2, and 6 are discussed in the text. The sources for column 3 are: Baird (1834): 61, 333; The Bankers' Magazine and State Financial Register, vol. 1, pt. 1: 213; Berry (1943): 36–37; Bishop (1864): vol. 2: 403; Chevalier (1961): 210; Cist (1841): 255; Cist (1845): vol. 2, 258, 304; Dayton (1925): 349; DeBow (1854): vol. 3, 154; DeBow's Review, vol. 9, 651; vol. 18, 505; Embree (1848–49): 315; Gould (1951): 127; Hall (1848a): 12, 129, 131, 166, 169, 170, 208, 217, 220; The Western Monthly Magazine, vol. 4, 411; Huber (1959): 97; Hunt's Merchants' Magazine, vol. 1, 457; vol. 4, 411; Huber (1959): 97; Hunt's Merchants' Magazine, vol. 1, 457; vol. 12, 290; vol. 14, 385; vol. 19, 589; Hunter (1949): 110–12; Jenkins (1841): 366; Lippincott (1916): 106; Morrison (1958): 230–31; Quick (1926): 175; Niles' Register, vol. 43, 23; vol. 63, 325; vol. 64, 64; vol. 65, 384; vols. 66, 378; vol. 71, 63; vol. 75, 45; Ringwalt (1888): 138; Stuart (1833): vol. 2, 507; Thurston (1888): 76; Walker (1880): 251; The American Pioneer, vol. 1, 70; Serial set 359, Senate Doc. 284, 14, 31, 33, 35, 48; Serial set 415, Sen. Doc. 137, 3; Serial set 421, House Doc. 126, 4; Serial set 434, Sen. Doc. 179, 9–10; Serial set 434, Sen. Doc. 185, 28–31; Serial set 442, House Doc. 154, 7; Serial set 527, House Report 741, 96, 162; Serial set 619, Sen. Exec. Doc. 42, 108, 110; Serial set 900, House Exec. Doc. 48, 9.

in Table C–1, along with our estimates of average costs per ton. Typically, we have given the most weight-to-cost estimates based on a number of steamboats. In general, the estimates for single boats have been viewed with suspicion because these boats may have been newsworthy for reasons that affected their costs.

The average construction cost of the vessels operating in the Louisville–New Orleans trade as reported in the 1850 census was $90.36 per ton. The vessels were constructed between the years of 1843 and 1850, but most of them were built during the latter part of the decade.

There are many methods that can be used to calculate the annual depreciation charge, but regardless of the method used, the cost of the steamboat should be recovered over its lifetime. Thus, the average annual depreciation charge (as listed in column 5 of Table C–1) is the initial cost of the steamboat divided by its average life span.

Repairs were an important item of expense. Most minor repairs could be handled without undue delay by the ship's engineer or carpenter using the tools and supplies on hand. Major repairs, however, required that the boat be brought, or towed, to the nearest boatyard. Unfortunately, repair costs were rarely listed separately in the statements of operating costs. In 1829, Morgan Neville estimated that repairs to a steamboat during its lifetime amounted to one-half of the original cost of the vessel.[13] Consequently, with an average life span of four to five years, the annual repair cost was 10 to 12.5 percent of the original cost. In 1834 it was estimated that 16 percent of a steamboat's operating expenses were for "contingencies,"[14] which probably included repairs, canal tolls, wharfage charges, etc. A steamboat's annual operating expenses were generally a little more than its original cost, so annual repairs were probably somewhat less than 16 percent of the original cost. For example, the *Franklin* was a luxurious 200 ton steamboat and was built in 1836 at a cost of $30,000. Repairs were calculated to have been $21,500 over the first four years of its lifetime, or about 18 percent of its original cost each year.[15] By comparison, in 1847, a 249 ton steamboat reported "expenses" of $223.10 during an 18 day voyage, which was 8.7 percent of the boat's operating expenses for the voyage.[16] Recalling that a steamboat's annual operating expenses were generally a little more than its original cost indicated that the annual repairs for this boat were probably over 8.7 percent of its original cost. Finally, Davis Embree gave $1,200 as the annual repair cost of a steamboat that cost almost $20,000. In this case, annual repairs were about 6 percent of the original cost.[17] Somewhat arbitrarily, our estimates of the annual repairs for steamboats in the Louisville–New Orleans trade (column 6, Table C–1) are placed at 12 percent of the original cost of the vessel.

INSURANCE

The short life span of steamboats and the hazardous conditions under which they operated are reflected in the insurance rates. Many steamboat operators carried no insurance,[18] and those that did purchase commercial insurance were limited to two-thirds or three-quarters of the value of the

[13] Hall (1848a): 129, and Hunter (1949): 369–70.

[14] Hall (1848a): 132; Serial set 421, House Doc. 126, 5.

[15] Morrison (1958): 232–33, gives $10,500 as the annual charge for depreciation and repairs. The total charge for repairs and depreciation for four years was $42,000. The original cost of the boat was $30,000, and it had a value of $9,492 after four years. Thus, the depreciation during the first four years was $20,508 and the repairs during this period were $42,000–$20,508=$21,492.

[16] Serial set 527, House Report 741, 117.

[17] Embree (1848–49): 313–15.

[18] Hunter (1949): 367. J. L. Wilmers of Neare, Gibbs & Co., River Marine Underwriters, Cincinnati, Ohio, in a letter date March 20, 1967 estimated that of the steamboats five years old or less 45 percent carried insurance prior to 1830, 60 percent carried insurance between 1830 and 1850, and 80 percent carried insurance after 1850. He estimated that of the vessels over five years old 20 percent carried insurance prior to 1830, 40 percent carried insurance between 1830 and 1850, and 55 percent carried insurance after 1850.

boat.[19] However, the cost of full coverage is the appropriate insurance cost for our purposes. The period insurance coverage was customarily about nine months.[20]

Neare, Gibbs & Co., river marine underwriters, report that the annual insurance premiums for steamboats in the Louisville–New Orleans trade were 31 percent of the boat's value prior to 1830, 22 percent of its value from 1830 to 1850, and 18 percent of its value after 1850.[21] These rates appear rather high when compared to contemporary quotations. James Hall, for example, quotes an average rate of 15 percent for the early forties.[22] Hunter reports that rates of 1 or 2 percent per month (or 8 to 18 percent per season) prevailed during most of the ante-bellum period.[23] Another source used 12 percent as the average premium for steamboat insurance for the operating season during the the late forties.[24] About the same time, Embree used 12 percent as the average annual premium for steamboat insurance, and his calculations showed the insurance companies to be losing money at this rate.[25]

These latter quotations do not seem reasonable, given the average life spans of the steamboats. For example, with a life span of six years the expected insurance costs should average about 17 percent of the average value. Yet none of the contemporary quotations are this high.

The 1850 census reports on vessels in the Louisville–New Orleans trade provide the answer to this dilemma. The insurance costs reported for those vessels range from 6 to 11 percent *of the construction cost,* regardless of the age of the vessel. In other words, it appears that the insurance premiums were calculated on the original cost rather than the value of the vessel at the time the insurance was purchased. The average premium paid by the census vessels was 7.7 percent. Assuming that this provided two-thirds or three-quarters coverage, gives a rate of 10.0 to 11.5 percent of the original cost for full coverage.

We have placed the cost of full coverage at 18 percent of the construction cost prior to 1820, 15 percent during the 1820–29 decade, 12 percent during the 1830–39 decade, 10 percent during the 1840–49 decade, and 9 percent for the 1850–60 period.

---

[19] Hunter (1949): 366.

[20] Embree (1848–49): 313–14.

[21] Letter from James L. Wilmers, Neare, Gibbs & Co., River Marine Underwriters, Cincinnati, Ohio, March 20. 1967.

[22] Hall (1848a): 168; also Serial set 421, House Doc. 126, 5.

[23] Hunter (1949): 367.

[24] Serial set 527, House Report 741, 96.

[25] Embree (1848–49): 315. Embree compared the premiums paid over the life of a steamboat to the claim paid when (as he assumed) half the steamboats were abandoned to the underwriters after two years. He found that the premiums covered less than three-fourths of the claim. He ignored all other claims and explained that the insurance companies could make money, since the boats abandoned to them were often only partially damaged.

CREW SIZE AND COMPOSITION

A number of sources give information that makes it possible to calculate the relationship between boat size and crew size. The results range from about 7 crewmen per hundred tons[26] to 19 crewmen per hundred tons,[27] and averaged about 12 crewmen per hundred tons.[28] We have used this average in conjunction with our estimates of given average boat sizes (in Table C-1 above) to determine crew sizes.

The composition of the crew varied from boat to boat, but generally "The crew of the steamboat fell into three groups: officers, cabin crew, and deck crew. The minimum staff of officers on most steamboats included, in addition to the captian, a clerk, two pilots, two engineers, and a mate."[29] A cook, a steward, and a carpenter were sometimes found on a steamboat with a larger complement of officers, but "the deck crew generally comprised half or more of the entire crew."[30] In addition, there was the cabin crew, which was about one-half the size of the deck crew.[31] In combination, these formed about three-quarters of the total crew, and we have grouped these together because their salaries (per man) were roughly the same. Estimating on this basis, a 220 ton steamboat employed approximately 7 officers and 19 crewmen, a 290 ton boat employed about 9 officers and 26 crewmen, a 310 ton steamboat used around 9 officers and 28 crewmen, and a 360 ton vessel employed approximately 10 officers and 33 crewmen.

The 1850 census returns indicate that the vessels in the Louisville–New Orleans trade had an average of 47 crewmen. However, as noted above the average size of these vessels was relatively large. The crew size was found to be proportional to vessel size, giving an average crew of 40 for a 310 ton vessel and of 44 for a 360 ton boat.

WAGES

Our estimates of the wages paid to the officers and crew are given in Table C-2, along with our calculations of the average annual labor costs by decade. The total labor costs are based on payments to the officers (except the

---

[26] *Niles' Register,* vol. 23: 275; Serial set 2552, House Exec. Doc. 6, pt. II, 194.

[27] Morrison (1958): 230–32.

[28] *The Bankers' Magazine and State Financial Register,* vol. 1, pt. 1: 213; Callender (1909): 279; Hall (1848a): 166, 219; Huber (1959): 97; Hulbert (1906): 333; *Hunt's Merchants' Magazine,* vol. 1: 457; Hunter (1949): 443; *The Louisville Directory* (1832) 127; Morrison (1958): 234–35; *Niles' Register,* vol. 43: 23; vol. 44; 64; Serial set 415 Senate Doc. 137, 3; Serial set 434, Senate Doc. 185, 6; Serial set 527, House Report 741, 96; Serial set 547, Senate Doc. 4, 9; Serial set 619, Senate Exec. Doc. 42, 13–16 Serial set 1018, House Report 141, 14 and 15.

[29] Hunter (1949): 443.

[30] Ibid., p. 446.

[31] Ibid.

Table C–2. Average Annual Labor Cost of Steamboats in the Louisville–New Orleans Trade, 1810–60

Crew member	Before 1820			1820–29			1830–39		
	No.	Salary	Total	No.	Salary	Total	No.	Salary	Total
Captain	1	$1,000*	$1,000	1	$1,000*	$1,000	1	$1,250*	$1,250
Clerk	1	600*	600	1	600*	600	1	750*	750
Engineer	1	50	300	1	75	450	1	100	900
2nd engineer	1	40	240	1	50	300	1	50	450
Pilot	2	50	600	2	60	720	2	150	2,700
Mate	1	50	300	1	50	300	1	60	540
Steward				1	30	180	1	40	360
Cook				1	30	180	1	40	360
Carpenter									
Deck and Cabin Crew	19	20	2,280	26	20	3,120	28	25	6,300
Total	26		5,320	35		6,850	37		13,610

Crew member	1840–49			1850–60		
	No.	Salary	Total	No.	Salary	Total
Captain	1	$1,250*	$1,250	1	$1,500*	$1,500
Clerk	1	800*	800	1	900*	900
Engineer	1	75	675	1	100	900
2nd engineer	1	50	450	1	50	450
Pilot	2	125	2,250	2	150	2,700
Mate	1	50	450	1	75	675
Steward	1	40	360	1	45	405
Cook	1	40	360	1	40	360
Carpenter				1	45	405
Deck and Cabin Crew	28	22.50	5,670	33	25	7,425
Total	37		12,265	43		15,720

*Annual salaries; all other figures are monthly wages.

Note: Salaries are estimated from the following sources: DeBow's Review, vol. 26, 433; Embree (1848–49): 315–16; Flugel (1924): 436; Hunt's Merchants' Magazine, vol. 1, 457; Hunter (1949): 445, 465–67; Merrick (1909): 163; Morrison (1958): 229, 232–35; Sellers (1936): 247; Serial set 178, House Report 213, 4; Serial set 619, Senate Exec. Doc. 42, 112.

captain and clerk) and crew for the entire navigation season of six month
before 1829 and nine months thereafter.[32] The captain and clerk, however
were retained for the full year.

Three checks on the estimates presented in Table C–2 are available. Embree
calculated the monthly wages of a crew of 34 men to be $1,175 in 1849.[33]
This corresponds to an annual wage bill of $10,575 and compares to ou
estimates of $9,475 for a crew of 35 men during the 1820–29 decade, whe■
wages were lower. Another source found the monthly wage bill of a large
luxury boat with a crew of 40 to 50 men to be $2,225 in 1838.[34] This i■
equivalent to an annual wage bill of $20,295 and compares to our estimate
of $15,720 for a crew of 43 men during the 1850–60 period. This compari
son is meaningful because wages were approximately the same for botl
periods.

The 1850 census reports on the Louisville–New Orleans trade provide the
third check. They are not totally accurate, since they provide only the
monthly wage bill and the number of months in operation, thus excluding the
wages of the captain and clerk during the nonoperating months. The annua■
wage costs were found to vary directly with crew size. The estimated annua■
wages for a 37 man crew is $14,730 and for a 43 man crew is $17,120.

TRAVELING TIMES AND NUMBERS OF VOYAGES PER YEAR

Before 1820, many of the voyages were made in record time and mos■
were completed at least close to the fastest times recorded. Therefore, for thi
early period we have assumed that average traveling times were approximately
equal to the record times. For the other decades, after 1820, our estimates o■
average traveling times are based on record times marked up by one-quarte■
to one-third, as suggested by Hunter.[35] These adjustments give traveling time
estimates that closely compare to various traveling times given in contempo
rary references.[36] The record times and our estimates of average traveling
times, both upstream and downstream, are given in Table C–3.

In addition, Table C–3 gives estimates of the average number of round
trips completed each year, which when multiplied by the appropriate average

[32] Embree (1848–49): 316, and Hunter (1949): 445.

[33] Embree (1848–49): 316.

[34] *Hunt's Merchants' Magazine,* vol. 1: 457.

[35] Hunter (1949): 25.

[36] Bishop (1864), vol. 2: 282; Blowe (1820): 587; Bristed (1818): 66; Bullock
(1905): 118; Chapin (1843): 189; Chevalier (1961): 208; Dayton (1925): 337, 349;
Fearon (1818): 249; Ford (1881): 353; Hall (1848a): 147; Monette (1903): 503, 504;
Morrison (1958): 227, 229; *Niles' Register,* vol. 25: 95; vol. 48: 310; *Wholesale Prices
Current at Cincinnati, Ohio,* 1823: 3; *The American Pioneer* (1842), vol. 1: 70; Serial set
442, House Doc. 154, 7; Serial set 2136, House Misc. Doc. 42, vol. 8, 176; Serial set
2552, House Exec. Doc. 6, pt. II, 193.

Table C–3. Average Number of Round Trips per Year, the Record and Average Upstream and Downstream Traveling Times, and the Average Running Time per Year for Steamboats in the Louisville–New Orleans Trade, 1810–60

Period	Average number of round trips per year	Record time upstream (days)	Average time upstream (days)	Record time downstream (days)	Average time downstream (days)	Average round trip time (days)	Average running time per year (days)
	(1)	(2)	(3)	(4)	(5)	(6)	(7)
Before 1820	3	20	20.0	10	10.0	30	90
1820–29	5	10	12.5	6	7.5	20	100
1830–39	8	7	9.5	5	6.5	16	128
1840–49	10	6	7.5	4	5.5	13	130
1850–60	12	5	6.5	4	5.3	11.8	141

Sources: Baird (1834): 61; Berry (1943): 34–35; Chevalier (1961): 209; Cincinnati Daily Gazette, March 23, 1840; Dayton (1925): 335; Foreman (1928–29): 39; Gould (1951): 530–44; Hall (1838): 238; Hall (1848a): 131; Hunter (1943): 205; Hunter (1949): 24, 25; Lloyd (1856): 279; Mills (1820): 45–56; Morrison (1958): 47–52; Niles' Register, vol. 26, 48, 251; vol. 32, 151, 229; vol. 56, 352; vol. 59, 208; vol. 75, 320; Preble (1895): 83; Walker (1880): 252; Serial set 359, Senate Doc. 284, 13, 14, 33, 35, 48; Serial set 415, Senate Doc. 137, 3; Serial set 442, House Doc. 154, 7; Serial set 2552, House Exec. Doc. 6, pt. II, 206, 207.

round trip time gives the average yearly running time (column 7, Table C–3). For the most part, the sources used to estimate the average annual number of round trips are the same as those used to determine traveling times (see Table C–3). However, the evidence is taken from separate examples or statements on voyage times and the number of trips per year. They are not mutually derived from the same recorded passages. Consequently, each serves as a partial check on the other. An additional check stems from a comparison of our derived average running times per year with information on these times from contemporary sources.[37] This comparison tends to confirm our estimates.

The analysis of steamboat arrivals at New Orleans from Louisville during the period August 25, 1848 to August 30, 1849 provides additional evidence on the average round trip time and the average number of round trips. From the arrival dates for individual vessels it is possible to calculate round trip travel times (including time in port at both ends). These times range from a low of 13 days to a high of 30 days and average 21 days. There is a distinct pattern of shorter round trip times during the peak season. This is probably

[37] Embree (1848–49): 316; Hall (1848a): 129, 131, 167; Serial set 421, House Doc. 26, 4; Serial set 527, House Report 741, 96; Serial set 619, Senate Exec. Doc. 42, 113.

due to the availability of a larger volume of traffic and to the ability t
maintain higher speeds, given the higher water levels.

Some of the vessels only operated in the Louisville–New Orleans trade fc
part of the period. However, it is possible to estimate the number of roun
trips such vessels could have made had they continued in the trade for the ful
year. These estimates, together with the actual number of round trips fo
those vessels that did operate in the Lousiville–New Orleans trade for the ful
period, are available for 13 steamboats. They vary between 9 and 13 roun
trips per year. The average is 11 round trips per year.

Reductions in traveling times and port times increased the number c
yearly voyages completed by an average steamboat. However, the norma
season of navigation also was extended over the ante-bellum period becaus
of various improvements in the vessels, in the rivers, and in the handling o
steamboats. Throughout the period, vessels were "in operation" for abou
nine months each year, the remaining time being used to clean and repair th
boat out of water. But in the early period, the hazards of the river, particu
larly during periods of low water, in conjunction with the early physica
characteristics of steamboats, permitted a viable navigation season of onl
about six months.[38] Although we cannot determine the time exactly, some
where around 1830 this navigation season was extended to nine months an
came to coincide with the period of operation.[39]

FUEL COSTS

Yearly fuel costs depended on the yearly consumption rate of wood an
the price per cord of wood.[40] As the vessels grew in size, and as their engine
became more powerful and their yearly running time was increased, th
average annual consumption rate rose. We have based our estimates o

---

[38] Hunter (1949): 222–23.

[39] Ibid. Also see Appendix F.

[40] It has been assumed that wood was the only fuel used. There is evidence that som
steamboats in the Louisville–New Orleans trade used coal, particularly after 1850. Co
had advantages over wood but could not displace it on the steamboats of the Louisville
New Orleans trade. Hunter (1949): 268, 269, explains that:

> Before the advantages of coal could be fully realized there were obstacles to b
> overcome. In addition to the inertia of established practice and opinion there wer
> technical difficulties to be surmounted if coal was to come into general use. Coal wa
> quite different in character from wood and the proper methods of using it had to b
> determined and made known to steamboatmen. . . . Coal required a smaller an
> shallower firebox and larger grate openings than wood; yet to adopt a furnac
> designed solely for the use of coal was often not practicable, since on many parts c
> the river system coal was available only at exorbitant prices. . . . Along the low
> Mississippi in Mississippi and Louisiana the price of coal was so high as ordinarily t
> be prohibitive for steamboatmen.

umerous contemporary and other reports on the daily fuel consumption rate
or various sized vessels.

Morrison reports that in 1818 a 400 ton steamboat took twenty days to
ravel from New Orleans to Louisville, and that it consumed about 360
ords of wood in the process.[41] In this case, the consumption rate was
bout one cord of wood for each 22 tons every twenty-four hours. In
829, Morgan Neville estimated the average daily fuel consumption rate to be
ne cord for each 12 tons of the boat's measurement.[42] Shortly thereafter, the
uel consumption rate of the *Constitution* (400 tons) was reported to be
6 cords of wood per day, or one cord for each 15 tons every
wenty-four hours.[43] During the thirties, the *Franklin* (200 tons), a Louisville
nd Cincinnati packet, reportedly consumed 785 cords of wood and a few
ons of coal in a month.[44] Assuming that this boat ran every day and
gnoring the coal consumption, places the daily fuel conumption rate at one
ord for each 8 tons. Morrison reports that toward the end of the thirties a
00 ton boat took six days to travel from New Orleans to Louisville and
onsumed 360 cords of wood,[45] and that about this same time "larger boats"
onsumed 30 cords of wood every twelve hours.[46] If the "larger boats" were
bout 400 tons, then both cases indicate a fuel consumption rate of approxinately one cord for each 7 tons every twenty-four hours. Another source
laimed that a 325 ton steamboat consumed 24 cords of wood per day during
he late thirties.[47] This corresponds to a daily fuel consumption rate of
early one cord for every 13 tons. The average fuel consumption rate of New
Orleans boats (about 275 tons each) around 1840 was about 35 cords of
vood per day, or one cord for each 8 tons every twenty-four hours.[48]
Embree estimated that in 1849 a 211 ton boat required 32 cords for each
wenty-four hours, or approximately one cord per day for each 7 tons.[49] The
uel consumption of the *Bostona* (481 tons) on a round trip between
Louisville and New Orleans in 1850, with a total running time of eleven days,
vas 660 cords of wood.[50] This represents a daily fuel consumption rate of
pproximately one cord of wood for each 8 tons. From the evidence above,
ve estimate that the average daily fuel consumption rate was approximately
one cord for each 20 tons before 1820, one cord for each 12 tons during the

[41] Morrison (1958): 229.
[42] Gould (1951): 118; Hall (1848a): 129; Hunter (1949): 266.
[43] Hensahw (1911): 383.
[44] Morrison (1958): 232.
[45] Ibid., p. 229.
[46] Morrison (1958): 237.
[47] *Hunt's Merchants' Magazine*, vol. 1: 457.
[48] Serial set 361, Senate Doc. 284, 13 and 14.
[49] Embree (1848–49): 316.
[50] Hunter (1949); Table 7: 650, 651.

1820–29 decade, one cord for each 10 tons 1830–39, and one cord for eacl 8 tons 1840–60.

Data available from a variety of sources[51] places the price of wood a roughly $2.25 per cord prior to 1830 and $2.50 per cord from 1830 to 186(Therefore, the average annual fuel bill for each period is equal to the averag size of the Louisville–New Orleans steamboats divided by the fuel consump tion expressed in measured tons per cord per day and multiplied by th average running time per year and the average price of wood. On this basi: the average annual fuel bill was $2,228 prior to 1820, $5,445 1820–29 $9,920 during the 1830–39 decade, $12,594 1840–49, and $15,862 durin the period from 1850 to 1860. Walker reported that steamboats running i 1834 measured about 39,000 tons and spent nearly $1,500,000 annually o fuel,[52] for an annual expenditure of about $38.50 per year for fuel. On thi basis a 310 ton steamboat would have spent $11,935 per year for fuel, whicl compares favorably to our fuel expenditure estimates for the 1830–39 an 1840–49 decades.

The 1850 census reports for the vessels operating in the Louisville–Nev Orleans trade again provide a basis of comparison. Based on those returns th annual fuel costs of a 310 ton steamboat would be approximately $11,60(Those for a 360 ton steamboat would be approximately $12,250.

STORES AND "OTHER" COSTS

This cost category was rather ill defined, but the largest item was the cos of food for the cabin passengers and crew. In addition, however, there wer various supplies for the kitchen, dining hall, and passenger cabins, such a linen, dishes, utensils, and assorted other items. Also such items as ropes account ledgers, and receipt books, that were not part of repair costs, an other expenditures for wharfage charges, canal tolls, and advertising were als included. No direct estimates of these costs were available, but several source give information on the relative magnitudes of the various operating expense of wages, fuel costs, stores, and "other" costs. For instance, in 1834, Morga Neville estimated that wages and fuel costs accounted for 66 percent of th operating expenses,[53] and James Hall felt that this estimate was appropriat for 1842 as well.[54] In the 1870s, about 69 percent of the *Franklin*'

---

[51] Cobbett (1819): 209; Embree (1848–49): 316; Flugel (1924): 434; Hall (1836): 145; Hall (1848a): 129; Henshaw (1911): 383; Hulbert (1906): 333; *Hunt's Merchants Magazine*, vol. 1: 457; Hunter (1949), footnote to Table 1: 644; Morrison (1958): 229 Serial set 178, House Report 213, 4; Serial set 359, Senate Doc. 284, 13 and 14; Serial set 619, Senate Exec. Doc. 42, 113.

[52] Walker (1880): 252.

[53] Hall (1848a): 132.

[54] Ibid., p. 167.

perating expenses were for wages and fuel,[55] and in 1840, wages and fuel costs were estimated to account for 71 percent of the operating expenses.[56] Toward the end of the forties, wages and fuel costs were estimated separately at 73 percent of the operating expenses[57] and 70.7 percent of the operating expenses.[58] Finally, Hunter reports that wages and fuel costs amounted to only 62.8 percent of the operating expenses of an upper Missouri River steamboat in 1855 and 58.9 percent of the operating expenses of another boat in 1860.[59]

From the above we have assumed that wages and fuel costs represented 70 percent of the operating expenses of steamboats in the Louisville–New Orleans trade throughout the ante-bellum period, with stores and "other" costs accounting for the remaining 30 percent. Therefore, using the wages and fuel costs presented above, the estimates of average annual stores and "other" costs are $3,255 prior to 1820, $5,269 for the 1820–29 decade, $10,084 for the 1830–39 decade, $10,653 for the 1840–49 decade, and $13,535 for the period from 1850 to 1860.

Our estimates of repairs and stores and other costs may be combined and compared to the total of provisions and general expenses as reported by the Louisville–New Orleans boats in the 1850 census. Our estimates for the 1840–49 and 1850–60 periods are $14,001 and $17,855 respectively. The estimates obtained from the census reports are $13,817 for a 310 ton boat and $14,576 for a 360 ton boat.

TOTAL COSTS AND COMPARATIVE ESTIMATES

The total costs as estimated above are $23,616; $31,494; $47,481; $47,230; and $58,677 respectively for the five periods. Several rules-of-thumb and independent estimates of the annual cost of operating a steamboat are available as checks on these figures.

In 1829 the annual operating expenses of steamboats were estimated at $71.40 per ton, or $20,706 for a 290 ton boat.[60] Our estimate is $21,314. During the thirties, steamboats over 200 tons were estimated to operate for 180 days per year at a cost of $140 per day for wages, fuel, stores, and other expenses.[61] This annual expenditure of $25,200 compares to our estimated costs of $33,614. In 1832 an expenditure of $153 per ton per year was

[55] Morrison (1958): 232
[56] Serial set 359, Senate Doc. 284, 13 and 14.
[57] Serial set 527, House Report 741, 117.
[58] Embree (1848–49): 315, 316.
[59] Hunter (1949): 362.
[60] Hall (1848a): 130; Walker (1880): 251.
[61] Hall (1848a) 131; Serial set 421, House Doc. 126, 4.

estimated to be sufficient to cover all of the boat's expenses.[62] This meant an annual expenditure of $47,430 for a 310 ton boat, which is very close to the estimated total cost of $47,481. In 1834 a steamboat's running expenses were estimated at $119 per ton per year.[63] On this basis a 310 ton steamboat would have running expenses of $36,890 per year, which compares to our estimates of $33,614 per year. Hunter estimated that from 1830 through 1860 a steamboat's annual wages, fuel, insurance, stores, and "other" expenditures were from 1.25 to 2.0 times the boat's original cost.[64] Thus, Hunter would have expected these costs to be between $42,625 and $68,200 per year during the thirties. We estimated them at $37,706 per year for the 1830–39 decade.

Hunter's rule-of-thumb would have the annual wages, fuel, insurance, stores, and "other" costs between $34,875 and $55,800 during the forties. We estimated them at $38,302. There was a report that a 498 ton steamboat had running expenses of $325 per day during the forties.[65] This amounts to $42,250 for the 130 running days. Another report gave the annual running expense as $131.40 per ton, or $40,734 for a 310 ton boat.[66] It was not clear whether these figures were comparable to the estimated operating expenses of $35,512 or the variable costs of $41,650. Hunter's rule-of-thumb also holds for the 1850–60 period. The estimated costs of $48,357 fall within the range of $45,000 to $72,000 calculated using his rule-of-thumb.

The 1850 census reports also provide a check on the total cost estimates for all costs, excluding depreciation. These amount to $44,564 for a 310 ton boat and $48,060 for a 360 ton boat. Our estimates are $41,650 for the 1840–49 decade and $52,677 for the 1850–60 period.

[62] *The Louisville Directory,* 1832: 126.
[63] Walker (1880): 252.
[64] Hunter (1949): 362.
[65] Serial set 527, House Report 741, 117.
[66] Serial set 547, Senate Doc. 4, 72.

APPENDIX D

The Revenue Determinants of Steamboating in the Louisville — New Orleans Trade, 1810 — 1860

SOURCES OF REVENUE

Steamboats obtained the vast bulk of their revenues from the transportation of passengers and freight. Some slight revenues were earned on mail contracts and barroom concessions, but these were only minor sources of income. Mail contracts were awarded only to the fastest and safest boats, which were allowed to paint the slogan "United States Mail" on their paddleboxes. These boats were paid a small fee for each shipment of mail and were assessed penalties for late delivery. [1]

Because the number of steamboats with mail contracts was relatively small, the earnings from such contracts were insignificant when averaged over all boats. Hunter reports a similar finding for revenues from barroom concessions: "The sale of liquor or of barroom concessions was common steamboat practice, but this, except on the finer and faster vessels, brought in relatively

[1] Morrison (1958): 233, 234, reports that the fee for carrying the mail between Cincinnati and Louisville was $4.00 per trip. Maximilian (1906), part 3: 145, reports that the fee for this trip was $5.00 in the early thirties. Serial set 783, House Exec. Doc. 22, 2, reports that the steamboats conveying mail between Louisville and New Orleans supplied Cairo, Memphis, Napoleon, Vicksburg, and Natchez six times per week. They were paid $25 per trip for this. In addition, there were two trips per week that supplied all other offices of importance for which the boats were paid $100. Thus, the average fee for carrying the mail between Louisville and New Orleans was less than $50 per trip. Serial set 366, House Doc. 159, 7 and 8, reports that there was tri-weekly mail service between Louisville and New Orleans. It also reports that from July 1 to Dec. 31, 1839, fines of $3,550 were levied for irregularities in the delivery of mail on this route. If we assume that navigation between Louisville and New Orleans was possible for the entire six months, despite the low water of July, August, and September, then there would have been 72 upstream and 72 downstream shipments on this route for a total of no more than $7,200 in fees. Thus, the penalties were about 50 percent of the fees. A steamboat in the Louisville–New Orleans trade, with a mail contract, making ten round trips per year would have collected about $1,000 in fees and paid about $500 in fines. Its annual income from the mail contract would have been about $500, a very small fraction of its annual revenue.

small sums."[2] Again, when averaged over all steamboats the importance of these revenues becomes very small. Therefore, we have concentrated our analysis on revenues from the carriage of passengers and freight. This is consistent with the practice by contemporary sources chronicling the operation of steamboats to ignore the other insignificant sources of revenue.[3]

FREIGHT RATES

As noted by Dixon, wide seasonal fluctuations in freight rates make it difficult to calculate a representative series of average rates: "There were no such things as typical freight rates during the era of steamboating. Rates varied widely with the supply and demand of boats, the stage of the water and the quantities of freight offered, and it is difficult to give any idea of them at all."[4]

As shown in Figure 6–7 in Chapter 6, both the freight rates and steamboat activity varied with the stage of the river. When the water was low, only the smallest steamboats carrying only partial loads could operate, and freight rates were high. When the water was high, even the largest steamboats could carry full loads, thus, loads were large and freight rates were low. Because of this, trade was concentrated in the spring and fall.[5]

However, "from Cincinnati, Louisville, and St. Louis southward, low water presented a less serious restriction upon navigation than from upriver ports and seasonal rate fluctuations were less extreme."[6] Navigation in the Louisville–New Orleans trade was usually most restricted on the Ohio River between Cairo and Louisville. During periods of low water on this portion of the route, a steamboat would sometimes carry part of its cargo in a keelboat lashed to its side. When it got to Cairo this cargo was transferred on board and the keelboat was disposed of.[7] In this manner steamboats were able to carry full loads for a greater portion of the year, thus reducing the seasonal fluctuations. A seasonal pattern did prevail in the freight rates of the Louisville–New Orleans trade, but the fluctuations in these rates were less extreme than in other trades.

Because of their variability and the relatively small volume of traffic perhaps, rates were not published during the early part of the ante-bellum

[2] Hunter (1949): 373–74. Government charters of steamboats on a per diem basis during wartime were profitable but rare occurrences.

[3] Callender (1909): 279; Embree (1848–49): 317, 319; Hall (1848a): 208–10; Mill (1820): 45, 46; Serial set 619, Senate Exec. Doc. 42, 114.

[4] Dixon (1909): 27.

[5] Hunter (1949): 375.

[6] Ibid.

[7] *The Cincinnati Daily Chronicle,* November 20, 1841, makes mention of this practice.

period. Consequently, rates from that period are difficult to obtain and evidence stems largely from freight or "way" bills. After 1840, however, rates were fairly well established for the major trades and were published weekly.

1850–1860

The most complete information available on freight rates and traffic volume pertains to the Cincinnati to New Orleans traffic from 1850 to 1860. Rates were published monthly for flour, pork, whiskey, and pound freight.[8] Steamboat departures were also published monthly.[9] Average annual rates for each of the four categories were calculated as weighted averages of the monthly rates, using the number of departures as weights.

The use of departures as an index of the volume shipped introduces a slight upward bias into the calculations. During periods of low water the departures consisted of smaller boats carrying partial loads, so the high rates that prevailed during such periods are overemphasized somewhat.

Inspection of the weighted annual freight rates indicates that they compare favorably to the monthly rates during the first half of the year. In other words, as Hunter noted, "the important rates ... were those which ruled during the active seasons of navigation."[10]

The weighted annual rates for each of the four categories of freight for the years 1850 through 1860 were averaged again, using the number of departures as weights. These decade averages were found to be 27.1 cents per hundred pounds for flour, 32.9 cents per hundred pounds for pork, 33.4 cents per hundred pounds for whiskey, and 36.1 cents per hundred pounds for pound freight. These were combined to give an overall average of 32.5 cents per hundred pounds.[11] This is the rate we have accepted for down-

---

[8] The monthly rates are obtained primarily from *Hunt's Merchants' Magazine.* They were supplemented by quotations drawn from the other sources listed below. The rates obtained are shown in Haites (1969): 229–30. They are similar but not identical to those given by Berry (1943), Tables 3–6: 558–59, despite his use of the same primary sources. The differences are explained by our having access to more reports than did Berry. The downstream freight rates are obtained from Berry (1943): 558–59; Callender (1909): 340; *Hunt's Merchants' Magazine,* vol. 23: 545; vol. 25: 489; vol. 27: 617; vol. 29: 750; vol. 43: 616; Meyer (1917): 581; W. Smith (1860): 11; F. Way, Jr. (unpaged); *Western Christian Advocate* (all available issues containing relevant freight rate data); Serial set 811, Senate Exec. Doc. 1, pt. II, 359 and 361; Serial set 920, Senate Exec. Doc. 11, pt. II, 343.

[9] See *Hunt's Merchants' Magazine,* vol. 21: 468; vol. 23: 469; vol. 25: 506; vol. 27: 635; vol. 29: 751; vol. 31: 636; vol. 37: 759; vol. 41: 607; W. Smith (1860): 51.

[10] Hunter (1949): 375.

[11] The use of this average makes the implicit assumption that equal weights of flour, pork, whiskey, and pound freight were shipped. It was not possible to test this assumption, but it is unlikely that this was the case. However, many other goods were shipped at rates between those for flour and pound freight so that the "true" average was probably not much different from that calculated.

stream shipments in the Lousiville—New Orleans trade for 1850 to 1860.[12]

Sources quoting upstream freight rates between 1850 and 1860 are scarce. Captain Way's collection contains a receipt for a shipment of salt from New Orleans to Cincinnati in 1852 at 35 cents per sack (about 15 cents per hundred pounds) and a receipt for a shipment of wine from New Orleans to Louisville in 1852 at 30 cents per hundred pounds.[13] Hunter states that the downstream rate during this period was from 25 to 50 percent higher than the upstream rate.[14] Thus, given the downstream rate of 32.5 cents per hundred pounds, the upstream rate was probably between 21.5 and 26 cents per hundred pounds. We have accepted 25 cents per hundred pounds as the rough average of steamboat freight rates for upstream shipments in the Louisville—New Orleans trade, 1850–60.

1840–1849

Steamboat freight rates for pound freight, flour, pork, and whiskey shipped from Cincinnati to New Orleans were also published monthly during the 1840–49 period.[15] However, data on steamboat departures are not available for most of this period. Thus a new weighting must be used.

The method adopted deletes the two highest monthly freight rates and uses the simple average of the remaining monthly rates as the average rate for the year. For those years where monthly rates were available for only seven months, only the highest has been deleted. If six or fewer monthly rates are available, none have been deleted. The annual rates are all given equal weight in the calculation of the decade average. When this method was applied to the 1850–60 data it produced a freight rate of 32.3 cents per hundred pounds as compared to 32.5 cents per hundred pounds, using the number of departures as weights. The procedure described above, therefore, is judged to be consistent with that used for the 1850–60 period.

The average rate for each category of freight for the entire decade is 55.2 cents per barrel of flour (26.1 cents per hundred pounds), 67.3 cents per

---

[12] Freight rates downstream, Cincinnati to New Orleans and Louisville to New Orleans, were similar throughout most of the ante-bellum period and hence justify the use of Cincinnati—New Orleans freight rate data for the Louisville—New Orleans route. Compare, for instance, *Louisville Prices Current 1860* to Berry (1943): 558–59. Also, see Berry (1943): 45, and Gould (1951): 598.

[13] F. Way, Jr., unpaged, both shipments sent by the steamboat *Winfield Scott.*

[14] Hunter (1949): 376–77.

[15] See the comments in footnote 8 regarding the comparability of the rates presented in Haites (1969): 229–30, which are used here, and those presented by Berry (1943): 558–59. The downstream rates are obtained from Berry (1943): 558–59; *DeBow's Review,* vol. 6: 64; Dixon (1909): 28; Embree (1848–49): 109; *Hunt's Merchants' Magazine,* vol. 23: 545; Hunter (1949): 376; Meyer (1917): 574; Serial set 415, Senate Doc. 129, 55.

barrel of pork (30.6 cents per hundred pounds), 76.7 cents per barrel of whiskey (27.4 cents per hundred pounds), and 31.6 cents per hundred pounds of pound freight. The average rate for all four types of freight is 29.0 cents per hundred pounds. We have taken 30.0 cents per hundred pounds as the average rate for downstream shipments in the Louisville–New Orleans trade for the 1840–49 decade.

Sources quoting upstream freight rates for the 1840–49 decade are relatively scarce. The rate from New Orleans to Louisville was occasionally as low as 15 cents per hundred pounds,[16] but during the early forties the rate was as high as 63 cents per hundred pounds.[17] Captain Embree has suggested that the average rates for this period ranged from 20 to 30 cents per hundred pounds,[18] and Hunter and Berry both claim that the downstream rate was higher than the upstream rate during this decade.[19] Thus, we have accepted 25 cents per hundred pounds as the average rate for upstream shipments, 1840–49.

1830–1839

Prior to 1840 there are only scattered quotations available on freight rates. The data presented above demonstrate that for the 1840–60 period average freight rates downstream were similar to the rates for pound freight during periods of high water. They also indicate that the highest rates generally can be ignored. This suggests two guidelines for the analysis of the scattered freight rate quotations prior to 1840. First, freight rates on commodities such as flour, pork, corn, salt, etc. (expressed in cents per hundred pounds) would tend to be below the average rate. Second, rates that prevailed during periods of low water would tend to be above the average rate. We rely on these considerations frequently.

One of the sources giving downstream freight rates for the 1830s indicates that the cost of sending a barrel of port from Cincinnati to New Orleans fell from $1.50 to 37.5¢ during this decade.[20] This represents an average cost of 93.75 cents per barrel, or 42.6 cents per hundred pounds. Another source reports that brandy was shipped downstream in 1834 for 75 cents per barrel (about 35 cents per hundred pounds).[21] Henry Shreve gave $15 per ton (75 cents per hundred pounds) as the average low water freight rate in 1830,[22] and another contemporary described a shipment from Louisville to New

[16] See Berry (1943): 57; and *The American Pioneer*, vol. 1: 70.
[17] Hunt's Merchants' Magazine, vol. 8: 457.
[18] Embree (1848–49): 109.
[19] Berry (1943): 56–57; and Hunter (1949): 376.
[20] Ambler (1932): 163.
[21] Dexter (no date): 9.
[22] Serial set 208, House Doc. 74, 1.

Orleans in 1836 at a rate of 50 cents per hundred pounds.[23] Finally, Berry presents some monthly freight rates for whiskey, pork, flour, and pound freight for the last three years of this period. The average rate for these four categories of freight, 1837–39, is 42.3 cents per hundred pounds.[24]

The rates for the shipments of pork and brandy were probably below the average rate, and the average rate for the last three years of the decade was undoubtedly below the decade average, because rates were declining. Alternatively, the rate for the low water period was likely above the average rate. Our estimate of the approximate average rate for all downstream freight shipments by steamboat in the Louisville–New Orleans trade during the 1830–39 decade is 50 cents per hundred pounds.

Both Berry and Hunter claim that the upstream freight rates were approximately the same as the downstream rates during the 1830–39 decade.[25] Among the Wallace Family Papers are eight bills of lading for shipments from Louisville to New Orleans in December 1834, and they show a rate of 50 cents per hundred pounds.[26] Other bills of lading covered shipments made toward the end of May 1835 at rates of 62.5 cents and one dollar per hundred pounds. Dixon also quotes a rate of 50 cents per hundred pounds for the year 1839.[27] During the latter part of 1839, 50 cents per hundred pounds was the rate quoted for heavy articles.[28] However, heavy articles were usually charged a low rate. Morrison states that during 1838, the freight rate on shipments from New Orleans to Louisville varied from 33 cents to $1.50 per hundred pounds and averaged 62.5 cents per hundred pounds.[29] Shreve placed the upstream rate during periods of low water at $20 per ton ($1.00 per hundred pounds).[30] We have accepted 50 cents per hundred pounds as the rough average rate for upstream freight shipments in the Louisville–New Orleans trade, 1830–39. This is consistent with the above evidence and Hunter's and Berry's assertions that upstream and downstream rates were about equal during this decade.

1820–1829

The Hunt Papers contain several receipts for various downstream shipments during the early portion of the 1820–29 decade.[31] For instance, they indicate that the charges on a shipment of rope and yarn made in August

[23] Bohannan (no date): unpaged.
[24] Berry (1943): 558–59.
[25] Ibid., p. 56; and Hunter (1949): 376.
[26] Wallace Family Papers, unpaged.
[27] Dixon (1909): 27.
[28] *Hunt's Merchants' Magazine,* vol. 1: 457.
[29] Morrison (1958): 228.
[30] Serial set 208, House Doc. 74, 1.
[31] J. W. Hunt, unpaged.

1820 were $1.00 per hundred pounds, and a similar shipment was sent during January 1821 for 75 cents per hundred pounds. Meyer gives the cost of shipping a barrel of flour as $1.25 (62.5 cents per hundred pounds) in 1820.[32] For 1822 the *Wholesale Prices Current at Cincinnati* places the average downstream rate between 75 cents and $1.25 per barrel (37.5 cents to 62.5 cents per hundred pounds).[33] Two years later the cost of sending a barrel of flour downstream was reportedly $1.00 (50 cents per hundred pounds).[34] Berry's collection of rate quotations indicates that pound freight was shipped from Cincinnati to New Orleans at the rate of 62.5 cents per hundred pounds, July 1827–January 1828.[35] During February and March this rate fell to 50 cents per hundred pounds, and during April and May 1828 it rose to 55 cents per hundred pounds. Lee White, in a speech in 1827, assumed the rate between New Orleans and Louisville to be 0.5 cents per pound (50 cents per hundred pounds) in either direction.[36]

Clearly, the rates during the early part of the decade were above the average rate, since freight rates fell during this period. The rates on flour shipments, however, were probably below the average rate. We have placed the approximate rate for all downstream freight shipments at 62.5 cents per hundred pounds, 1820–29.

There was a major reduction in the upstream freight rates during the 1820–29 decade. A number of sources give the upstream rate in 1820 as $2.00 per hundred pounds (or more).[37] In 1822 the *Wholesale Prices Current at Cincinnati* places average upstream rates between 75 cents to $1.25 per hundred pounds.[38] "The charges on general merchandise from New Orleans to Louisville or Cincinnati was given in June 1824 as 75 cents per hundred pounds."[39] Niles Weekly Register reports that the cost of shipping a barrel of flour upstream in 1826 was $1.75 (87.5 cents per hundred pounds).[40] By the end of the period, freight was being shipped upstream at a rate of 50 cents per hundred pounds.[41] Hunter reports that in 1820 the upstream rate was only one-third greater.[42] Taking the upstream rate to average from one-half to two-thirds greater than the downstream rate, gives an upstream rate of

[32] Meyer (1917): 88.
[33] *Wholesale Prices Current at Cincinnati* (1823): 3
[34] Gephart (1909): 96.
[35] Collected from various editions of the *Liberty Hall and Cincinnati Gazette* and kindly provided by Thomas S. Berry.
[36] Reported in Berry (1943): 56
[37] Dixon (1909): 27; Flint (1904): 286; Gephart (1909): 98; Meyer (1917): 88, 111; Mills (1820): 45, 46.
[38] *Wholesale Prices Current at Cincinnati* (1823): 3.
[39] Berry (1943): 55.
[40] *Niles' Register* (July 8, 1826): 331: "From the *Louisiana Advertiser,* of a late date."
[41] Berry (1943): 56; Chevalier (1961): 208; Thruston (no date): unpaged.
[42] Hunter (1949): 376.

between 95 cents and $1.05 per hundred pounds. We have accepted $1.00 per hundred pounds as the overall average rate for all upstream shipments during the 1820–29 decade.

1810–1819

The upstream freight rates prior to 1820 were very high. In 1812 the Louisiana legislature established rates of 4.5 cents per pound for heavy goods and 6 cents per pound for light goods.[43] These rates prevailed until 1819 and the average charge was said to be 5 cents per pound ($5.00 per hundred pounds).[44] The rates quoted by most other sources range from $4.00 to $6.50 per hundred pounds.[45] The only exceptions are quotes of 2 cents per pound ($2.00 per hundred pounds)[46] and 50 cents per bushel (70 cents per hundred pounds)[47] for salt, both in 1819, and a quote of $6.00 to $7.00 per hundred pounds in 1811.[48] We have taken the average rate for upstream freight for the 1810–19 decade to be about $5.00 per hundred pounds.

Some sources report that the downstream rates during this decade were one-half the upstream rates, thus ranging from $2.25 to $3.00 per hundred pounds.[49] Receipts for actual shipments did not bear these sources out, however, and most shipments covered by the Hunt Papers were made at one cent per pound ($1.00 per hundred pounds).[50] Others were made at 90 cents per hundred pounds and $1.02.5 per hundred pounds. The Thruston accounts contain records of a shipment made in April 1817 at 80 cents per hundred pounds,[51] and the report that flour was shipped downstream in 1814 for $1.50 per barrel (75 cents per hundred pounds) was repeated several times. [52] Meyer reported that corn was shipped downstream in 1819 for 25 cents per bushel (about 50 cents per hundred pounds).[53] Fearon reported the down-

---

[43] Dixon (1909): 13, reports that these rates were specified in the Louisiana charter to Fulton and Livingston.

[44] Dayton (1925): 338.

[45] Berry (1943): 53, 54; Birkbeck (1819): 5, 6; Burnet (1847): 400; Dayton (1925): 338; Depew (1895), vol. 1: 26; Dixon (1909): 12, 13; Elder (1873): 16; Embree (1848–49): 109; E. Evans (1904): 314; Fearon (1818): 249; Flint (1904): 164; Hunter (1949): 26; Meyer (1917): 87; Morrison (1958): 218, 228; Ringwalt (1888): 13; Sterns (1900): 36: Wade (1964): 56.

[46] Birkbeck (1819): 6.

[47] Meyer (1917): 87.

[48] Chevalier (1961): 208.

[49] Depew (1895), vol. 1: 26; Dixon (1909): 13; Evans (1904): 314; Meyer (1917): 87; Serial set 2552, House Exec. Doc. 6, part II. 195.

[50] J. W. Hunt, "Papers 1792–1849," contains records of thirteen shipments from Louisville to New Orleans at one cent per pound ($1.00 per hundred pounds), one shipment at $1.02 1/2 per hundred pounds, and four shipments at 90 cents per hundred pounds made during the 1810–19 period.

[51] Thruston (no date): unpaged.

[52] Dixon (1909): 12; Ringwalt (1888): 13; and Sterns (1900): 36.

[53] Meyer (1917): 87.

stream freight charge to be $0.75 to $1.00 per hundred pounds in 1818. [54]
The *Aetna* took freight for her downstream trip in 1815 at $1.00 per hundred
pounds.[55] The Cincinnati *Western Spy* reported that the rates on upstream
shipments ranged from four to six times the downstream shipments in
1819.[56] The upstream rates ranged from $4.00 to $6.50 per hundred pounds,
thus implying a downstream rate of approximately $1.00 per hundred
pounds. Our guidelines suggest that the rates for the corn and flour shipments
and the rate during the spring navigation season (April) 1814 were probably
below the average rate. Therefore, we have accepted $1.00 per hundred
pounds as the approximate average rate for downstream freight for the
1810–19 decade. Our estimates of average upstream and downstream rates
for each decade are summarized in Table D–1.

CARGO CAPACITY AND AVERAGE UTILIZATION

As indicated in Appendix C, Table C–3, the average size of steamboats on
the Louisville–New Orleans route grew from approximately 220 tons before
1820 to nearly 360 tons by the decade of the 1850s. This substantial
increase, however, understates the growth of cargo-carrying capacity for an
average steamboat on this route, 1810–60. Early in the century, cargo-
carrying capacity was considerably less than measured tonnage, but as the
physical characteristics of the boats were altered the ratio of carrying capacity to measured tonnage rose.

The carrying capacity of a steamboat was greater when traveling down-
steam than when traveling upstream, primarily because it was easier to travel
with the current than against it. There are numerous sources relating downstream carrying capacity to measured tonnage. Our estimates of this ratio
range from 0.50 in the 1810–19 decade to 1.75 in the 1850–60 period. These
ratios and the estimates of the downstream carrying capacity are shown in
Table D–2.

Table D–1. Average Steamboat Freight Rates by Decade in the Louisville–New Orleans
Trade, 1810–60 (per hundred pounds)

Period	Upstream	Downstream
Before 1820	$5.00	$1.00
1820–29	1.00	0.625
1830–39	0.50	0.50
1840–49	0.25	0.30
1850–60	0.25	0.325

---

[54] Fearon (1818): 246, quoted in Meyer (1917): 87.
[55] Hunter (1949): 26.
[56] Reported in Hunter (1949): 375–76.

Table D-2. Average Carrying Capacity of Steamboats in the Louisville–New Orleans Trade, by Decade, 1810–60

Period	Average measured tonnage (tons)	Ratio of downstream carrying capacity to measured tonnage	Average downstream carrying capacity (tons)	Average upstream carrying capacity (tons)
	(1)	(2)	(3)	(4)
Before 1820	220	.50	110	55
1820–29	290	.80	232	116
1830–39	310	1.00	310	155
1840–49	310	1.60	496	248
1850–60	360	1.75	630	315

Sources: Column (1)–from Table C–1, Appendix C.

Column (2)–Chevalier (1961): 210; Dayton (1925): 349; *De Bow's Review,* vol. 18, 505; Hall (1838): 239; Hall (1848a): 221; *Hunt's Merchants' Magazine,* vol. 1, 449 Hunter (1943): 212–13; Hunter (1949): 82–3, 652; *The Louisville Directory* (1855–56): xii; *Niles' Register,* vol. 63, 325; Noble, unpaged; Ringwalt (1888): 114; Thurstor (1857): 76; Serial set 329, House Doc. 185, 7; Serial set 527, House Report 741, 117 164; Serial set 619, Senate Exec. Doc. 42, 113; Serial set 656, House Report 166, 4 Serial set 900, House Exec. Doc. 48, 7–9.

Column (3) is the product of column (1) and column (2).

Column (4) is one-half column (3)–see the text and footnote 57.

There are relatively few sources relating upstream carrying capacity to measured tonnage or to downstream capacity.[57] Based on the available data, we have estimated the upstream carrying capacity at half the downstream capacity throughout the period.

Having derived estimates of average carrying capacity we must now determine the approximate average percentage of that capacity that was utilized by cargo during each decade on the Louisville–New Orleans route. Two important considerations bear on our estimates. First, the vast bulk of all freight was through-freight. It went the entire journey from Louisville to New Orleans, and there was very little way-freight shipped by trunk route steam boats. Contemporary reports[58] strongly suggest that way-freight was excep tional, and Shreve argues the same for a later period in the nineteenth century:

[57] *Niles' National Register,* vol. 63: 325; Noble (no date): unpaged; Hall (1838): 239 Serial set 619, Senate Exec. Doc. 42, 113.

[58] Callender (1909): 317; Dixon (1909): 16; Johnson (1915), vol. 1: 213, 242.

The western produce shipped down the river never stopped at the plantation, but was sent direct to New Orleans, and thence transshipped up the river over the same route it had just gone.[59]

Two factors primarily account for the lack of way-freight. First, beside selling crops, the sugar and cotton commission houses in New Orleans served as the plantation owner's agents in New Orleans. Their services included the selling of crops, arrangement of credit, and the purchase of supplies for the plantations.[60] Because New Orleans was the major market for most plantation supplies, goods were first shipped downstream to New Orleans, sold, and then shipped back upstream to the plantation. The second reason for the lack of way-freight was that landing a large steamboat to take on or unload such freight was expensive. A steamboat could land only when facing the current. When traveling downstream the steamboat had to go below the landing site, turn around, and travel back upstream to the landing site. Upon departure, it had to turn around again before proceeding downstream. Such maneuvers were costly for the large steamboats of the Louisville–New Orleans trade.

Our second consideration is the assumption that steamboats on the Louisville–New Orleans trade typically did not embark on a downstream run until they had a "paying" load on board. Contemporary reports[61] support this, and these considerations, in conjunction with numerous accounts of utilization, suggest that downstream loads averaged about 75 percent of capacity throughout the ante-bellum period.[62] Admittedly, there were probably great variations around this average.

The average downstream freight revenues for a single trip are calculated as the product of the downstream freight rates (expressed in dollars per ton) and 75 percent of the steamboat's downstream carrying capacity. Estimates of the average annual downstream freight revenues are obtained by multiplying the average downstream freight revenues for a single trip by the appropriate number of round trips per year (see Table C–3 Appendix C). This our estimates of average annual downstream freight revenues are $4,900 before 1820, $10,900 during the 1820–29 decade, $18,600 1830–39, $22,300 during the 1840–49 decade, and $36,900 for the 1850–60 period.

There is very little direct evidence on which an estimate of the upstream utilization can be based. According to Johnson the upstream Mississippi trade

---

[59] Serial set 2552, House Exec. Doc. 6, part II, 205.
[60] Babin (1953) contains a good discussion of the commission house system in New Orleans before the Civil War.
[61] Hall (1848a): 135; Hunter (1933–34): 95.
[62] Callender (1909): 279; *DeBow's Review,* vol. 2: 58; Frantz (1960): 148; *Hunt's Merchants' Magazine,* vol. 19: 589; Mills (1820): 45, 46; Morrison (1958): 231, *Niles' Register,* vol. 56: 278; Serial set 170, House Doc. 11, 5; Serial set 178, House Report 213, 3; Serial set 619, Senate Exec. Doc. 42, 113; Serial set 656, House Report 166, 9; Serial set 900, House Exec. Doc. 48, 8.

volume was at most one-half of that downstream.[63] If we allow for the difference in upstream and downstream carrying capacity, this suggests that the upstream utilization rates were at most equal to the downstream rates. We have assumed that upstream utilization averaged 75 percent of capacity before 1840.

For the two decades after 1840 the upstream utilization estimates are derived as residuals. The procedure used is as follows. Given total costs and the downstream freight and total passenger revenues, what upstream freight revenue would have been required to provide a 10 percent return on invested capital? For the 1840s this utilization is 44 percent; for the 1850s it is only 12 percent. Though imprecise, these esimates are consistent with observations on the serious backhaulage problem[64] that developed in the late ante-bellum period.

Upstream cargo revenues are derived in the same manner as the downstream revenues. Our average annual estimates of these revenues are $12,400 for the decade before 1820, $8,700 1820–29, $9,300 from 1830 to 1839, $5,300 during the 1840s, and $2,000 from 1850 to 1860.

PASSENGER FARES AND PASSENGER TRAFFIC

If there was sufficient water to navigate, a steamboat could usually carry a full complement of passengers, even if it often could not carry a full load of freight. Thus the seasonal variation of passenger fares was less than that of freight rates. As noted by Hunter: "The passenger business was in many respects similar to the freight business and followed much the same course. Fares like rates fell rapidly from the high initial levels; they fluctuated with the stage of the rivers and responded quickly to other factors affecting the competitive situation. Neither the long-range decline, however, nor the spread between high-water and low-water fares was as pronounced as in the case of freight rates."[65]

There was, however, another important dimension to passenger fares. Steamboats varied widely in the quality of their accommodations and service, with the result that even though almost all steamboats carried passengers, a disproportionately large share of the business fell to the newer, larger, and more elaborately furnished vessels. These vessels also commanded higher fares. This fare differential was most pronounced during the latter part of the

---

[63] Johnson (1915), vol. 1: 213. This must refer to steamboat freight only, since before the 1830s over half the downstream freight was carried by flatboats. Thus, if the statement referred to total freight, the upstream freight (all by steamboat) would be greater than the downstream freight shipped by steamboat. Furthermore, the upstream freight would exceed the average capacity of the steamboats.

[64] Morrison (1958): 248; and Embree (1848–49): 109.

[65] Hunter (1949): 380.

period, when "first class" boats charged $20 to $30 for cabin passage
between Louisville and New Orleans, while lesser boats were charging only
$12 to $15.[66]

Two general types of accommodations were available to steamboat passengers, deck and cabin passage. "The cabin passengers formed the aristocracy of
the steamboat, a leisure class which by virtue of money enjoyed all the
comforts and luxuries which the boat might afford, and escaped most of the
hardships and hazards which fell to the lot of the occupants of the lower
deck."[67] Cabin passage included stateroom and meals for the duration of the
voyage, regardless of the delays encountered.

It was frequently remarked that one could travel in a good steamboat at little
more than the cost of spending the same time in a first-class hotel, and with
accommodations which on the best boats were quite comparable.[68]

Steamboat owners were primarily concerned with space for freight and
roomy, attractive quarters for cabin passengers. What space remained after all
other needs were met was placed at the disposal of the deckers.[69]

On many steamboats little if any space was reserved even nominally for their
use; often the decker was obliged to find a resting place on or about the piles
of boxes, barrels, bales, and other freight.[70]

In the provision of meals, too, the deck passengers were left largely to their
devices. Except for the stove supplied for the combined purposes of cooking
and heating, the management provided nothing.[71]

The chief and almost only virtue of deck passage was its cheapness.[72]

Not only was the cost of deck passage low, but the spread between deck and
cabin fares was remarkably wide. . . . Deck fare was frequently only one-fifth
or one-sixth of the cabin fare; sometimes it rose to as much as one-third or
one-half. The more common ratio in the middle years of the steamboat era
was approximately one to four.[73]

Very little seasonal variation in passenger fares in the Louisville–New
Orleans trade is evident in the fares quoted by the various sources, and when
the premium rates charged by the first class boats are ignored, the passenger
fare quotations appear remarkably uniform. Our estimates of average passen-

[66] Ibid., p. 381; and Robertson (1855): 106.
[67] Hunter (1949): 391, 392. Hunter's Chapter 9 (pp. 390–418) discusses the experience of cabin passengers in detail.
[68] Ibid., p. 418.
[69] Ibid., p. 422. Deck passenger experiences are discussed in detail on pp. 419–41.
[70] Ibid., pp. 422–23.
[71] Ibid., p. 424.
[72] Ibid., p. 420.
[73] Ibid., p. 421.

Table D–3. Average Upstream and Downstream Fares for Deck and Cabin Passage
between Louisville and New Orleans, 1810–60

	Upstream		Downstream	
Period	Cabin	Deck	Cabin	Deck
Before 1820	$125	$25	$75	$18
1820–29	50	10	25	6
1830–39	25	6	25	6
1840–49	20	4	20	4
1850–60	15	3	15	3

Sources: American Almanac (1836): 127; Berry (1843): 57; Birkbeck (1819): 5;
Casseday (1852): 253; Chevalier (1961): 211; *Cincinnati Daily Gazette,* Oct. 18, 1845;
Nov. 15, 1845 ; and Dec. 13, 1845; Crittenden (1857): 190; Dayton (1925): 337–38,
351; *De Bow's Review,* vol. 6, 62; Depew (1895): vol. 1, 26; Elder, 16; Faux (1904):
164; J. Flint (1904): 164; T. Flint (1832): 212; Gilleland (1820): 272; Grayson, 22; Hall
(1848a): 146; *The Western Monthly Magazine,* vol. 4, 411, 413; Hunter (1949): 380–82,
419–21; *Liberty Hall and Cincinnati Gazette,* July 17, 1851; Aug. 21, 1851; Meyer
(1917): 77, 129; Mills (1820): 45, 46: Morrison (1958): 218, 227, 228; *Niles' Register*
vol. 25, 95; Robertson (1855): 106; Turner (1907): 83; Welby (1904): fn. 147, 279–80;
The American Pioneer, 70; Serial set 920, Senate Exec. Doc. 11, pt. II, 343; Serial set
2552, House Exec. Doc. 6, pt. II, 195.

ger fares by class for each decade are presented in Table D–3. The sources on
which the estimates are based are also presented there.

To calculate passenger revenues it is also necessary to estimate the average
number of deck passengers and cabin passengers that traveled in each direction. Most reports of passenger loads were for steamboats involved in accidents or record journeys, and most of these were for upstream voyages. These
reports are given in Table D–4, along with our estimates of the average
number of passengers in each class, each way, for one trip.

From the reports cited we have tabulated the number of passengers on a
per ton basis. For those reports not giving the steamboat's tonnage this
information has been obtained from the "Lytle List." At various times during
the ante-bellum period statistics on average passenger loads were collected, or
estimates were made, and these have been used directly or as a check on the
calculations. Reports of passenger loads for steamboats not traveling in the
Louisville–New Orleans trade also have been used as checks. The use of these
reports is tempered by the knowledge that the average passenger loads of
steamboats in the shorter trades were generally larger than those of steamboats in the longer trades, and that the disproportion between deck and cabin
passengers was, in general, least in the short local trades.

Having calculated the average number of upstream passengers per ton per
trip for each period, it is possible to calculate the average annual number of
upstream passengers per trip for each period. Throughout the ante-bellum
period large numbers of immigrants and flatboatmen traveled upstream from

Table D–4. Average Number of Deck and Cabin Passengers Carried per Upstream Trip and Downstream Trip by Steamboats in the Louisville–New Orleans Trade, 1810–60

Period	Average measured tonnage (tons)	Average number of upstream passengers per ton per trip	Average number of upstream passengers per trip	Average number of downstream passengers per trip	Number of cabin passengers as a fraction of the total
Before 1820	220	.30	66	50	.30
1820–29	290	.35	102	76	.35
1830–39	310	.40	124	93	.40
1840–49	310	.40	124	93	.40
1850–60	360	.40	144	108	.40

Period	Average number of upstream cabin passengers per trip	Average number of upstream deck passengers per trip	Average number of downstream cabin passengers per trip	Average number of downstream deck passengers per trip
Before 1820	20	46	15	35
1820–29	36	66	27	49
1830–39	50	74	37	56
1840–49	50	74	37	56
1850–60	58	86	43	65

Sources: Ambler (1932): 173; Baird (1834): 341; Banta (1949): 298; Callender (1909): 279; *The Cincinnati Directory* (1829): 166; Crittenden(1857): 193; Dayton (1925): 339, 341; DeBow (1854): vol. 3, 154; *DeBow's Review,* vol. 2, 58; Embree (1848–49): 5, 87, 317; Flugel (1924): 433–34; Hall (1848*a*): 219; Henshaw (1911): 382–85; *Hunt's Merchants' Magazine,* vol. 18, 494; vol. 26, 506; vol. 28, 263; Hunter (1949): 420–22; *Liberty Hall and Cincinnati Gazette,* March 23, 1819; Lloyd (1856): 285–91; Mc-Dermott (1951): 44–45; Mills (1820): 45–46; Morrison (1958): 231, 235; *Niles' Register,* vol. 20, 224; vol. 24, 32; vol. 26, 48; vol. 30, 267; vol. 34, 235; vol. 38, 68; vol. 42, 153; vol. 52, 202; vol. 54, 145; vol. 56, 162 and 278; vol. 60, 32; vol. 64, 144 and 256; vol. 67, 352; vol. 69, 288, 352; vol. 73, 288; vol. 75, 320; Ringwalt (1888): 114; Robertson (1855): 103; Shepard (1948): 18; D. Smith (1957): 276, 279, 281; Serial set 208, House Doc. 74, 1; Serial set 345, House Doc. 21, 309; Serial set 490, House Report 661, 5; Serial set 529, Senate Exec. Doc. 18, 59–65; Serial set 547, Senate Doc. 4, 9; Serial set 619; Senate Exec. Doc. 42, 16–21, 114; Serial set 841, House Exec. Doc. 1, pt. II, 364, 365; Serial set 900, House Exec. Doc. 48, 8; Serial set 2132, House Misc. Doc. 42, vol. 4, 665.

New Orleans; thus the number of passengers moving upstream was greater than the number moving downstream. We have assumed that the number of downstream passengers per trip for each period averaged about three-quarters of the number of upstream passengers. The proportion of passengers in each class has been derived from the several sources listed in Table D–4 that provide such information.[74] As indicated in Table D–4: "the proportion of passengers traveling by cabin increased slowly, no doubt largely in response to the steady reduction of fares, which in terms of dollars was much more significant for cabin than for deck passage."[75]

We have assumed that the proportion in each class was the same in each direction. Consequently, average annual passenger revenue for each period is the product of the average number of round trips and round trip passenger revenues per year (the sum of fares times the number in each class, each way, respectively). The final estimates of average annual total passenger revenues are $16,100, $17,000, $23,600, $22,600, and $23,600 for each respective decade, 1810–60.

Three pieces of data are available to check these estimates. One estimate gives $6,000 as the annual passenger revenue of steamboats in the Louisville–New Orleans trade in 1820.[76] An 1842 report estimated that steamboats on the western rivers measured 126,278 tons and estimated the annual value of the passenger traffic at $2,595,108.[77] Accordingly, the value of the passenger traffic was about $20.58 per ton per year, or $6,380 per year for a 310 ton steamboat. Hall reports two estimates of the total value of passenger traffic in 1846; the first has been discarded as being too low, but the second was $5,118,269.[78] Steamboat tonnage in 1846 has been estimated at 249,055 tons[79] for passenger earnings of about $20.55 per ton per year, or $6,370 per year for a 310 ton boat. All of these estimates are substantially below ours.

The 1850 census reports do not show a significant relationship between passenger revenue and vessel size for steamboats in the Louisville–New Orleans trade. However, they do indicate that the ratio of passenger to freight revenue was about 0.8. This ratio holds for our estimates as well.

---

[74] Hunter (1949): 421–22, reports that in the late forties and early fifties passenger lists for 60 steamboats arriving in Cincinnati averaged 96 cabin and 150 deck passengers. Steamboats running in the Pittsburg and Cincinnati Packet Line in the fifties carried about 100 cabin and 125 deck passengers. In both cases the cabin passengers are about 40 percent of the total.

[75] Ibid., p. 421.

[76] Mills (1820): 45, 46.

[77] Hunt's Merchants' Magazine, vol. 18: 494.

[78] Hall (1848a): 208, 210.

[79] Ibid. The two estimates of the combined tonnage of steamboats operating on the western rivers would indicate that this tonnage doubled in the four years from 1824 to 1846. This was not the case, suggesting that one or both of the estimates is incorrect. We have assumed that each report was internally consistent.

APPENDIX E

The Cost and Revenue Determinants of Flatboating in the Louisville — New Orleans Trade, 1810 — 1860

Flatboats plying the Mississippi to New Orleans were among the largest and most solidly constructed flatboats in the West. They were covered over their entire length and were the most expensive flatboats on the river system. The average size of flatboats increased substantially during the antebellum period. Our estimates of the average size by decade are given in Table E-1. Except for the 1810–19 decade, the estimates are based on reports of flour-carrying flatboats arriving at New Orleans.

Construction costs, of course, depended on the vessel's size and the costs per ton. Various sources report that the costs remained at approximately $1.50 per ton throughout the period.[1] Therefore, average flatboat costs, by decade, 1810–60, would have been about $45, $62, $84, $140, and $219, respectively.

A flatboat generally had a crew of five or six men, including the captain.[2] A larger boat required a larger crew, but it was difficult to operate even a small boat with fewer than five men. Hunter states that one man for each 15

---

[1] Construction cost estimates are based on assertions by Baldwin (1941) and several government reports. For instance: "The price of flatboats all during the keelboat age can be placed definitely at between $1.00 and $1.50 a foot, depending somewhat upon the width desired and upon the equipment. The price would make an average flatboat of fourteen by fifty feet cost about $75." Baldwin (1941): 54. As a measure of capacity, apparently a foot and a ton were nearly the same. Goverment flatboats in the 1790's were, on the average, twelve or fourteen feet wide and forty-five or fifty feet in length. These figures seem to have held good in later years for the general run of flatboats. The average flat probably held between four and five hundred barrels, or forty to fifty tons." Ibid., p. 47. According to government reports, between 1822–27, there was a loss of 150 flatboats (30 each year) at $60 per ton (40 tons average boat); House Doc. No. 11, 1827, 5–6, and in 1842, it was estimated that there were 4,000 flatboats on the western rivers (75 tons each) valued at $105 per boat. Serial set 415 Senate Doc. 137, 3.

[2] Baldwin (1941): 48; Berry (1943): 44; Hall (1848a): 166; Hunter (1949): 54; Imlay (1792): 98–110; Kussart (1929), vol. 1: 6; Meyer (1917): 99; Ringwalt (1888): 11; Wallace Family Papers 1834–35, unpaged; Serial set 415, Senate Doc. 137, 3.

Table E–1. Average Costs of Flatboat Operation in the Louisville–New Orleans Trade, 1810–60

Period	Average flatboat capacity (tons)	Average flatboat cost	Average crew size	Average total wages	Average food costs	Average wharfage charges	Average total cost
1810–19	30	$45	5	$235	$5	$6	$291
1820–29	41	62	5	235	6	6	309
1830–39	56	84	5	235	9	10	338
1840–49	93	140	7	340	12	10	502
1850–60	146	219	10	520	22	15	776

Sources: All cost estimates are discussed in the text. The sources for the average flatboat capacity are: Ambler (1932): 49; Bishop (1864) vol. 2, 67; Chevalier (1961): 215; Hunter (1949): 54; Reiser (1951): 30; Serial set 2552, House Exec. Doc. 6, pt. II, 186, 195; and the *New Orleans Prices Current* for the commercial years 1825–26, 1834–35, 1843–44, and 1856–57.

tons can be used as a rough guide to the size of a flatboat crew.[3] Therefore, flatboats of 75 tons or less can be taken to have required a crew of five men. A 90–100 ton flatboat would have had a crew of six to seven men, and a 150 ton flatboat a crew of about ten men, including the captain.

Reports on the wages paid flatboatmen ranged from $30 to $50 per trip for crewmen and $50 to $200 per trip for the captain.[4] In addition, food was provided. Reports indicate that the wages remained constant from 1810 until the Civil War.[5] Since the voyage from Louisville to New Orleans by flatboat took about one month,[6] the estimates of average wages for a crewman are $40 per trip. We have assumed that the captain of a crew of four received $75 per trip, the captain of a crew of six $100 per trip, and the captain of a crew of nine $125 per trip, with the latter's second-in-command receiving $75 per trip. Thus, a flatboat with five men on board had a wage bill of $235, a flatboat with seven men had a wage bill of $340, and a boat with ten men had a wage bill of $520.

The only other costs were the food for the crew, wharfage charges, and interest, but this later cost was too small to be of concern. Insurance costs are treated below in the calculation of flatboat freight rates. Estimates of food costs for the crew are based on the diet of a male field hand slave in the

[3] Hunter (1949): 443.
[4] Baldwin (1941): 88, 89; *The Bankers' Magazine and State Financial Register,* vol II, part I: 188; Berry (1943): 44; Kussart (1929), vol. 1: 6; *The Louisville Directory* (1832): 127; Hall (1848a): 143; Ringwalt (1888): 11; "Wallace Family Papers 1834–35"; Serial set 415, Senate Doc. 137, 3; Serial set 2552, House Exec. Doc. 6, part II, 195.
[5] Baldwin (1941): 89, for example.
[6] Ibid., pp. 68, 89; Callender (1909): 416; Meyer (1917): 96, 99. See also Chapter 6, pp. 79–80 (above) for qualifications.

ante-bellum south.[7] Berry's Cincinnati prices have been used to convert these quantities into values. Based on the crew size, these estimates are $5, $6, $9, and $12, and $22 per voyage for each decade respectively.

The only other cost normally incurred by a flatboat in the Louisville–New Orleans trade was the wharfage charge at New Orleans. During the early part of the period the wharfage charge was $6,[8] and in 1836 the wharfage charge was changed to $10,[9] with changes occurring again several times during the early fifties.[10] After 1851 flatboats less than 80 feet long were charged $10, flatboats from 80 to 100 feet long were charged $12, and flatboats over 100 feet long were charged $15.[11] These charges, along with the other average costs of flatboat operation in the Louisville–New Orleans trade, are summarized by decade in Table E–1.

A flatboat had two sources of revenues, the freight revenue and the salvage revenue from the sale of the boat. All reports on the disposal of flatboats indicate that they brought less than $25 and were often cast loose and allowed to drift downriver.[12] It has been assumed that the average amount paid for a flatboat at New Orleans was about 10 percent of its cost, thus $5 to $6 is the salvage revenue for a 30 to 41 ton flatboat, $8 for a 56 ton flatboat, $14 for a 93 ton flatboat, and $23 for a 146 ton flatboat.

Flatboat freight rates are known to have been consistently lower than steamboat freight rates,[13] but there are not sufficient citations available to calculate a series of average flatboat freight rates directly. On flatboats the shipper paid both the shipping charges and the costs of the insurance on his goods. It is assumed that the freight rate and insurance premium together were the same for both flatboats and steamboats; hence flatboat freight rates are calculated by subtracting the difference between steamboat and flatboat insurance costs from steamboat freight rates. The results give an upward bias for several reasons. First, flatboat travel was slower than steamboat travel, so

---

[7] Fogel and Engerman (1974), vol. 2: 97, gives the per capita food consumption of slaves in 1860. This diet is shown to have a higher caloric value than the diet of the average person in 1879. The slave diet represents a per capita food cost of about $30 per year or $2.50 per month. Prices of all the foodstuffs included in the diet are not available for the ante-bellum period. Our food cost estimates are therefore based on the assumption that corn and pork constituted 40 and 60 percent respectively of the total food cost (see *De Bow's Review*, vol. 12: 291–92). Thus, Berry's price indices for corn and pork can be combined to give a food price index (Berry [1943], Table 16: 183, 549.). When converted (Haites [1969]: 78–79), the index gives food costs of $1.00, $1.15, $1.76, $1.68, and $2.17 per man per month respectively for each period.

[8] Baldwin (1941): 189.

[9] Hunt's *Merchant's Magazine*, vol. 2: 425.

[10] Ibid., vol. 22: 219; vol. 24: 90; vol. 25: 347; and vol. 27: 234.

[11] Ibid., vol. 27: 234.

[12] Baldwin (1941): 49; Berry (1943): 24; Dunbar (1915), vol. 1: 284; Hall (1848a): 328; Meyer (1917): 88.

[13] Berry (1943): 45, 88, 89; *Cincinnati Daily Chronicle*, Sept. 18, 1941; Hunter (1949): 25, 56.

shippers were probably willing to pay some premium for steamboat transportation, at least on perishable cargos. Second, flatboats traveled only when the water was highest, at a time when rates in general were typically lower than average. Thus, using the average steamboat freight rates to calculate the average flatboat freight rates gives an upward bias to the flatboat rates Finally, there were possible qualitative differences in the services that favored steam, at least after the early trial period for steamboats.

Although information on the actual premiums for insurance on freight shipped by steamboat and flatboat are not required for our purposes, evidence on the difference between these premiums is important. Quotations of actual insurance premiums are relatively scarce,[14] but insurance premiums apparently did not vary significantly from month to month,[15] and they were approximately halved from 1810 until 1845.[16] More important for our calculations, premiums on freight sent by flatboat were at least twice those for insurance on freight sent by steamboat.[17] From these relationships and the available quotations, it is possible to find the difference between the premiums for insurance on common freight shipped by flatboat and by steamboat for each decade prior to 1860. These differences were 3 percent, 2 percent, and 1.5 percent for the three respective decades 1810–39, and 1 percent, 1840–60.

Table E–2. Average Flatboat Freight Rates in the Louisville–New Orleans Trade, by Decade, 1810–60

Period	Average steamboat freight rate downstream[a] ($/ton)	Average value of freight shipped ($/ton)	Difference in insurance premiums on freight (percent)	Difference between steamboat and flatboat freight rates ($/ton)	Average flatboat freight rate ($/ton)
1810–19	$20.00	$115	3	$3.45	$16.55
1820–29	12.50	100	2	2.00	10.50
1830–39	10.00	90	1.5	1.35	8.65
1840–49	6.00	80	1	.80	5.20
1850–60	6.50	95	1	.95	5.55

[a]From Appendix D, Table D–1.

---

[14] Baldwin (1941): 183, 230; Berry (1943): 68, 69, 70, 89; *Cincinnati Daily Chronicle,* June 17, 1843; *DeBow's Review,* vol. 8: 161–63; *Hunt's Merchants' Magazine,* vol. 22: 216–19; Hunter (1949): 368, 369; "Wallace Family Papers 1834–35," unpaged.
[15] Berry (1943): 69.
[16] Ibid., pp. 68, 70.
[17] Ibid., p. 68; Hunter (1949): 369.

The tons of freight received and the value of produce received by river annually at New Orleans are given by Callender.[18] From these annual figures he estimates of the average value of downstream freight are $117 per ton from 1816 through 1819, $105 per ton for the 1820–29 decade, $95 per ton for 1830–39, $83 per ton for the 1840–49 decade, and for the period from 1850 through 1860 it was $98.33 per ton.[19] The lower the value per ton the higher the flatboat freight rate, so the value per ton has been rounded downward, and thus the flatboat freight rates are again given a slight upward bias. The calculations of average flatboat freight rates for each period are shown in Table E–2.

Average revenues by decade are the product of these rates and average flatboat capacity in each period, because according to contemporary observers,[20] flatboats typically carried capacity loads.

---

[18] Callender (1909): 315.

[19] When each of the annual figures was given a weight equal to the number of tons of produce received at New Orleans by river during the year, the results were 1816–19: $118.27 per ton; 1820–29: $101.47 per ton; 1830–39: $95.51 per ton; 1840–49: $81.75 per ton; and 1850–60: $97.41 per ton.

[20] Hall (1848a): 204, for example.

APPENDIX F

*Characteristics of Trunk
and Tributary Vessels, 1850*

CENSUS DATA, 1850

Recent work by Bateman, Foust, and Weiss on nineteenth-century industrial development has uncovered data on forty-five steamboats that called at Louisville during the year 1850. The data exist because Schedule 5 of the census was not completed properly. The data include:

- the name of the steamboat;
- the route on which it operated;
- the construction cost of the vessel;
- the number of crewmembers;
- the monthly wage bill;
- the annual expenditures for provisions, fuel, insurance, general expenses, and lockage;
- the number and horsepower of the engines;
- the annual freight and passenger revenues; and
- the number of months per year during which the boat operated.

This information was supplemented by the registered tonnage, the date of construction, and the date of cessation of service from the "Lytle List." Finally, references in Hunter made it possible to identify five of the boats as packet-boats.[1]

[1] Hunter (1949): 320–35.

The census data reflects the contemporary practice of designating steam-boats by the trade in which they operated. The trades of the boats in the census data, and the number of boats in each, are summarized in Table F–1. We have further classified the trades as being on trunk routes or tributaries. Trunk routes are essentially those on the Mississippi and Ohio rivers down-stream of St. Louis and Pittsburgh respectively. Five trunk routes are repre-sented in the data. One, the Louisville–New Orleans route, includes almost half the boats. The other four have a total of nine steamboats–five of them packets. There are five tributary routes with a total of fourteen boats.

This assignment of boats to routes should not be regarded as fixed. We have mentioned elsewhere that boats could and did move from one trade to another in response to market conditions. Our data on steamboat arrivals at New Orleans between August 25, 1848 and August 31, 1849 illustrates this. There were a total of 213 arrivals from Louisville by 66 different vessels. Thirty-eight of the boats made the trip only once; the other twenty-eight made the trip at least twice. Some made as many as fourteen round trips.

COST ESTIMATES

To estimate the total annual costs for the census vessels, which are comparable to the costs estimated in Appendix C, requires three adjustments to the reported cost data. First, the insurance cost must be raised to the level of full coverage. To do this it was assumed that the reported insurance cost represented three-quarters coverage, so that the cost of full coverage would be 1.333 times the reported cost.

Second, annual wages must be estimated. The annual wages were calcu-lated as the monthly wages times the number of months operated plus $175 per month for the nonoperating months. The latter is the wages paid to the

Table F–1. Steamboat Trades Represented in the 1850 Census Data

Route	No. of boats	Trunk or tributary	Comments
1. Louisville–New Orleans	22	Trunk	
2. Louisville–St. Louis	4	Trunk	3 Packets
3. Louisville–Tennessee River	5	Tributary	
4. Louisville–Henderson	2	Trunk	
5. Louisville–Frankfort	2	Tributary	
6. Louisville–Cincinnati	2	Trunk	2 Packets
7. Louisville–Green River	3	Tributary	
8. Louisville–Wabash River	3	Tributary	
9. Louisville–Kninhaus River	1	Tributary	
10. Louisville–Madison	1	Trunk	

Table F–2. Sensitivity of Profit Rate to Cost Adjustment Assumptions, 1850

Category	Preferred assumptions (in %)	Range obtained using alternative assumptions (in %
Louisville–New Orleans	7.8	6.7–10.0
Other trunk	10.4	9.7–12.0
All trunk	8.5	7.6–10.5
Tributary	23.6	22.1–27.1

captain and clerk, who were customarily retained during the off-season. Finally, annual depreciation costs were calculated as the original cost of the boat divided by the average life span of all boats in the same category—where vessels were categorized as Louisville–New Orleans, other trunk, or tributary.

To test the sensitivity of the costs, and hence profits, to the assumptions underlying the cost adjustments the following alternatives were tested:

• no adjustment to reported insurance costs;
• reported insurance costs raised by 50 percent on the assumption that they represent the cost of two-thirds coverage;
• annual wages calculated as the product of the number of months operated and the monthly wages;
• depreciation calculated on the basis of a six-year life for boats operating on trunk rivers and a five-year life for boats on the tributaries.

The various combinations of assumptions tested produced eleven different estimates of the profit rate. The profit rate corresponding to the preferred assumptions together with the range of profit rates obtained as a result of changing the assumptions is shown in Table F–2 for the various categories of vessels.

ROUTE CHARACTERISTICS

Tables F–3 to F–5 present the calculated means and standard deviations of seventeen variables which bear upon the operations of the steamboats. We have grouped these calculations in three separate tables in order to compare vessel characteristics under three separate route categories. In Table F–3, we compare characteristics between packets and all other trunk river steamboats. In Table F–4 we compare the characteristics of steamboats operating on the Louisville–New Orleans route to those operating on other trunk routes. And finally, in Table F–5, we compare the characteristics of steamboats operating on all trunk rivers to those operating on tributary rivers.

To determine whether or not there are significant differences between two given categories of vessels, we conducted tests of difference between means. In each case the hypothesis under test is

$$H : \mu_1 = \mu_2$$

That is, the two universes actually have the same mean. Accordingly, we present the calculated t-statistics in Tables F–3 to F–5. For the tests of significance, we have chosen a two-tailed test and a level of acceptance at $\alpha = 0.05$.

PACKETS VS. ALL OTHER TRUNK STEAMBOATS

As noted in Table F–1, the 1850 census data contain information on five packet steamboats—two on the prestigious Louisville–Cincinnati route and three on the Louisville–St. Louis route. Thus, all five operated on trunk rivers. Yet, Table F–3 draws out some striking, though not always unexpected, differences between packet and nonpacket steamboats operating on the trunk rivers.

A comparison of the data in Table F–3 shows that packet steamboats carried relatively more passengers than freight, reflecting, as expected, the greater importance of schedule regularity in the passenger business than in the freight business. Also, not surprisingly, the greater importance of speed in the passenger business meant that packets had more powerful engines, and they were more lavishly built, as indicated by their higher construction cost per ton.

Our calculations also indicate that the packets in our sample had longer operating months per year, higher general expenses and provisions costs, but significantly lower average monthly wage per crewman and insurance cost.

In spite of these observed differences between packets and other trunk river vessels, our calculations show quite clearly that there was no significant difference in the rate of return to capital between packets and other vessels operating on the trunk rivers of the ante-bellum west.

LOUISVILLE–NEW ORLEANS ROUTE
VS. ALL OTHER TRUNK ROUTES

Table F–4 indicates that there were only three significant differences between vessels that operated on the Louisville–New Orleans route and all other trunk river steamboats. These differences are in the operating months per year and in the ratios of monthly wages/crewman and passenger revenue/ton. We attribute them to the fact that among the nine vessels categorized as "other trunk" vessels, five were packets (noted in the preceding section). Given the small sample size from this class of vessels, the calculated means are heavily weighted by the characteristics of the five packet boats. Thus, the three differences observed between the Louisville–New Orleans vessels and

Table F–3. Means, Standard Deviations, and T-Statistics of Packets and Trunk River Steamboats,[a] 1850

Variables	Packets Mean	Packets s.d.	All other trunk vessels Mean	s.d.	T-statistics
1 Size (tons)	353	127	387	152	.46
2 Number of crewmen	49	3	45	12	.71
3 Crewmen/ton	15	5	12	3	1.86
4 Horsepower/ton	2.34	.61	1.72	.43	2.74[b]
5 Age of vessel (years)	2.50	1.23	2.81	1.83	.36
6 Length of life (years)	5.60	1.51	6.39	3.60	.47
7 Operating months/year	10.40	1.52	8.65	1.62	2.22[b]
8 Construction cost/ton ($)	114.20	16.75	87.69	21.66	2.58[b]
9 Fuel cost/ton/month ($)	3.51	.98	4.12	1.10	1.15
10 Monthly wages/crewman ($)	32.53	.97	42.26	4.15	5.14[b]
11 Provisions cost/crewman/month ($)	30.38	3.92	25.66	5.92	1.70
12 Provisions cost/ton/month ($)	4.58	1.28	3.11	.79	3.46[b]
13 Insurance cost/construction cost/month ($)	.009	.003	.013	.003	2.67[b]
14 General expenses/ton/month ($)	2.06	.76	1.57	.36	2.28[b]
15 Freight revenue/ton ($)	51.54	18.64	91.33	23.23	3.60[b]
16 Passenger revenue/ton ($)	160.70	46.29	73.28	28.55	5.66[b]
17 Rate of return (%)	8.32	2.72	8.52	5.97	.07

[a]Trunk river steamboats are defined in this table as: all trunk river steamboats minus packet boats.
[b]Indicates variable with significant mean difference, for α = 0.05 and using a two-tailed test.

Table F–4. Means, Standard Deviations, and T-Statistics of Louisville–New Orleans and Other Trunk River Steamboats, 1850

Variables	Louisville–New Orleans vessels		All other trunk vessels		T-statistics
	Mean	s.d.	Mean	s.d.	
1 Size (tons)	412	150	308	117	1.85
2 Number of crewmen	47	12	43	10	.96
3 Crewmen/ton	12	3	15	4	1.97
4 Horsepower/ton	1.75	.45	2.00	.63	1.24
5 Age of vessel (years)	2.59	1.88	3.17	1.32	.84
6 Length of life (years)	6.36	3.75	6.00	2.24	.27
7 Operating months/year	8.27	1.28	10.56	1.59	4.20[a]
8 Construction cost/ton ($)	90.36	22.04	95.89	25.98	.60
9 Fuel cost/ton/month ($)	4.12	1.08	3.76	1.13	.84
10 Monthly wages/crewman ($)	43.06	2.49	34.89	5.87	5.50[a]
11 Provisions cost/crewman/month ($)	27.27	4.71	24.34	7.97	1.28
12 Provisions cost/ton/month ($)	3.53	.75	3.57	1.53	.77
13 Insurance cost/construction cost/month ($)	.013	.003	.011	.004	1.39
14 General expenses/ton/month ($)	1.56	.37	1.86	.63	1.65
15 Freight revenue/ton/month ($)	88.98	24.34	74.97	31.28	1.34
16 Passenger revenue/ton ($)	71.31	29.38	126.60	53.96	3.70[a]
17 Rate of return (%)	7.75	5.50	10.36	5.31	1.21

[a]Indicates variable with significant mean difference, for $\alpha = 0.05$ and using a two-tailed test.

Table F–5. Means, Standard Deviations, and T-Statistics of Trunk and Tributary Steamboats, 1850

Variables	All trunk river vessels		All tributary river vessels		T-statistics
	Mean	s.d.	Mean	s.d.	
1 Size (tons)	381	147	149	34	5.83[a]
2 Number of crewmen	46	11	30	7	4.74[a]
3 Crewmen/ton	13	3	20	3	6.96[a]
4 Horsepower/ton	1.82	.51	1.46	.54	2.16[a]
5 Age of vessel (years)	2.76	1.73	1.64	1.17	2.19[a]
6 Length of life (years)	6.26	3.35	5.36	2.95	.87
7 Operating months/year	8.94	1.71	9.93	1.00	2.01[a]
8 Construction cost/ton ($)	91.97	22.94	77.86	16.77	2.06[a]
9 Fuel cost/ton/month ($)	4.02	1.09	4.21	1.01	.55
10 Monthly wages/crewman ($)	40.69	5.27	36.15	4.12	2.85[a]
11 Provisions cost/crewman/month ($)	26.42	5.86	20.10	3.33	3.76[a]
12 Provisions cost/ton/month ($)	3.35	1.02	4.09	.74	2.43[a]
13 Insurance cost/construction cost/month ($)	.012	.004	.026	.015	5.00[a]
14 General expenses/ton/month ($)	1.65	.47	1.83	.85	.91
15 Freight revenue/ton ($)	84.92	26.78	176.10	48.42	8.41[a]
16 Passenger revenue/ton ($)	87.38	45.08	107.90	55.64	1.32
17 Rate of return (%)	8.51	5.49	23.62	14.12	5.20[a]

[a]Indicates variable with significant mean difference, for $a = 0.05$ and using a two-tailed test.

he other trunk river vessels actually reflect the most significant differences etween trunk and packet vessels described in the previous section. Once hese unique features of packets are removed, the Louisville–New Orleans essels appear characteristically not to be different from vessels operating on ll trunk river routes.

This supports our claim that our findings and conclusions relative to the ouisville–New Orleans route have general applicability to all trunk river outes.

TRUNK VS. TRIBUTARY

Although the 1850 census data show no significant differences among teamboats operating on different trunk routes, they do clearly show that here were marked differences between trunk and tributary river routes. /hen the means of each of the seventeen variables on trunk and tributary vers are compared (Table F–5), the means of thirteen variables stand out as eing significantly different from one another. These differences suggest that ay attempt to analyze the economics of steamboating on the ante-bellum estern rivers requires separate analyses of the trunk and tributary compo- ents.

APPENDIX G

Measures and Indexes of Total Factor
Productivity Changes of Steamboats and Flatboats

Measures of total factor productivity change show the rate of change o output per unit of all inputs, appropriately weighted. Because of data limita tions, historical studies of productivity change frequently impose problems o measurement. This being true in this case, we have employed two measures i the hope of capturing the approximate range of productivity advance tha occurred over the period.

Our first measure compares the growth of physical output relative to th growth of the inputs. The second measure is based on a comparison o changes in the input prices relative to changes in the output price. Ideally where the data are perfectly consistent, both measures should give the sam findings. To illustrate our measures and this consistency algebraically w define the following terms:

$$Q = \text{output}$$
$$P_Q = \text{price of } Q$$
$$K = \text{capital inputs}$$
$$L = \text{labor inputs}$$
$$P_K = \text{the price of } K$$
$$P_L = \text{the price of } L$$

We begin with the accounting identity that total revenues equal total payments to the factors of production; thus

(1) $$P_Q \cdot Q = P_K \cdot K + P_L \cdot L.$$

By taking the total derivative of (1) we have

(2) $$\dot{P}_Q Q + \dot{Q} P_Q = \dot{P}_K K + \dot{K} P_K + \dot{P}_L L + \dot{L} P_L,$$

where dots denote rates of change in the variable with respect to time. Now divide (2) by the accounting identity (1) and multiply each term on the right side of the equation by 1 $(= \dfrac{P_K}{P_K} = \dfrac{K}{K} = 1)$. Thus we obtain

(3) $$\frac{\dot{P}_Q}{P_Q} + \frac{\dot{Q}}{Q} = \frac{P_K}{P_K} \cdot \frac{\dot{P}_K K}{(P_K K + P_L L)} + \frac{K}{K} \cdot \frac{\dot{K} P_K}{(P_K K + P_L L)}$$

$$+ \frac{P_L}{P_L} \cdot \frac{\dot{P}_L L}{(P_K K + P_L L)} + \frac{L}{L} \cdot \frac{\dot{L} P_L}{(P_K K + P_L L)},$$

which shows that the rate of growth of output and output price equals the rate of growth of inputs and input prices. The capital and labor shares of total costs respectively are

(4) $$\alpha = \frac{P_K K}{P_K K + P_L L} \text{ and } 1 - \alpha = \frac{P_L L}{P_K K + P_L L}.$$

By selecting a specific base year or time period, α and $1-\alpha$ are treated as constants and equation (3) becomes

(5) $$\frac{\dot{P}_Q}{P_Q} + \frac{\dot{Q}}{Q} = \alpha \left(\frac{\dot{P}_K}{P_K} + \frac{\dot{K}}{K} \right) + (1 - \alpha) \left(\frac{\dot{P}_L}{P_L} + \frac{\dot{L}}{L} \right).$$

To derive an index of inputs let $I = \hat{P}_K K + \hat{P}_L L$ where $\hat{P}_K$ and $\hat{P}_L$ are base year prices of K and L respectively and also are treated as constants. Thus

(6) $$\dot{I} = \hat{P}_K \dot{K} + \hat{P}_L \dot{L}$$

and dividing (6) by the index I we get

(7) $$\frac{\dot{I}}{I} = \frac{\hat{P}_K \dot{K}}{\hat{P}_K K + \hat{P}_L L} + \frac{\hat{P}_L \dot{L}}{\hat{P}_K K + \hat{P}_L L} = \frac{K}{K} \cdot \frac{\hat{P}_K \dot{K}}{(\hat{P}_K K + \hat{P}_L L)} + \frac{L}{L} \cdot \frac{\hat{P}_L \dot{L}}{(\hat{P}_K K + \hat{P}_L L)}.$$

When the same base years are chosen for $\hat{P}_K$, $\hat{P}_L$, α, and $1 - \alpha$, then (7) becomes

$$(8) \qquad \frac{\dot{I}}{I} = \alpha \frac{\dot{K}}{K} + (1-\alpha)\frac{\dot{L}}{L},$$

which states that the rate of growth of the input index is determined by the rates of growth of each input weighted by its share of total costs. To obtain an index of input prices (P_I) we define P_I by equation (9).

$$(9) \qquad P_I = P_K^{\alpha} \cdot P_L^{1-\alpha};$$

$$(9') \qquad \log(P_I) = \alpha \log P_K + (1 - \alpha) \log P_L .$$

Now we can differentiate $(9')$ to obtain,

$$(10) \qquad \frac{\dot{P}_I}{P_I} = \alpha \frac{\dot{P}_K}{P_K} + (1 - \alpha)\frac{\dot{P}_L}{P_L}.$$

We can now define the productivity measure P as

$$(11) \qquad P = \frac{Q}{I} .$$

By differentiating (11), and then multiplying each side of the equation by $1/P = I/Q$ we obtain our *first measure* of productivity *change:*

$$(12) \qquad \frac{\dot{P}}{P} = \frac{\dot{Q}}{Q} - \frac{\dot{I}}{I} = \frac{\dot{Q}}{Q} - \alpha\frac{\dot{K}}{K} - (1-\alpha)\frac{\dot{L}}{L}.$$

From (5) we see that

$$(13) \qquad \frac{\dot{Q}}{Q} - \alpha\frac{\dot{K}}{K} - (1 - \alpha)\frac{\dot{L}}{L} = \alpha\frac{\dot{P}_K}{P_K} + (1 - \alpha)\frac{\dot{P}_L}{P_L} - \frac{\dot{P}_Q}{P_Q};$$

therefore noting (10) we have our *second measure* of productivity *change:*

$$(14) \qquad \frac{\dot{P}}{P} = \alpha\frac{\dot{P}_K}{P_K} + (1-\alpha)\frac{\dot{P}_L}{P_L} - \frac{\dot{P}_Q}{P_Q} = \frac{\dot{P}_I}{P_I} - \frac{\dot{P}_Q}{P_Q} .$$

Although both measures (12) and (14) should give identical results, data limitations impose some inexactness to the estimates. The indexes for our two measures of steamboat productivity change are given in Tables G–1 and G–2 respectively, and the same for flatboats are given in Tables G–3 and G–4.

The indexes are derived from the data in Appendixes C, D, and E, and explanatory notes, where needed, are given in the tables.

Finally, it should be made explicit that the assumption underlying the choice of weights in equations (12) and (14) is that of long-run competitive equilibrium prevailing during the beginning and ending periods of measurement. Despite market imperfections, there was considerable competition among the keelboat and flatboat operators prior to the steamboat. As indicated in Chapter 3, long-run competitive equilibrium was once again achieved perhaps within a decade and certainly within two decades of the advent of the steamboat.

Table G–1. Indexes of Inputs, Outputs, and Total Factor Productivity per Steamboat on the Louisville–New Orleans Route 1815–60 (1840–49 = 100)

Years	Capital[a] series	Labor[b] series	Fuel[c] series	Weighted[d] inputs series (I)	Downstream[e] freight series	Upstream[e] freight series
(1)	(2)	(3)	(4)	(5)	(6)	(7)
1815–19	71	79	20	62	7	15
1820–29	94	97	48	84	23	53
1830–39	100	100	79	95	50	114
1840–49	100	100	100	100	100	100
1850–60	116	103	126	112	152	42

	Downstream passenger series		Upstream passenger series			
Years	Cabin[f]	Deck[f]	Cabin[f]	Deck[f]	Weighted[g] output series (Q)	Q/I × 100
	(8)	(9)	(10)	(11)	(12)	(13)
1815–19	12	19	12	19	11.	17
1820–29	36	44	36	45	33	40
1830–39	80	80	80	80	71	75
1840–49	100	100	100	100	100	100
1850–60	139	139	139	139	134	120

Source: Appendixes C and D.

[a]The capital series is an index of the average measured tonnage of a steamboat on the Louisville–New Orleans route. This series is a reasonably good proxy of the annual input of capital expressed as a flow, because the expected life and opportunity cost of capital remained almost constant over the period.

[b]The labor series is based on the calculation that there were 48 equivalent deck hands per average steamboat, 1815–19; 59, 1820–29; 61, 1830–49; and 63, 1850–60. Each cabin attendant has been rated equivalent to one deck hand. All other staff have been rated in multiple equivalent deck hand units on the basis of the ratio of their respective wage rates to that of the deck hand's (1840–49 base year wages are used).

[c]The fuel series is based on the average annual consumption of wood per steamboat

[d]The weights for the inputs equal the total annual outlay in current prices for a particular input divided by the total annual costs; insurance and repair costs are assigned to capital, while "stores and others" are assigned to labor. The shares for 1840 to 1849 are as follows: Capital 0.25, Labor 0.49, Fuel 0.26.

[e]The freight output series are indexes of the freight (in tons) carried per year Constant mileage and no "way freight" is assumed.

[f]The passenger series are indexes of the number of passengers carried per year Constant mileage and no "way passengers" are assumed.

[g]The weighted output index is calculated by using weights for each freight and passenger series, equal to its contribution to total revenue. These shares for 1840–49 are

Downstream freight	.44	Downstream deck passengers	.04
Upstream freight	.11	Upstream cabin passengers	.20
Downstream cabin passengers	.15	Upstream deck passengers	.06

Table G–2. Indexes of Input and Output Prices and Total Factor Productivity per Steamboat on the Louisville–New Orleans Route 1815–60 (1840–49 = 100)

Year	Capital[a] price series	Wage[b] series	Fuel[c] price series	Insurance[d] rate series	Berry's[e] price index	Weighted[f] input price series (P_I)	Downstream[g] freight series	Upstream[g] freight series	Downstream[g] cabin fare series	Downstream[g] deck fare series	Upstream[g] cabin fare series	Upstream[g] deck fare series	Weighted[h] output price series (P_O)	$P_I/P_O \times 100$
(1)	(2)	(3)	(4)	(5)	(6)	(7)	(8)	(9)	(10)	(11)	(12)	(13)	(14)	(15)
1815	100	74	90	180	217	129	342	1538	375	450	625	625	556	23
1816	100	74	90	180	239	136	342	1538	375	450	625	625	556	24
1817	100	74	90	180	250	139	342	1538	375	450	625	625	556	25
1818	100	74	90	180	232	134	342	1538	375	450	625	625	556	24
1819	100	74	90	180	235	134	342	1538	375	450	625	625	556	24
1820	100	79	90	150	171	115	256	615	125	150	250	250	270	43
1821	100	79	90	150	105	96	256	578	125	150	250	250	266	36
1822	100	79	90	150	120	101	214	542	125	150	250	250	243	41
1823	100	79	90	150	123	102	214	505	125	150	250	250	239	42
1824	100	79	90	150	120	101	214	468	125	150	250	250	235	43
1825	100	79	90	150	122	101	214	431	125	150	250	250	231	44
1826	100	79	90	150	113	99	214	394	125	150	250	250	227	43
1827	100	79	90	150	111	98	214	357	125	150	250	250	223	44
1828	100	79	90	150	112	98	214	320	125	150	250	250	219	45
1829	100	79	90	150	120	101	214	283	125	150	250	250	215	47
1830	100	112	100	120	113	108	219	269	125	150	125	150	185	59
1831	100	112	100	120	121	110	227	231	125	150	125	150	184	60
1832	100	112	100	120	123	111	216	194	125	150	125	150	175	63
1833	100	112	100	120	124	111	201	181	125	150	125	150	167	67
1834	100	112	100	120	116	109	189	170	125	150	125	150	161	68
1835	100	112	100	120	143	117	178	154	125	150	125	150	154	76
1836	100	112	100	120	177	127	171	154	125	150	125	150	151	84

(continued)

Table G–2 cont.

Year	Capital[a] price series	Wage[b] series	Fuel[c] price series	Insurance[d] rate series	Berry's[e] price index	Weighted[f] input price series (P_I)	Downstream[g] freight series	Upstream[g] freight series	Downstream[g] cabin fare series	Downstream[g] deck fare series	Upstream[g] cabin fare series	Upstream[g] deck fare series	Weighted[h] output price (P_O) series	Weighted price P_I/P_O × 100
(1)	(2)	(3)	(4)	(5)	(6)	(7)	(8)	(9)	(10)	(11)	(12)	(13)	(14)	(15)
1837	100	112	100	120	160	122	142	154	125	150	125	150	138	88
1838	100	112	100	120	157	121	148	154	125	150	125	150	141	86
1839	100	112	100	120	168	124	137	154	125	150	125	150	136	91
1840	100	100	100	100	127	108	112	154	100	100	100	100	111	97
1841	100	100	100	100	109	103	125	138	100	100	100	100	115	89
1842	100	100	100	100	88	97	103	123	100	100	100	100	104	93
1843	100	100	100	100	88	97	105	108	100	100	100	100	103	94
1844	100	100	100	100	94	98	77	92	100	100	100	100	89	110
1845	100	100	100	100	107	102	88	77	100	100	100	100	92	111
1846	100	100	100	100	93	98	98	77	100	100	100	100	96	102
1847	100	100	100	100	110	103	121	77	100	100	100	100	107	96
1848	100	100	100	100	91	97	87	77	100	100	100	100	92	106
1849	100	100	100	100	94	98	84	77	100	100	100	100	90	109
1850	100	117	100	90	105	105	89	77	75	75	75	75	81	129
1851	100	117	100	90	110	107	114	77	75	75	75	75	92	116
1852	100	117	100	90	113	108	97	77	75	75	75	75	85	127
1853	100	117	100	90	127	112	97	77	75	75	75	75	85	131
1854	100	117	100	90	134	114	157	77	75	75	75	75	111	102
1855	100	117	100	90	150	118	107	77	75	75	75	75	89	132
1856	100	117	100	90	148	118	163	77	75	75	75	75	114	103
1857	100	117	100	90	158	121	132	77	75	75	75	75	100	120
1858	100	117	100	90	124	111	94	77	75	75	75	75	84	132
1859	100	117	100	90	139	115	97	77	75	75	75	75	85	135
1860	100	117	100	90	134	114	117	77	75	75	75	75	94	121

Sources: Columns (3), (4), (5), (8), (9), (10), (11), (12), (13) are derived from Appendixes C and D. Column (6) is derived from Berry's index of wholesale commodity prices (all commodities) in *U.S. Historical Statistics* (1960): 121.

[a]The price of capital is defined as the interest cost, or the borrowing cost, to the industry and is assumed to have remained unchanged over the period. This assumption is made for want of specific evidence, but testing for the sensitivity of this assumption by letting the interest rate change by as much as one-third over the period only changes the final productivity measure by one-tenth of one percent. By and large, then, the final measure is insensitive to this assumption. The same insensitivity is found true for an alternative definition of capital that includes depreciation as well as interest costs. This "rental price" for the firm would be adequate for certain analyses, but ours is from the industry perspective.

[b]The wage series is an index of the total wage bill for 7 officers and 19 crewmen.

[c]The fuel price series is based on our estimates that the price of a cord of wood was $2.25 before 1830 and $2.50 for 1830 and thereafter.

[d]The insurance rate series is based on our calculations that the rate was approximately 18% on the original construction cost of an average steamboat 1815–19, 15% 1820–29, 12% 1830–39, 10% 1840–49, and 9% 1850–60.

[e]We have assumed that Berry's price index adequately represents changes in the other costs, such as food expenditures for the crew and expenditures for repairs and other miscellaneous expenses.

[f]The (1840–49) weights used for the input prices of capital, labor, fuel, insurance, and other costs (Berry's index) equal their individual shares in the total annual cost. They are, respectively, 0.12, 0.26, 0.27, 0.06, and 0.29.

[g]These are indexes of freight rates and passenger fares contained in Appendix D, Tables D–1 and D–3. The most complete freight data are from 1815–19 and 1840–60, which fortunately are the terminal periods of the study.

[h]For weights used, see note (g) in Table G–1.

Table G–3. Indexes of Inputs, Outputs, and Total Factor Productivity per Flatboat in the Louisville–New Orleans Routes, 1815–60 (1840–49 = 100)

Year	Capital[a] series	Labor[b] series	Weighted[c] inputs series (I)	Output[d] series (Q)	Q/I × 100
(1)	(2)	(3)	(4)	(5)	(6)
1815–19	32	278	204	32	16
1820–29	44	139	111	44	40
1830–39	60	93	83	60	72
1840–49	100	100	100	100	100
1850–60	156	153	154	156	101

Sources: Appendix E.

[a]The capital series is an index of the average size of flatboats.

[b]The labor series is an index of equivalent man days per round trip, based on the number of round trip days times the number of equivalent men; the number of equivalent men is obtained by weighting each crewman in multiple units, using wage rates as weights:

	Equivalent number of men		Time components		Days per
	Crew size	Men equivalents	Days downstream	Days upstream	round trip
Before 1820	5	5.9	30	90	120
1820–29	5	5.9	30	30	60
1830–39	5	5.9	20	20	40
1840–49	7	8.5	20	10	30
1850–60	10	13.0	20	10	30

[c]The 1840–49 weights for labor and capital are 0.70 and 0.30 respectively. The labor share is equal to the wages paid plus food costs plus the opportunity cost of the return trek upstream (computed only for the first three periods) divided by total revenue. The opportunity cost component is equal to total revenues minus total costs. The capital weight includes construction costs and wharfage fees.

	Weights	
	Labor share	Capital share
Before 1820	.90	.10
1820–29	.84	.16
1830–39	.81	.19
1840–49	.70	.30
1850–60	.72	.28

[d]The output series is an index of annual freight ton miles per flatboat. Full utilization and constant mileage per voyage are assumed.

Table G–4. Indexes of Input and Output Prices and Total Factor Productivity per Flatboat on the Louisville–New Orleans Routes, 1815–60 (1840–49 = 100)

Year	Capital[a] price series	Labor[b] price series	Weighted[c] input price series (P_I)	Price of[d] output series (P_Q)	P_I/P_Q × 100
(1)	(2)	(3)	(4)	(5)	(6)
1815–19	100	45	62	264	23
1820–29	100	64	75	202	37
1830–39	100	111	108	166	65
1840–49	100	100	100	100	100
1850–60	100	129	120	107	112

Sources: Appendix E.

[a]See note (a), Table G–2.

[b]The labor price series is an index of the money wages of four crewmen and a captain, plus their food costs, plus their computed opportunity costs for the longer, more expensive upriver journey, 1815–39, minus the expense of the return deck passage on a steamboat, 1820–60, all put on a per day basis. The opportunity cost for the period 1815–39 is a sum equal to the difference between total revenues and total costs (for each decade):

	Total net labor cost of four crewmen and a captain	Days per round trip	Price of labor per day (1)/(2)	Index of labor price
	(1)	(2)	(3)	(4)
Before 1820	$450	120	$3.75	45
1820–29	318	60	6.13	64
1830–39	368	40	9.95	111
1840–49	249	30	8.96	100
1850–60	321	30	11.20	129

[c]See note (c), Table G–3 for the weights used.

[d]The price of output series is an index of our estimates of flatboat freight rates in Chapter 3, p. 000.

BIBLIOGRAPHY

Albion, Robert G. *The Rise of New York Port.* New York: Charles Scribner's Sons, 1939.

Albion, Robert G. *Square-Riggers on Schedule.* Princeton: Princeton University Press, 1938.

Ambler, Charles H. *A History of Transportation in the Ohio Valley.* Glendale, California: The Arthur H. Clark, Co., 1932.

The American Almanac and Repository of Useful Knowledge. Boston: Gray and Bowen, 1836, 1841, 1845, 1849.

Andreano, Ralph L., ed. *New Views on American Economic Development.* Cambridge, Mass.: Schenkman Publishing Co., 1965.

Appleton, John B. "The Declining Significance of the Mississippi as a Commercial Highway in the Middle of the Nineteenth Century." *Philadelphia Geographical Society Bulletin.* Vol. 28. Philadelphia: Philadelphia Geographical Society, 1930.

Atwater, Caleb. *A History of the State of Ohio, Natural and Civil.* Cincinnati: Glezen and Shepard, 1838.

Babin, Claude Hunter. "The Economic Expansion of New Orleans Before the Civil War." Ph.D. thesis, Tulane University, New Orleans, 1953.

Baird, Robert. *View of the Valley of the Mississippi.* 2nd ed. Philadelphia: H. S. Tanner, 1834.

Baldwin, Leland D. *The Keelboat Age on Western Waters.* Pittsburgh: University of Pittsburgh Press, 1941.

Baldwin, Leland D. "Rivers in the Early Development of Western Pennsylvania." *The Western Pennsylvania Historical Magazine.* Vol. 16. Pittsburgh: The Historical Society of Western Pennsylvania, 1933.

The Bankers' Magazine and State Financial Register. 15 vols. Baltimore: J. S. Homans, 1846–1860.

Banta, R. E. "The Ohio." In *Rivers of America,* edited by Hervey Allen and Carl Carmer. New York: Rinehart and Company, 1949.

Bateman, Fred, Foust, J., and Weiss, T. "Profitability in Southern Manufacturing: Estimates for 1860." *Explorations in Economic History* 12, no. 3 (Summer 1975).

Berry, Thomas S. *Western Prices Before 1861.* Vol. 74, Harvard Economic Studies. Cambridge: Harvard University Press, 1943.

Bidwell, Percy W., and Falconer, John I. *History of Agriculture in the Northern United States, 1620–1860.* Washington: Carnegie Institute, 1925.

Birbeck, Morris. *Extracts from a Supplementary Letter from the Illinois dated January 31st 1819.* New York: C. Wiley and Co., 1819.

Birbeck, Morris. *Notes on a Journey in America from the Coast of Virginia to the Territory of Illinois.* London: James Ridgway, 1818. Reprinted: *March of America Facsimile Series.* No. 62. Ann Arbor, Michigan: University Microfilms, 1966.

Bishop, James L. *A History of American Manufactures from 1608 to 1860.* 2 vols. Philadelphia: Edward Young and Co., 1864.

Blowe, Daniel. *A Geographical, Historical, Commercial and Agricultural View of the United States of America.* London: Edwards and Knibb, 1820.

Blunt, Joseph. *The Shipmaster's Assistant and Commercial Digest.* New York: E. and G. W. Blunt, 1837.

Bogart, Ernest L. *Internal Improvements and State Debt in Ohio.* New York: Longmans, Green and Co., 1924.

Bohannan, Thomas. Mercantile Records 1834–1841. Manuscript. Filson Club Library, Louisville, Kentucky.

Boucher, John N. *A Century and a Half of Pittsburgh and Her People.* 4 vols. Pittsburgh: The Lewis Publishing Co., 1908.

Boyd, J. Hayden, and Walton, Gary M. "The Social Savings from Nineteenth Century Rail Passenger Services." *Explorations in Economic History* 9 (Spring 1972): 233–54.

Bradbury, Robert W. "The Water-Borne Commerce of New Orleans." *Louisiana Business Bulletin.* Vol. 1. Jackson, Mississippi: Louisiana State University, 1937.

Breck, Samuel. *Sketch of the Internal Improvements Already Made by Pennsylvania.* Philadelphia: M. Thomas, 1818.

Bristed, John. *America and Her Resources.* London: Henry Colburn, 1818.

Bromwell, William J. *History of Immigration to the United States.* New York: Redfield, 1856.

Broude, Henry W. "The Role of the State In American Economic Development, 1820–1890." *The State and Economic Growth.* H. G. J. Aitken, ed. New York: Social Science Research Council, 1959, pp. 4–25.

Brown, Paul W. "The Collapse of the Steamboat Traffic Upon the Mississippi: An Inquiry into Causes." *Proceedings of the Mississippi Valley Historical Association.* Vol. 9. Cedar Rapids, Iowa: Mississippi Valley Historical Association, 1918.

Brown, Samuel R. *The Western Gazetter, or Emigrants' Directory.* Albany: H. C. Southwick, 1817.

Bruchey, Stuart. *The Roots of American Economic Growth 1607–1861.* New York: Harper and Row, 1965.

Buck, Solon J., and Buck, Elizabeth H. *The Planting of Civilization in Western Pennsylvania.* Pittsburgh: University of Pittsburgh Press, 1939.

Bullock, William. *Sketch on a Journey Through the Western States of North America, from New Orleans to New York in 1827.* Vol. 19 of Early

Western Travels, 1748–1846. Edited by Reuben F. Thwaites. 34 vols
    Cleveland: The Arthur H. Clark Co., 1905.

Burke, John G. "Bursting Boilers and the Federal Power." *Technology and
    Culture* 7 (1966): 1–23.

Burnet, Jacob. *Notes on the Early Settlement of the Northwestern Territory.*
    Cincinnati: Derby, Bradley and Co., 1847.

Buttrick, Tilly, Jr. *Voyages, Travels and Discoveries of Tilly Buttrick Jr.* Vol
    8 of *Early Western Travels, 1748–1846.* Edited by Reuben G. Thwaites
    34 vols. Cleveland: The Arthur H. Clark Co., 1904.

Byrd, Douglas. *Steamboating on the Cumberland.* Nashville, Tenn.: Tennessee
    Book Co., 1961.

Callender, Guy S. "The Early Transportation and Banking Enterprises of the
    States in Relation to the Growth of the Corporation." *Quarterly Journal
    of Economics* 17 (November 1902): 111–62.

Callender, Guy S. *Selections from the Economic History of the United States
    1765–1860.* Boston: Ginn and Company, 1909.

Cammack, Eleanore A. "Notes on Wabash River Steamboating: Early Lafay-
    ette." *Indiana Magazine of History.* Vol. 50. Bloomington, Indiana: The
    History Department of Indiana University, 1954.

Campbell, Thomas J. *The Upper Tennessee.* Chattanooga: T. J. Campbell
    1932.

Carson, W. Wallace. "Transportation and Traffic on the Ohio and the Missis-
    sippi Before the Steamboat." *The Mississippi Valley Historical Review.*
    Vol. 7. The Mississippi Valley Historical Association, 1920–21.

Casseday, Ben. *The History of Louisville from its Earliest Settlement Till the
    Year 1852.* Louisville: Hull and Brother, 1852.

Chapin, William. *A Complete Reference Gazetteer of the United States of
    North America.* New York: T. and E. H. Ensign, 1843.

Chevalier, Michel. *Histoire et Description des Voies de Communication aux
    États–Unis et des Travaux D'Art qui en Dependent.* 2 vols. Paris: Librairie
    de Charles Gosselin, 1840–41.

Chevalier, Michel. *Society, Manners and Politics in the United States.* Re
    printed: Garden City, New York: Doubleday and Company, 1961.

Chittenden, Hiram M. *History of Early Steamboat Navigation on the Mis-
    siouri River.* 2 vols. New York: Francis P. Harper, 1903.

Chittenden, Hiram M. "Forests and Reservoirs in their Relation to Stream
    Flow with Particular Reference to Navigable Rivers." *Transactions of the
    American Society of Civil Engineers.* Vol. 62. New York: American
    Society of Civil Engineers, 1909.

Cincinnati Daily Chronicle. 1839–43, 1849.

Cincinnati Daily Gazette. 1827–60.

The Cincinnati Directory. Cincinnati: Oliver Farnsworth, 1819. Cincinnati
    Robinson Fairbank, 1829, 1831.

Cist, Charles. *Cincinnati in 1841: Its Early Annals and Future Prospects*
    Cincinnati: Charles Cist, 1841.

Cist, Charles. *The Cincinnati Miscellany, or Antiquities of the West.* 2 vols
    Cincinnati: Caleb Clark, 1845. Cincinnati: Robinson and Jones, 1846.

Cist, Charles. *Sketches and Statistics of Cincinnati in 1851.* Cincinnati: Wm
    H. Moore and Co., 1851.

Claiborne, John F. H. *Mississippi as a Province, Territory and State.* Vol. 1
    Reprinted Jackson, Mississippi: Louisiana State University Press, 1964.

Clark, John G. *The Grain Trade in the Old Northwest.* Urbana, Illinois: University of Illinois Press, 1966.

Clark, Victor S. *History of Manufactures in the United States.* 3 vols. New York: McGraw–Hill Book Co. for The Carnegie Institution, 1929.

Cobbett, William. *A Year's Residence in America.* 2nd. ed. London: Chapman and Dodd, 1819.

Cole, A. H. *Wholesale Commodity Prices in the United States, 1700–1861.* Cambridge, Mass.: Harvard University Press, 1938.

Collins, Gabriel, ed. *The Louisville Directory.* Louisville: Prentice and Weissenger, 1836. Louisville: Henkle Logan and Co., 1841.

Coman, Katherine. *The Industrial History of the United States.* New York: The Macmillan Company, 1918.

Cooley, L. V. "On River Transportation and Its Relation to New Orleans: Past, Present, and Future." Address Before the Tulane Society of Economics. New Orleans, 1911.

Covington, Samuel T. "Pioneer Transportation on the Ohio River." *Indiana Quarterly Magazine of History.* Vol. 4. Indianapolis: The Indiana Historical Society, 1908.

Coxe, Tench. *A Statement of the Arts and Manufactures of the United States of America for the Year 1810.* Philadelphia: A. Cornman Jr., 1814.

Cramer, Zadock. *The Navigator.* 8th ed. Pittsburgh: Cramer, Spear and Eichbaum, 1814. Reprinted: *March of America Facsimile Series.* No. 61. Ann Arbor, Michigan: University Microfilms, 1966.

Crittenden, S. W. *An Inductive and Practical Treatise on Book-Keeping.* Philadelphia: E. C. and J. Biddle, 1857.

David, Paul A. "The Growth of Real Product in the United States Before 1840: New Evidence, Controlled Conjectures." *The Journal of Economic History* 27 (June 1967): 151–97.

Davis, Lance E. "Capital Immobilities and Finance Capitalism." *Explorations in Entrepreneurial History* 1 (Fall 1963). Reprinted in *Purdue Faculty Papers in Ecomonic History, 1956–66.* Homewood, Ill.: R. D. Irwin, 1967.

Davis, Lance E., Easterlin, R. A., Parker, W. N., et al. *American Economic Growth.* New York: Harper and Row, 1972.

Dayton, Fred Erving. *Steamboat Days.* New York: Frederick A. Stokes Company, 1925.

Dean, William H., Jr. "The Theory of the Geographic Location of Economic Activities, with Special Reference to Historical Change." Ph.D. thesis, Harvard University, Cambridge, Mass., 1938.

De Bow, James D. B., ed. *The Commercial Review of the South and West.* (Title varies.) Also known as *De Bow's Commercial Review.* 34 vols. New Orleans, January 1846–July 1864.

De Bow, James D. B. "A Southern Farm, Louisiana." *The Commercial Review of the South and West* (De Bow's *Commercial Review*), Vol. 12, New Orleans, 1852.

De Bow, James D. B. *The Industrial Resources, Statistics, etc. of the United States and More Particularly of the Southern and Western States.* 3 vols. New York: D. Appleton and Co., 1854. Reprinted, New York: Augustus M. Kelley, 1966.

De Pew, Chauncey, M., ed. *One Hundred Years of American Commerce 1795–1895.* 2 vols. New York: D. O. Haynes and Company, 1895.

Dexter, Edmund. Bill of Lading Book. Manuscript. Filson Club Library, Louisville, Kentucky.

Dickens, Charles. *American Notes and Pictures from Italy.* London: Oxford University Press, 1957.

Dixon, Frank H. *A Traffic History of the Mississippi River System.* National Waterways Commission, Doc. No. 11. Washington: Government Printing Office, 1909.

Donovan, Frank R. *River Boats of America.* New York: Thomas Y. Crowell Co., 1966.

Drake, B., and Mansfield, E. D. *Cincinnati in 1826.* Cincinnati, 1827.

Duane, William, reporter. *Debate on Mississippi Question,* (7 Congress, 2 Session, Feb. 23–25, 1803). Philadelphia: Wm. Duane, 1803. *Duane Collection of Pamphlets,* Vol. 72. Library of Congress.

Dunbar, Seymour. *History of Travel in America.* 4 vols. Indianapolis: Bobbs–Merrill Company, 1915.

Elder, John Scott, Jr. The Autobiography of "An Old Steamboatman." Manuscript. Filson Club Library, Louisville, Kentucky, 1873.

Ellet, Charles, Jr. *An Essay on the Laws of Trade in Reference to the Works of Internal Improvement in the United States.* Richmond, Va.: P. D. Bernard, 1839. Reprinted, New York: August M. Kelley, 1966.

Embree, Davis, ed. *The Western Boatman.* Vol. 1, Nos. 1–11. Cincinnati: A. Nelson and Co., January 1848–August 1849.

Evans, Estwick. *A Pedestrious Tour of Four Thousand Miles, Through the Western States and Territories During the Winter and Spring of 1818.* Vol. 8 of *Early Western Travels, 1748–1846.* Edited by Reuben G. Thwaites. 34 vols. Cleveland: The Arthur H. Clark Co., 1904.

Evans, George H., Jr. *Business Incorporations in the United States, 1800–1943.* New York: National Bureau of Economic Research, 1948.

Fatout, Paul. *Indiana Canals.* West Lafayette, Indiana: Purdue University Studies, 1972.

Faux, William. *Memorable Days in America, Being a Journal of a Tour to the United States Nov. 1818–July 1820.* Vols. 11 and 12 of *Early Western Travels, 1748–1846.* Edited by Reuben G. Thwaites. 34 vols. Cleveland: The Arthur H. Clark Co., 1904.

Fearon, Henry B. *Sketches of America.* London: Longman, Hurst, Rees, Orme and Brown, 1818.

Fisher, Richard, S. *A New and Complete Statistical Gazetteer of the United States of America.* New York: J. H. Colton, 1853.

Fishlow, Albert. "Antebellum Interregional Trade Reconsidered." *American Economic Review* 54 (May 1964): 352–64.

Fishlow, Albert. *American Railroads and the Transformation of the Ante-Bellum Economy.* Cambridge, Mass.: Harvard University Press, 1965.

Fishlow, Albert. *Productivity and Technological Change in the Railroad Sector, 1840–1910.* Output, Employment and Productivity in the United States after 1800. N.B.E.R., New York, 1966.

Flagg, Edmund. *The Far West: Or a Tour Beyond the Mountains.* Vols. 26 and 27 of *Early Western Travels, 1748–1846.* Edited by Reuben G. Thwaites. 34 vols. Cleveland: The Arthur H. Clark Co., 1905.

Flint, James. *Letters from America, Containing Observations on the Climate and Agriculture of the Western States, the Manners of the People, the Prospects of Emigrants, etc.* Vol. 9 of *Early Western Travels, 1748–1846.* Edited by Reuben G. Thwaites. 34 vols. Cleveland: The Arthur H. Clark Co., 1904.

Flint, Timothy. *The History and Geography of the Mississippi Valley to Which is Appended a Condensed Physical Geography of the Atlantic United States and the Whole American Continent.* 2 vols. 2nd ed. Cincinnati: E. H.Flint and L. R. Lincoln, 1832.

Flint, Timothy. *Recollections of the Last Ten Years.* Boston: Cummings, Hilliard, and Co., 1826.

Flugel, Felix. "Pages from a Journal of a Voyage Down the Mississippi to New Orleans in 1817." *The Louisiana Historical Quarterly.* Vol. 7. New Orleans: Louisiana Historical Society, January—October 1924.

Fogel, Robert W. "A Provisional View of the 'New Economic History'." *American Economic Review* 54 (May 1964): 377—89.

Fogel, Robert W., *Railroads and American Economic Growth: Essays in Econometric History.* Baltimore: The Johns Hopkins Press, 1964.

Fogel, Robert W., and Engerman, S. L. *The Reinterpretation of American Economic History.* New York: Harper and Row, 1971.

Fogel, Robert W., and Engerman, S. L. *Time on the Cross.* 2 vols. Boston: Little, Brown & Co., 1974.

Folmsbee, Stanley, J. *Sectionalism and Internal Improvements in Tennessee, 1796—1845.* Philadelphia, 1939.

Ford, Henry A., and Ford, K. B. *History of Cincinnati.* Cleveland: L. A. Williams and Co., 1881.

Foreman, Grant. "River Navigation in the Early Southwest." *Mississippi Valley Historical Review.* Vol. 15. Cedar Rapids, Iowa: Mississippi Valley Historical Association, 1928—29.

Frantz, Joe B., ed. "Trips Up the River: 1855 and 1857." *Louisiana History.* Vol. 1. Baton Rouge, Louisiana: Louisiana Historical Association, 1960.

Gallagher, William D., and Curry, Otway, eds. *The Hesperian or Western Monthly Magazine.* Vol. 3. Cincinnati: John D. Nichols, 1839.

Gallman, Robert. "Change in Total U.S. Agricultural Factor Productivity in the Nineteenth Century," *Agricultural History* (1972).

Gamble, Jay M. *Steamboats on the Muskingum.* New York: Steamship Historical Society of America, 1971.

Geer, Curtis M. *The Louisiana Purchase and the Westward Movement.* Vol. 8 of *The History of North America.* Edited by Guy C. Lee. 2 vols. Philadelphia: George Barrie and Sons, 1904.

Gephart, William F. *Transportation and Industrial Development in the Middle West.* Vol. 34, No. 1, *Columbia University Studies in History, Economics and Public Law.* New York: Longmans, Green and Co. for Columbia University, 1909.

Gephart, William F. "Transportation in Ohio 1788—1830." M.A. thesis, The Ohio State University, Columbus, 1907.

Gilleland, J. C. *The Ohio and Mississippi Pilot.* Pittsburgh: R. Patterson and Lambdin, 1820.

Goodrich, Carter. *Government Promotion of American Canals and Railroads, 1800—1890.* New York: Columbia University Press, 1960.

Goodrich, Carter, ed. *Canals and American Economic Development.* New York: Columbia University Press, 1961.

Goodrich, Carter, ed. *The Government and the Economy, 1783—1861.* Indianapolis: The Bobbs-Merrill Co., 1967.

Goodrich, Carter. "Internal Improvements Reconsidered." *The Journal of Economic History* 30 (June 1970): 289—311.

Goodwin, Frank P. "Building a Commercial System." *Ohio Archaeological and Historical Publications.* Vol. 16. Columbus: Ohio State Archaeological and Historical Society, 1907.

Gould, E. W. *Fifty Years on the Mississippi.* St. Louis: Nixon–Jones Printing Co. Reprinted, Columbus: Long's College Book Co., 1951.

Graham, Gerald S. "The Ascendency of the Sailing Ship, 1850–85." *The Economic History Review,* 2 series, 9 (Aug. 1956): 74–88.

Gray, Lewis Cecil. *History of Agriculture in the Southern United States to 1860.* 2 vols. Washington: The Carnegie Institution, 1933. Reprinted, Gloucester, Mass.: Peter Smith, 1958.

Grayson, Frank Y. *Thrills of the Historic Ohio River.* Cincinnati: *Cincinnati Times–Star.*

Gregg, Dorothy. "The Exploitation of the Steamboat: The Case of Colonel John Stevens." Ph.D. thesis, Columbia University, New York, 1951.

Haites, Erik F. "Ohio and Mississippi River Transportation, 1810–1860." Ph.D. Thesis, Purdue University, 1969.

Haites, Erik, and Mak, James. "Ohio and Mississippi River Transportation: 1810–1860." *Explorations in Economic History* (Winter 1970–71): 153–80.

Haites, Erik, and Mak, James. "Steamboating on the Mississippi: A Study of a Purely Competitive Industry." *Business History Review* (Spring 1971): 52–78.

Haites, Erik, and Mak, James. "The Decline of Steamboating on the Antebellum Western Rivers." *Explorations in Economic History* (October 1973): 25–36.

Hall, James. *Notes on the Western States; Containing Descriptive Sketches of their Soil, Climate, Resources, and Scenery.* Philadelphia: Harrison Hall, 1838.

Hall, James. *Statistics of the West at the Close of the Year 1836.* Cincinnati: J. A. James and Co., 1836.

Hall, James. *The West: Its Commerce and Navigation.* Cincinnati: H. W. Derby and Co., 1848.

Hall, James. *The West: Its Soil, Surface and Productions.* Cincinnati: Derby, Bradley and Co., 1848.

Hall, James, ed. *The Western Monthly Magazine.* Vols. 2 and 4. Cincinnati: Corey and Fairbank, 1834–35.

Harlow, Alvin F. *Old Towpaths: The Story of the American Canal Era.* New York: D. Appleton and Co., 1926.

Harpster, J. W., ed. *Pen Pictures of Early Western Pennsylvania.* Pittsburgh: University of Pittsburgh Press, 1938.

Hart, Albert B., ed. *National Expansion 1783–1845.* Vol. 3 of *American History Told by Contemporaries.* 5 vols. New York: The Macmillan Company, 1908.

Hartsough, Mildred L. *From Canoe to Steel Barge on the Upper Mississippi.* St. Paul, Minneapolis: The University of Minnesota Press, 1934.

Hazard, Samuel. *United States Commercial and Statistical Register.* 6 vols. Philadelphia, July 1839–July 1842.

Healey, Kent T. "American Transportation Before the War Between the States." H. F. Williamson, ed. *The Growth of the American Economy* (1944).

Heller, John E. "A History of Ohio River Trade at Louisville from Its

Beginning Until 1840." M.A. thesis, University of Louisville, Louisville, Ky., 1922.

Henshaw, Leslie S. "Early Steamboat Travel on the Ohio River," *Ohio Archaeological and Historical Publications.* Vol. 20. Columbus: Ohio State Archaeological and Historical Society, 1911.

Hill, Forest G. *Roads, Rails and Waterways.* Norman: University of Oklahoma Press, 1957.

Holt, Charles, F. "The Role of State Government in the Nineteenth Century American Economy, 1820–1902: A Quantitative Study." Ph.D. thesis, Purdue University, 1970.

Howland, S. A. *Steamboat Disasters and Railroad Accidents in the United States.* Worcester, Mass.: Dorr, Howland and Co., 1840.

Huber, Leonard V. *Advertisements of Lower Mississippi River Steamboats 1812–1920.* West Barrington, Rhode Island: The Steamship Historical Society of America, 1959.

Hulbert, Archer B. *Waterways of Westward Expansion.* Vol. 9 of *Historic Highways of America.* Edited by Archer B. Hulbert. 16 vols. Cleveland: The Arthur H. Clark Co., 1903.

Hulbert, Archer B. *The Ohio River: A Course of Empire.* New York: G. P. Putnam's Sons, 1906.

Hulbert, Archer B. *The Paths of Inland Commerce.* Vol. 21 of *Chronicles of America Series.* Edited by Allen Johnson. New Haven: Yale University Press, 1920.

Hunt, Freeman, ed. *Merchants' Magazine and Commercial Review.* (Title varies.) Also known as *Hunt's Merchants' Magazine.* 63 vols. New York: July 1839–December 1870.

Hunt, John W. Papers 1792–1849. Manuscript. Filson Club Library, Louisville, Ky.

Hunter, Louis. "The Invention of the Western Steamboat." *The Journal of Economic History.* Vol. 3 (September 1943): 201–21.

Hunter, Louis C. *Steamboats on the Western Rivers.* Cambridge Mass.: Harvard University Press, 1949.

Hunter, Louis C. *Studies in the Economic History of the Ohio Valley.* Vol. 19, nos. 1–2. *Smith College Studies in History.* Northampton, Mass.: Department of History of Smith College, 1933–1934.

Hutchinson, William K., and Williamson, S. H. "The Self-Sufficiency of the Ante-Bellum South. Estimates of the Food Supply." *The Journal of Economic History* 31, no. 3 (September 1971): 591–612.

Imlay, Gilbert. *A Topographical Description of the Western Territory of North America.* London: J. Debrett, 1792.

Jenkins, Warren. *The Ohio Gazetteer and Travellers' Guide.* Columbus: Isaac N. Whiting, 1841.

Johnson, Emory R., et al. *History of the Domestic and Foreign Commerce of the United States.* 2 vols. Washington: Carnegie Institution, 1915.

Johnson, Emory R. *Ocean and Inland Water Transportation.* New York: D. Appleton and Company, 1906.

Jones, S. *Pittsburgh in the Year 1826.* Pittsburgh: Johnston and Stockton, 1826.

Keller, Vernon D. "The Commerical Development of Cincinnati to the Year 1860." Ph.D. thesis, University of Chicago, 1935.

Kimball, James. *Business Directory for the Mississippi Valley*. Cincinnati: Kendall and Bernard, 1844.

Kirkland, Edward C. *A History of American Economic Life*. New York: Appleton–Century–Crofts, 1969.

Knauerhase, Ramon. "The Compound Steam Engine and Productivity Changes in the German Merchant Marine Fleet, 1871–1887." *The Journal of Economic History* 27 (Sept. 1968): 390–403.

Knight, Frank H. "Investment and its Yield: Quantitative Relations." Reprinted in *Readings in the Theory of Income Distribution*. Homewood, Ill.: R. D. Irwin, 1951, pp. 409–17.

Kohlmeier, Albert L. *The Old Northwest as the Keystone of the Arch of Federal Union*. Bloomington, Indiana: The Principia Press, 1938.

Krenkel, John H. *Illinois Internal Improvements 1818–1848*. Cedar Rapids, Iowa: The Torch Press, 1958.

Kussart, S. *Navigation on the Monongahela River*. 2 vols. Pittsburgh: Daily Republican, 1929.

Kuznets, Simon. *Secular Movements in Production and Prices*. Boston: Houghton Mifflin Co., 1930.

Landon, Charles E. "Technological Progress in Transportation on the Mississippi River System." *The Journal of Business* 33 (January 1960).

Lanman, James H. "American Steam Navigation." *Hunt's Merchants' Magazine and Commercial Review* 4 (1841): 124.

Lass, William E. *A History of Steamboating on the Upper Missouri River*. Lincoln: University of Nebraska Press, 1962.

Latrobe, John H. B. *The First Steamboat Voyage on the Western Waters*. Maryland Historical Society Fund Publication, no. 6. Baltimore: The Maryland Historical Society, 1871.

Leahy, Ethel C. *Who's Who on the Ohio River and Its Tributaries*. Cincinnati: The E. C. Leahy Publishing Co., 1931.

Leavitt, Charles T. "Transportation and Livestock of the Middle West." *Agricultural History* 8 (1934): 20–33.

Liberty Hall and Cincinnati Gazette. (Title varies.) 1806–61.

Lippincott, Isaac. "Internal Trade of the United States 1700–1860." Vol. 4, part II, no. 1. *Washington University Studies*. St. Louis: Washington University, 1916.

Lippincott, Isaac. "A History of River Improvement." *The Journal of Political Economy*, Vol. 22. Chicago: University of Chicago Press, 1914.

Lively, Robert A. "The American System, A Review Article." *Business History Review* 29 (1955): 81–96.

Lloyd, James T. *Lloyd's Steamboat Directory and Disasters on the Western Waters*. Cincinnati: James T. Lloyd and Co., 1856.

Lord, Daniel. *The Effect of Secession upon the Commercial Relations Between the North and South, and Upon Each Section*. New York: Office of the New York Times, 1861.

Louisiana. *The Ship Registers and Enrollments of New Orleans, Louisiana*. Vol. 1. The Survey of Federal Archives in Louisiana Division of Community Service Programs Work Projects Administration. Baton Rouge: Louisiana State University.

Louisville Directory. (Title varies.) Richard W. Otis, ed. Louisville: W. Lee White and Co., 1832.

Lytle, William M. *Merchant Steam Vessels of the United States 1807–1868*. Publication no. 6. Mystic, Connecticut: The Steamship Historical Society of America, 1952, and *Supplements* No. 2 and No. 3. Edited by Forrest R. Holdcamper. Mystic, Connecticut: The Steamship Historical Society of America, 1954 and 1958.

Mabry, William A. "Ante-Bellum Cincinnati and its Southern Trade." *American Studies in Honor of William Kenneth Boyd*. Edited by David Kelley Jackson. Durham, North Carolina: Duke University Press, 1940.

Mak, James, and Walton, Gary M. "Steamboats and the Great Productivity Surge in River Transportation." *Journal of Economic History* (September 1972): 619–40.

Mak, James, and Walton, Gary M. "On the Persistence of Old Technologies: The Case of Flatboats." *Journal of Economic History* (June 1973): 444–51.

Marestier, John B. *Memoir on Steamboats of the United States of America*. Translated by Sidney Withington. No. 31. Mystic, Connecticut: The Marine Historical Association, 1957.

Martin, William E. *Internal Improvements in Alabama*. The Johns Hopkins University Studies on Historical and Political Science. No. 20, 1902, pp. 127–208.

Maximilian, Prince of Wied. *Travels in the Interior of North America*. Translated by H. Evans Lloyd. Vols. 12, 13, 14, and 15 of *Early Western Travels 1748–1846*. Edited by Reuben G. Thwaites. 34 vols. Cleveland: The Arthur H. Clark Co., 1904.

McDermott, John F. *Up the Missouri with Audubon*. Norman, Oklahoma: University of Oklahoma Press, 1951.

Mace, Ellis C. *River Steamboats and Steamboat Men*. Cynthia, Kentucky: The Hobson Book Press, 1944.

MacGregor, John. *Commercial Statistics*. 5 vols. London: Whittaker and Co., 1847.

McMurtrie, Henrico. *Sketches of Louisville and Its Environs*. Louisville: S. Penn, Jr., 1819.

Melish, John. *Travels in the United States of America in the Years 1806 and 1807 and 1809, 1810, and 1811*. Philadelphia: J. Melish, 1812.

Merrick, George B. *Old Times on the Upper Mississippi*. Cleveland: The Arthur H. Clark Co., 1909.

Meyer, Henry B. *History of Transportation in the United States Before 1860*. Washington: The Carnegie Institution, 1917.

Mills, Robert. *A Treatise on Inland Navigation*. Baltimore: F. Lucas, Jr., 1820.

Mitchell, Samuel A. *Illinois in 1837*. Philadelphia: S. Augustus Mitchell and Grigg and Elliot, 1837.

Monette, John W. "The Progress of Navigation and Commerce on the Waters of the Mississippi River and the Great Lakes A.D. 1700 to 1846." *Publications of the Mississippi Historical Society*. Vol. 7. Oxford, Mississippi: Mississippi Historical Society, 1903.

Morris, Charles N. "Internal Improvements in Ohio, 1825–1850." *Papers of the American Historical Association* 3 (1889): 107–36.

Morrison, John H. *History of American Steam Navigation*. New York: Stephen Daye Press, 1958.

National Ship-Canal Convention. *Proceedings of the National Ship-Canal Convention, Held at the City of Chicago, June 2 and 3, 1863.* Chicago, 1863.

New Orleans Prices Current and Commerical Intelligencer. George B. Young, ed. New Orleans: Benjamin Levy, 1822, 1837–1861.

New Orleans. *Register of Flatboats.* Archives of the New Orleans Public Library.

Niles, Hezekiah. Niles, W. A., and Hughes, J., eds. *Niles' National Register.* (Title varies.) Vols. 1–75. Baltimore: H. Niles, 1811–49.

Noble, James F. Notes of a "Steamboat Man." Manuscript. Historical and Philosophical Society of Ohio Library, Cincinnati.

North, Douglass C. "International Capital Flows and the Development of the American West." *Journal of Economic History* 16 (December 1956): 493–505.

North, Douglass C. "Ocean Freight Rates and Economic Development, 1750–1913." *Journal of Economic History* 18 (December 1958): 537–55.

North, Douglass C. "The Role of Transportation in the Economic Development of North America." *Les Grandes voies Maritimes dans le Monde XVe–XIXe Siecles.* Paris: SEVPEN, 1965.

North, Douglass C. *Growth and Welfare in the American Past.* Englewood Cliffs, N.J.: Prentice Hall, 1966.

North, Douglass C. "Sources of Productivity Change in Ocean Shipping, 1600–1850." *The Journal of Political Economy* 76, no. 5. (Sept.–Oct. 1968): 953–70.

Odle, Thomas D. "The American Grain Trade of the Great Lakes, 1825–1873." *Inland Seas,* Pt. V, Vol. 7 (1952): 248–54.

Page, Thomas W. "Distribution of Immigrants in the United States before 1870." *The Journal of Political Economy* 20 (1912): 676–94.

Palmer, Charles K. "Improvement and Navigation of the Ohio River, 1787 to 1925." M.A. thesis, Indiana University, Bloomington, Ind., 1932.

Palmer, Charles K. "Ohio Valley Commerce, 1787–1936." *Indiana Magazine of History,* vol. 33. Bloomington, Indiana: Department of History of Indiana University, 1937.

Parish, Randall. *Historic Illinois.* Chicago: A. C. McClurg and Co., 1906.

Parker, William N., ed. *The Structure of the Cotton Economy of the Ante-Bellum South.* Washington, D.C., Agricultural History Society, 1970.

Petersen, William J. *Steamboating on the Upper Mississippi.* Iowa City: The State Historical Society of Iowa, 1937.

Poor, Henry V. "Sketch of the Rise and Progress of the Internal Improvements and of the Internal Commerce of the United States." *The Manual of the Railroads of the United States for 1881.* New York: H. V. & H. W. Poor, 1881.

Preble, George H. *A Chronological History of the Origin and Development of Steam Navigation.* 2d edition. Philadelphia: L. R. Hamersley & Co., 1895.

Primm, James N. *Economic Policy in the Development of a Western State, Missouri, 1820–1860.* Cambridge: Harvard University Press, 1954.

Quick, Herbert, and Quick, Edward. *Mississippi Steamboatin'.* New York: Henry Holt and Company, 1926.

Ransom, Roger L. "Social Returns from Public Transport Investment: A Case Study of the Ohio Canal." *Journal of Political Economy* 77 (Sept./Oct. 1970): 1041–60.

Ransom, Roger L. "Canals and Development: A Discussion of the Issues." *American Economic Review* 54 (May 1964): 365–76.

Ransom, Roger L. "Interregional Canals and Economic Specialization in the Ante-Bellum United States." *Explorations in Entrepreneurial History,* 2nd series, 5 (Fall 1967): 12–35.

Reiser, Catherine E. *Pittsburgh's Commercial Development 1800–1850.* Harrisburg, Pennsylvania: Pennsylvania Historical and Museum Commission, 1951.

Richardson, James D. *A Compilation of the Messages and Papers of the Presidents, 1789–1907.* New York: Bureau of National Literature and Art, 1908.

Ringwalt, J. L. *Development of Transportation Systems in the United States.* Philadelphia: J. L. Ringwalt, 1888.

Robertson, James. *A Few Months in America: Containing Remarks on Some of Its Industrial and Commercial Interests.* London: Longman & Co. 1855.

Rosenberg, Nathan. "Factors Affecting the Diffusion of Technology." *Explorations in Economic History* 10 (1972): 3–34.

Sadove, Abraham H. "Transport Improvement and the Appalachian Barrier." Ph.D. thesis, Harvard University, Cambridge, Mass., 1950.

Savage, Stephen G. "James Howard of Jeffersonville, Master Builder of Steamboats." M.A. thesis, Department of History, Indiana University, 1952.

Scheiber, Harry N. *Ohio Canal Era: A Case Study of Government and the Economy, 1820–1861.* Athens, Ohio: The Ohio University Press, 1969.

Scheiber, Harry N. "The Ohio Mississippi Flatboat Trade: Some Reconsiderations." In, David M. Ellis, ed., *The Frontier in American Development.* Essays in Honor of Paul Wallace Gates. Ithaca: Cornell University Press, 1969.

Schmidt, Louis B. "Internal Commerce and the Development of National Economy Before 1860." *The Journal of Political Economy.* Vol. 47. Chicago: The University of Chicago Press, 1939.

Schmidt, Louis B. "The Internal Grain Trade of the United States 1850–1860." *The Iowa Journal of History and Politics.* Vol. 18. Iowa City, Iowa: The State Historical Society of Iowa, 1920.

Scott, J. W. "Internal Trade." *The Hesperian or Western Monthly Magazine.* Vol. 3. Cincinnati: John D. Nichols, 1839.

Sellers, Elizabeth M. "The Pittsburgh and Cincinnati Packet Line: Minute Book 1851–1853." *The Western Pennsylvania Historical Magazine.* Vol. 19. Pittsburgh: The Historical Society of Western Pennsylvania, 1936.

Seybert, Adam. *Statistical Annals.* Philadelphia: Thomas Dobson & Son, 1818.

Shepard, Lee. "Early Steamboat Building at Cincinnati." *Bulletin of the Historical and Philosophical Society of Ohio.* Vol. 6. Cincinnati: The Historical and Philosophical Society of Ohio, 1948.

Shepherd, James F., and Walton, G. M. *Shipping, Maritime Trade and the Economic Development of Colonial North America.* New York: Cambridge University Press, 1972.

Shetler, Douglas. "Foodstuff Demands by the Cotton South in the Western Market: 1818–1841." Unpublished Paper. Department of Economics, U.C.L.A., 1972.

Short, Lloyd M. *Steamboat-Inspection Service.* New York: D. Appleton & Co., 1922.

Smith, Ophia D. "Cincinnati: From Keelboat to Steamboat." *Bulletin of the Historical and Philosophical Society of Ohio.* Vol. 15. Cincinnati: The Historical and Philosophical Society of Ohio, 1957.

Smith, Richard. "Review of the Trade and Commerce of Cincinnati for the Commercial Year Ending August 31, 1853." In *Cincinnati Prices Current* and *Hunt's Merchants' Magazine,* vol. 29, p. 694.

Smith, William. *Annual Statement of the Commerce of Cincinnati.* Cincinnati: Cincinnati Chamber of Commerce, Commercial Years Ending August 31, 1860 and 1861.

Snepp, Daniel W. "Evansville's Channels of Trade and the Secession Movement 1850–1865." *Indiana Historical Society Publications.* Vol. 8. Indianapolis: Indiana Historical Society, 1928.

Soltow, James H. "American Institutional Studies: Present Knowledge and Past Trends." *The Journal of Economic History* 31 (1971): 87–105.

Sterns, Worthy P. "The Foreign Trade of the United States from 1820 to 1840." *The Journal of Political Economy* 8. Chicago: The University of Chicago Press, 1900.

Stryker, James, ed. *Stryker's American Register and Magazine.* Vols. 1–6. Philadelphia: E. C. and J. Biddle, May 1848–December 1851.

Stuart, James. *Three Years in North America.* 2 vols. Edinburgh: Robert Cadell, 1833.

Supple, Barry E. *The Experience of Economic Growth.* New York: Random House, 1963.

Tarascon, J. A. *An Address to the Citizens of Philadelphia on the Great Advantages which Arise from the Trade of the Western Country to the State of Pennsylvania at Large, and to the City of Philadelphia in Particular.* Philadelphia: J. A. Tarascon and James Berthoud & Co., 1806.

Taylor, George R. *The Transportation Revolution 1815–1860.* Vol. 4 of *The Economic History of the United States.* New York: Holt, Rinehart and Winston, 1957.

Temin, Peter. *The Jacksonian Economy.* New York: W. W. Norton & Co., 1969.

Thompson, David Whittet. "The Great Steamboat Monopolies, Part I: The Mississippi." *American Neptune* 16 (1956): 28–40.

Thompson, James Howard. "A Financial History of the City of Pittsburgh, 1810–1910." Ph.D. thesis, University of Pittsburgh, 1948.

Thruston, Charles W., and Alfred. Accounts with Steamboats. Manuscript. Filson Club Library, Louisville, Kentucky.

Thurston, George H. *Alleghany County's Hundred Years.* Pittsburgh: A. A. Anderson & Son, 1888.

Thurston, George H. *Pittsburgh As It Is.* Pittsburgh: W. S. Haven, 1857.

Thurston, George H. *Pittsburgh's Progress, Industries and Resources.* Pittsburgh: A. A. Anderson & Son, 1886.

Trescott, Paul B. "The Louisville and Portland Canal Company, 1825–1874." *Mississippi Valley Historical Review* 44 (1957–58): 686–708.

Tucker, George. *Progress of the United States in Population and Wealth in Fifty Years, as Exhibited by the Decennial Census from 1790 to 1840.* New York: Press of Hunt's Merchants' Magazine, 1855.

Turner, Frederick J. *Rise of the New West, 1819–1829.* Vol. 14 of *The American Nation: A History.* Edited by Albert B. Hart. 27 vols. New York: Harper & Brothers, 1907.

U.S. Congress. House. Committee on Roads and Canals. *Navigation of the Ohio and Mississippi Rivers and a Bill to Improve the Navigation of the Ohio and Mississippi Rivers.* House Report 75, 18 Cong., 1 sess., 1824, Serial Set No. 105.

U.S. Congress. House. *Navigation of the Mississippi River.* Henry M. Shreve. House Doc. 11, 20 Cong., 1 sess., 1827, Serial Set No. 170.

U.S. Congress. House. President's Message. *Report of the Board of Engineers on the Ohio and Mississippi Rivers Made in the Year 1821.* House Doc. 35, 17 Cong., 2 sess., 1823, Serial Set No. 78.

U.S. Congress. House. Department of War. *Information . . . Respecting the Harbor of St. Louis.* House Doc. 298, 25 Cong., 2 sess., 1838, Serial Set No. 329.

U.S. Congress. House. Department of the Treasury. *Imports–Exports– Drawbacks etc.* House Doc. 330, 25 Cong., 2 sess., 1838, Serial Set No. 330.

U.S. Congress. House. Department of the Treasury. *Information in Relation to Steam Engines.* House Doc. 21, 25 Cong., 3 sess., 1838, Serial Set No. 345.

U.S. Congress. Senate. *Report of the Committee on Roads and Canals on the Bill to Authorize the Purchase of Stock in the Louisville and Portland Canal Co.* Senate Doc. 284, 26 Cong., 1 sess., 1840, Serial Set No. 359.

U.S. Congress. House. Post Office Department. *Failures and Irregularities of the Mail from New York to New Orleans.* House Doc. 159, 26 Cong., 1 sess., 1840, Serial Set No. 366.

U.S. Congress. Senate. Committee on Commerce. *Memorials Asking Congress to Make an Appropriation to Improve the Navigation of the Mississippi River and its Principals Tributaries.* Senate Doc. 137, 27 Cong., 3 sess., 1843, Serial Set No. 415.

U.S. Congress. House. *Memorial of the Citizens of the City of Cincinnati Relative to the Improvement of the Navigation of the Ohio and Mississippi Rivers.* House Doc. 126, 27 Cong., 3 sess., 1843, Serial Set No. 421.

U.S. Congress. Senate. *Memorial of a Number of Citizens of Cincinnati, Ohio Praying the Removal of Obstructions in the Navigation of the Ohio and Mississippi Rivers.* Senate Doc. 179, 28 Cong., 1 sess., 1844, Serial Set No. 434.

U.S. Congress. Senate. *Memorial of a Number of Citizens of the City of St. Louis, Missouri Praying an Appropriation for the Removal of Obstructions in the Western Rivers and for the Improvement of the Harbor of that City.* Senate Doc. 185, 28 Cong., 1 sess., 1844, Serial Set No. 434.

U.S. Congress. House. Department of the Treasury. *Documents Giving Information Relative to the Louisville and Portland Canal.* House Doc. 154, 28 Cong., 1 sess., 1844, Serial Set No. 442.

U.S. Congress. Senate. *Report of the Special Committee to Whom was Referred the Memorial of the Memphis Convention.* Mr. Calhoun. Senate Doc. 410, 29 Cong., 1 sess., 1846, Serial Set No. 477.

U.S. Congress. House. Committee on Roads and Canals. *Report on the Bill "to Remove Obstructions to the Navigation of the Falls of the Ohio."* House Report 661, 29 Cong., 1 sess., 1846, Serial Set No. 490.

U.S. Congress. House. Committee on Commerce. *Report on Harbor and River Improvements.* House Report 741, 30 Cong., 1 sess., 1848, Serial Set No. 527.

U.S. Congress. Senate. *Documents Relating to the Preservation and Protection of Passengers from Injuries Resulting from Steamboat Accidents.* Submitted by Mr. Davis. Senate Doc. 4, 31 Cong., Special Session of the Senate, 1849, Serial Set No. 547.

U.S. Congress. House. Department of the Treasury. *The Statistics and History of the Steam Marine of the U.S.* Senate Exec. Doc. 42, 32 Cong., 1 sess., 1852, Serial Set No. 619.

U.S. Congress. House. Department of the Treasury. *Report . . . on the Trade and Commerce of the British American Colonies . . . Great Lakes and Rivers.* I. D. Andrews. Senate Exec. Doc. 112, 32 Cong., 1 sess., 1853, Serial Set No. 622 (same as Serial Set No. 651, House Exec. Doc. 136).

U.S. Congress. Senate. *Investigation into the Causes of the Explosion of Steam-Boilers.* Alfred Guthrie. Senate Misc. Doc. 32, 32 Cong., 1 sess., 1852, Serial Set No. 629.

U.S. Congress. House. Committee on Roads and Canals. *Report on the Improvement of the Navigation of the Ohio River at the Falls.* House Report 166, 32 Cong., 1 sess., 1852, Serial Set No. 656.

U.S. Congress. Senate. Post Office Department. *Report on the Measures Taken to Establish Daily Mail Between Certain Places on the Mississippi.* Senate Exec. Doc. 31, 33 Cong., 1 sess., 1854, Serial Set No. 698.

U.S. Congress. House. Post Office Department. *Mail on the Mississippi River.* House Exec. Doc. 22, 33 Cong., 2 sess., 1854, Serial Set No. 783.

U.S. Congress. Senate. "Proceedings of the Annual Meeting of the Board of Supervising Inspectors." *Report on the State of the Finances.* Senate Exec. Doc. 3, 34 Cong., 3 sess., 1856, Serial Set No. 874 (same as Serial Set No. 896, House Exec. Doc. 2).

U.S. Congress. House. Department of War. *Commerce, Tonnage, etc. of the Ohio and Other Western Rivers.* House Exec. Doc. 48, 34 Cong., 3 sess., 1857, Serial Set No. 900.

U.S. Congress. House. Committee on Commerce. *Security of the Lives of Passengers on Board Vessels Propelled in Whole or in Part by Steam.* House Report 9, 35 Cong., 1 sess., 1858, Serial Set No. 964.

U.S. Congress. Senate. President's Message. *A Digest of the Statistics of Manufactures According to the Returns of the Seventh Census.* Senate Exec. Doc. 39, 35 Cong., 2 sess., 1859, Serial Set No. 984.

U.S. Congress. House. Committee on Commerce. *Better Security of Life on Board of Vessels Propelled by Steam.* House Report 141, 35 Cong., 2 sess., 1859, Serial Set No. 1018.

U.S. Congress. House. Committee on Commerce. *Security of Lives of Passengers on Board of Vessels Propelled in Whole or Part by Steam.* House Report 9, 36 Cong., 1 sess., 1860, Serial Set No. 1067.

U.S. Congress. House. Department of the Treasury. "Annual Report of the Board of Supervising Inspectors." *Report on the State of the Finances.* House Exec. Doc. 2, 36 Cong., 2 sess., 1860, Serial Set No. 1093.

U.S. Congress. House. "Memorial by the National Canal Convention, Chicago, 1863." *Message from the President of the U.S. to the Two Houses of Congress.* House Exec. Doc. 1, part V, 38 Cong., 1 sess., 1864, Serial Set No. 1184.

U.S. Congress. Senate. *Memorial of a Committee Appointed at the River Improvement Convention Held in St. Louis Feb. 13, 1867 Praying for an Appropriation for the Improvement of the Mississippi and Ohio Rivers.* Senate Misc. Doc. 5, 40 Cong., 1 sess., 1867, Serial Set No. 1309.

U.S. Congress. House. Committee on Commerce. *Report on the Louisville and Portland Canal.* House Misc. Doc. 83, 40 Cong., 2 sess., 1868, Serial Set No. 1349.

U.S. Congress. House. Department of the Treasury. *Security of Life on Steam Vessels.* House Exec. Doc. 175, 41 Cong., 2 sess., 1870, Serial Set No. 1418.

U.S. Congress. Senate. *Report of the Select Committee on Transportation Routes to the Seaboard.* Senate Report 307, Vol. I, 43 Cong., 1 sess., 1874, Serial Set No. 1588.

U.S. Congress. Senate. *Report of the Select Committee on Transportation Routes to the Seaboard.* Senate Report 307, Vol. II, 43 Cong., 1 sess., 1874, Serial Set No. 1589.

U.S. Congress. Senate. *Statement of Appropriations and Expenditures for Public Buildings, Rivers and Harbors, Forts, Arsenals, Armories, and Other Public Works from March 4, 1789 to June 30, 1882,* Sen. Exec. Doc. No. 196, 47th Cong., 1st sess. (1881) Serial Set 1992.

U.S. Congress. House. Department of the Interior. *Report on the Agencies of Transportation in the U.S.,* vol. IV of *Report of the Tenth Census,* T. C. Purdy, "History of Steam Navigation in the United States." House Misc. Doc. 42, vol. IV, 47th Cong. 2nd sess. 1883, Serial Set 2132.

U.S. Congress. House. Department of the Interior. "Report on the Shipbuilding Industry of the U.S." Henry Hall. Vol. VIII of *Report of the Tenth Census.* House Misc. Doc. 42, Vol. VIII, 47 Cong., 2 sess., 1884, Serial Set No. 2136.

U.S. Congress. House. Department of the Treasury. *Report on the Internal Commerce of the U.S. 1887.* Part II of *Report on the Commerce and Navigation of the U.S.* William F. Switzler. House Exec. Doc. 6, part II, 50 Cong., 1 sess., 1888, Serial Set No. 2552.

U.S. Congress. House. Department of the Interior. Census Office. "Transportation by Water." Henry C. Adams. Part II of *Report on Transportation Business in the United States.* Vol. XIV of *Report of the Eleventh Census.* House Misc. Doc. 340, Vol. XIV, part II, 52 Cong., 1 sess., 1894, Serial Set No. 3023.

U.S. Congress. Senate. Department of the Treasury. *Roads and Canals.* Albert Gallatin. 1808. Reprinted in *American State Papers.* Class X. Miscellaneous. Vol. I. Washington: Government Printing Office, 1834.

U.S. Department of Commerce. Census Bureau. *Historical Statistics of the United States, Colonial Times to 1957.* Washington: Government Printing Office, 1960.

U.S. Congress. Joint Economic Committee, "Historical and Comparative Rates of Production, Productivity and Prices," by G. R. Taylor, M. Abramovitz, and R. Goldsmith, *Hearings Before the Joint Economic Committee,* Part II, 86 Cong., 1 sess., April 7–10, 1959, pages 229–466.

Wade, Richard C. *The Urban Frontier: Pioneer Life in Early Pittsburgh, Cincinnati, Lexington, Louisville and St. Louis.* Chicago: The University of Chicago Press, 1964.

Walker, C. B. *The Mississippi Valley, and Prehistoric Events.* Burlington, Iowa: R. T. Root, 1880.

Wallace Family Papers. Manuscript. Filson Club Library, Louisville, Kentucky.

Walton, Gary M. "Productivity Change in Ocean Shipping after 1870: A Comment." *The Journal of Economic History* 30, no. 2 (June 1970) 435—41.

Warden, David B. *A Statistical, Political, and Historical Account of the United States of North America.* 3 vols. Edinburgh: Archibald Constable and Co., 1819.

Way, Frederick, Jr. A Collection of Freight Bills or "Way" Bills from Various Ohio and Mississippi River Steamboats. Manuscript. Inland Rivers Library Cincinnati Public Library, Cincinnati, Ohio.

Way, R. B. "The Commerce of the Lower Mississippi in the Period 1830—1860." *Proceedings of the Mississippi Valley Historical Association* Vol. 10, Extra No. Cedar Rapids, Iowa: The Mississippi Valley Historical Association, 1920.

Welby, Allard. *A Visit to North America and the English Settlements in Illinois.* Vol. 12 of *Early Western Travels 1748—1846.* Edited by Reuben G. Thwaites. 34 vols. Cleveland: The Arthur H. Clark Co., 1904.

Western Christian Advocate. Cincinnati, 1834—62.

Wholesale Prices Current at Cincinnati, Ohio. Cincinnati: Page & Robins, 1823.

Williams, John S., ed. *The American Pioneer.* 2 vols. Cincinnati: John S Williams, 1842 and 1843.

Williamson, Harold F. *The Growth of the American Economy.* New York Prentice—Hall, 1944.

Winston, James E. "Notes on the Economic History of New Orleans 1803—1836." *The Mississippi Valley Historical Review.* Vol. 11. Cedar Rapids, Iowa: Mississippi Valley Historical Association, 1924.

Woods, John. *Two Years Residence in the Settlement on the English Prairie in the Illinois Country.* Vol. 10 of *Early Western Travels 1748—1846* Edited by Reuben G. Thwaites. 34 vols. Cleveland: The Arthur H. Clark Co., 1904.

Wooldridge, John. *History of Nashville.* Nashville, 1890.

Yasuba, Yasukichi. "Birth Rates of the White Population in the United States 1810—1860, An Economic Study." *The Johns Hopkins University Studies in Historical and Political Science.* 79, no. 2 (1961).

INDEX

Library of Congress Cataloging in Publication Data

Haites, Erik F
   Western river transportation.

   (The Johns Hopkins University studies in historical
and political science; 93d ser., 2)
     Bibliography: pp. 188–204
     1. Inland water transportation–The West–History.
2. Shipping–Mississippi River–History. I. Mak,
James, joint author. II. Walton, Gary, M., joint author.
III. Title. IV. Series: Johns Hopkins University.
Studies in historical and political science;
93d ser., 2.
H31.J6 ser. 93, no. 2 [HE631.W4] 900'.8s
ISBN 0–8018–1681–5   [386'.3'0978]   75–12568